Digital Interfacing

This book takes the interface—or rather *to* interface, a process rather than a discrete object or location—as a concept emblematic of our contemporary embodied relationship with technological artefacts. The fundamental question addressed by this book is: how can we understand what it means to perceive or act upon the world as a body–artefact assemblage? Black works to clarify the role of artefacts of all kinds in human perception and action, then considers the ways in which new digital technologies can expand and transform this capacity to change our mode of engagement with our environment. Throughout, the discussion is grounded in specific technologies—some already familiar and some still in development (new virtual reality and brain–machine interface technologies, natural user interfaces, etc.). In order to develop a detailed, generalisable theory of how we interface with technology, Black assembles an analytical toolkit from a number of different disciplines, including media theory, ethology, clinical psychology, cultural theory, philosophy, science and technology studies, cultural history, aesthetics and neuroscience.

Daniel Black teaches Communications and Media Studies in the School of Media, Film and Journalism at Monash University, Australia.

Routledge Studies in New Media and Cyberculture

Digital Interfacing
Action and Perception through Technology

Daniel Black

Routledge
Taylor & Francis Group

NEW YORK AND LONDON

First published 2019
by Routledge
52 Vanderbilt Avenue, New York, NY 10017

and by Routledge
2 Park Square, Milton Park, Abingdon, Oxon OX14 4RN

First issued in paperback 2020

Routledge is an imprint of the Taylor & Francis Group, an informa business

Library of Congress Cataloging-in-Publication Data
Names: Black, Daniel (Daniel Ariad), author.
Title: Digital interfacing : action and perception through technology / Daniel Black.
Description: London ; New York : Routledge, 2018. | Series: Routledge studies in new media and cyberculture ; 43 | Includes bibliographical references and index.
Identifiers: LCCN 2018039388 (print) | LCCN 2018040828 (ebook) | ISBN 9780429425172 (ebook) | ISBN 9781138353886 (hardback : alk. paper) | ISBN 9780429425172 (ebk)
Subjects: LCSH: Human-machine systems—Philosophy. | Digital media—Psychological aspects.
Classification: LCC T14 (ebook) | LCC T14 .B47 2018 (print) | DDC 004.01/9—dc23
LC record available at https://lccn.loc.gov/2018039388

ISBN 13: 978-0-367-58367-5 (pbk)
ISBN 13: 978-1-138-35388-6 (hbk)

Typeset in Sabon
by Apex CoVantage, LLC

Contents

Epigraph

If all you have is a hammer, everything looks like a nail.

—origins unclear[1]

Note

1. While this principle is sometimes referred to as 'Maslow's hammer' (because of Maslow, 1966, pp. 15–16), it seems that Abraham Maslow was referencing an idea already in circulation at his time of writing.

Introduction

According to Erasmus's proverb, 'In the land of the blind, the one-eyed man is king.' But it seems to me that a more plausible scenario would be, 'In the land of the blind, the one-eyed man is diagnosed as psychotic'; after all, that's the likely fate of people in our own society who see things that don't feature in the perceptual experience of everyone around them. Even the technologically produced cyclops better known as the smartphone user, who looks at the world through a smartphone camera lens and Retina Display, while she might not be in danger of institutionalisation, still isn't attributed with superior powers of judgement or regal bearing. Take this quote from Edward Mendelson in *The New York Review of Books*:

> In popular culture, the zombie apocalypse is now the favored fantasy of disaster in horror movies set in the near future because it has already been prefigured in reality: the undead lurch through the streets, each staring blankly at a screen.
>
> (2016)

The smartphone user is regularly portrayed as an idiot or zombie who—robbed of spatial perception like all those lacking binocular vision—blunders around bumping into other people or inanimate objects, stepping into traffic or crashing their cars, and is inaccessible to social interaction. The behaviour of the smartphone user in public spaces or social settings can prompt remarks about the ironic tendency of a device ostensibly designed to increase our proficiency in tasks and facilitate social interaction through telecommunication to produce diametrically opposite results.

But of course the smartphone *is* increasing our proficiency in various ways and *is* facilitating social interaction; it's just that, as with the blind population listening to the one-eyed man and hearing only an irrational fixation with things that aren't there ('There are beautiful stars in the sky!'), the smartphone user who bumps into us in the street seems to lack mental or perceptual capacities because the focus of her attention is invisible to us. We don't see the text being read or video being watched, or the friend being interacted with.

While smartphone obsession is often characterised as an unhealthy fixation with a technological device, in most cases at least, the fixation is not on the device at all, but rather on things that are external to the device (other people, musical performances, Facebook pages), but which can only be acted upon or perceived *through* the device. The outside observer sees a strange relationship between human body and digital device, but for the user the digital device is the facilitator of a strange relationship between human body and something the observer isn't even aware of.

This problem of perspective is apparent in scholarship on our relationships with technological artefacts more generally. Attempts to understand our interactions with smartphones or personal computers tend to focus on the relationship between user and machine, when the experience of the user is often one in which the attributes of the machine simply inflect actions or perceptions that are directed somewhere else. This book is an attempt to understand, not how we experience technological artefacts, but rather how technological artefacts become integrated into our embodied experiences of the world around us.

The rise of digital culture took place against the backdrop of late twentieth-century thinking that often portrayed the impact of technological change on our bodies in bleak terms. While the massive cultural and economic success of digital technology has in the early twenty-first century counterbalanced this with the optimistic, cyber-libertarian narratives of personal transformation and empowerment influential in Silicon Valley (even if it hasn't completely stamped them out), discussions of technology at the end of the last millennium often portrayed the human body as being subjugated and turned into a commodity by plastic surgery or genetic engineering, or nullified by virtual reality's coming usurpation of physical existence. Scholars were heavily influenced by Michel Foucault's claim that the body, rather than being a product of nature and the private realm of an individual subjectivity, was in fact both integrated into and the product of technologies of social surveillance and control (1973, 1975, 1978).

This intellectual milieu is reflected in Vivian Sobchack's 1988 pronouncement that 'the electronic tends to marginalise and trivialize the human body' (in Sobchack, 2004, p. 161), and many thematically similar claims about a postmodern individual whose body is immobilised or rendered redundant as her mind is overwhelmed by a flood of electronic information. Jean Baudrillard's postmodern subject was locked inside a sterile apartment complex as if he were 'an astronaut in his bubble', tethered to the world only by the cables of communications networks; as a result, 'the human body, our body, seems superfluous in its proper expanse, in the complexity and multiplicity of its organs' (1988, pp. 15–18). Paul Virilio's postmodern subject was immobilised inside a car hurtling along a superhighway, over whose windscreen played flashes of contextless imagery that appeared and disappeared too rapidly to process (Virilio, 1995b; see also 1995a). Where the body had been a necessary part of the age of industry—even if it had only been a cog in a machine—in the postindustrial era it seemed surplus to requirements in a world where flows of energy had been supplanted by flows of information that could be piped in directly through the eyes. John Perry Barlow's famous (and now embarrassingly dated) 'A Declaration of the Independence of Cyberspace' (Barlow, 1996) described 'cyberspace' as 'the new home of Mind' (the body presumably being its previous, now vacant, one), and virtual reality was widely seen as a technology whose imminent arrival would allow us to literalise this pronouncement, stepping outside our bodily context entirely and taking up residence in a computer-generated world of information (Lanier and Biocca, 1992).

Such ideas seem naïve now, products of a fin-de-siècle propensity towards apocalyptic thinking, millenarianism and attitudes towards new technology that combined snobbery and superstitious fear. The millennium bug didn't cause personal computers to bring about the collapse of modern civilisation (Year 2000 Problem, n.d.), and we never were transformed into either mindless meat sacks twitching in response to an overabundance of electronic stimuli or demigods residing in a computer-generated fantasyland of pure information. The very idea of information as independent from bodily materiality has since been thoroughly critiqued (e.g. Hayles, 1999), and some authors have sought to unearth the hidden bodily dimension to our relationship with information technology (e.g. Hansen, 2004, 2006; Dourish, 2004; Munster, 2006).

However, when viewed from the perspective of the present moment, what is most striking about both the belief that information technologies might render the body obsolete and subsequent attempts to bring to light the hidden bodily dimensions of our relationship with these technologies is that, far from being absent from or even hidden in our relationships with digital technologies, the body has always been clearly prominent in them. I think there are multiple reasons why the centrality of the body to information technology use seems obvious to us today even as it was seemingly invisible to many twenty-five years ago. On one hand, the multi-user dungeons (an early form of online social space) famously described by Sherry Turkle as places where purely textual intercourse made physical identity irrelevant (Turkle, 1984) have spawned social networking services where concerns about the victimisation of people because of their race or gender, or the politics of bodily representation, are at least as strong as they ever were in older media. On the other hand, the physical technology itself has changed, and as it has become smaller and more mobile it has conspicuously attached itself to human bodies in ways that make the intimacy of the machine–body relationship particularly clear.

If we look at film of Doug Engelbart's famous 'mother of all demos' at the Fall Joint Computer Conference in San Francisco in 1968, in which he demonstrated the graphical user interface and other features that would become central to personal computing in future years,[1] it is clear that

Engelbart's own body is a key part of the demonstration, sitting at a work-station like the pilot of a science fiction spacecraft with eyes trained on a screen and hands playing over the keyboard and the newly invented computer mouse, and making expert manipulations of a 'chord board' that was never integrated into consumer computer setups. At the same time, however, Engelbart's body is immobilised, and perhaps overshadowed by an 'enormous video projector' (Moggridge, 2007, p. 33) that created a twenty-foot display screen, glowing with fascinating shapes that draw the eye away from the reality of Engelbart's virtuosic, embodied physical enactment of the commands that drive its output, encouraging a tendency to understand digital devices primarily in terms of what is on their screens that persists to the present. In contrast, watching a person walking down the street interacting with a smartphone or smartwatch today, or bumbling around in an immersive environment with one of a new generation of head-mounted displays clamped to her head, it is clear that the body is the key central component of these practices and physical assemblages, whose actions and perceptions, practices and habits make the digital device meaningful. While the size of Engelbart's screen perhaps made his body seem less significant, with these newer technologies the screens are small, perhaps making the human body seem proportionately larger.

While the research of the 1960s and 1970s that initiated the personal computing revolution produced new ways of understanding human–machine interaction, the physical hardware was nevertheless largely a grab bag of existing technologies. Users interacted with their personal computers using keyboards (a nineteenth-century technology that had been electrified around the turn of the twentieth century) and the cathode ray tube (an invention of the turn of the twentieth century that had become familiar as a feature of consumer appliances with the mass dissemination of television in the 1940s and 1950s). While the mouse was a new means of interaction called into being by the development of the graphical user interface, and would spawn optical and wireless versions with various additional buttons, wheels and so forth, our means of interaction with it has nonetheless not changed that much since its origins a half century ago, when it was not much more than a little toy car attached to a wire. Its mode of use—moving in two dimensions on a plane extending horizontally out from the user's body—is not a common one, and so would seem to spring directly from a habituation to the similar kinaesthetic experience of handwriting. Most significantly, perhaps, while the keyboard and mouse became the two mainstays of computer interaction, it is impossible to use both at the same time, requiring that the user move back and forth from one to the other as the need arises and so precluding any completely smooth, flowing mode of prolonged engagement with the machine.

The popularisation of the personal computer brought with it ancillary artefacts like the 'computer desk', and specialised knowledges like the ergonomic arrangement of computer equipment, enforced through occupational health requirements by organisations fearful of being held responsible for injury to their workers. While the new models of human–computer interaction made computers easier to use in all sorts of ways, the relationship between human user and physical hardware remained awkward enough that computers needed to be placed within physical spaces specifically designed to facilitate their use by living human bodies, and living bodies themselves had to be disciplined to assume postures and habits conducive to their effective use.

However, when digital devices became mobile, they inevitably began to shift between different contexts of use, and so could no longer be dependent upon a specialised, constrained spatial context. A mouse only functions as part of a larger assemblage that includes the surface over which the mouse moves, but smartphones, tablets and various other devices are not usually used on a flat surface that can support the peregrinations of a mouse, and are too small to allow touch-typing. Where the older personal computer required a user who was immobilised and heavily restricted in bodily movement and orientation, the popularisation of smaller and more mobile information technology has made it impossible to tailor the movements of the user to the device. Small screens, unified and minimised cases, operation by users who might be in a wide variety of physical postures and simultaneously engaged in other forms of physical activity, have all made it impossible to address a standardised user body holding itself in a prescribed attitude and situating itself in relation to a collection of input and output devices arrayed in a static configuration around her.

As computers have become more sophisticated and powerful, the limits of technology have become less and less constrained by what machines can do, and more and more constrained by what we can do with machines. As a result, our understanding of digital devices as physical artefacts has become more explicitly centred on the 'fit' between body and device; rather than digital technology being understood to render the body irrelevant, we are increasingly aware of what has always been the truth of the matter: these technologies are dependent upon the human body, just as we as embodied human beings are dependent upon them when we engage in certain kinds of activity.

This book is an investigation of this reciprocal relationship between our bodies and the technological artefacts we use. While I will be referring to various kinds of human–machine interfaces or user interfaces while doing this, my work arises from a rejection of 'the interface' as an object of study in favour of a focus on the kinds of human experience that allow specific modes of human–machine interaction to exist. The three central claims I will make about the tightly integrated engagements between bodies and technological artefacts that I refer to as interfacing are that they are *naturally artificial*; they *transform action and perception*; and they *create possibilities*. Exactly what I mean by these three claims can only become apparent over the course of the book, but I will here make some preliminary remarks about the first of them so as to make my starting position clearer.

When I say that close engagements between body and artefact are 'naturally artificial', the first word arises from a belief that our bodies and minds have evolved an intrinsic amenability to, and even dependence upon, the incorporation of objects into our capacity for action and sensory experience. I fully expect this claim to provoke in some readers an accusation that I am universalising and naturalising things that do not result from intrinsic human attributes (if these even exist at all) but rather are, in reality, historically contingent cultural productions that materialise certain ideologies. I am happy to plead partially guilty to this charge, even if I do so without any genuine feelings of remorse.

To get it out of the way, I will say now that I think interfacing with artefacts is natural. In the broadest sense, interfacing is natural because interfacing is a necessary part of being a living body in a world, and being a living body in a world is the natural state of human beings. But my claim is stronger than that, in that I believe that there is a particular human way of interfacing that is part of our evolutionary heritage, a natural way of engaging with our environment that is a crucial part of why our species has been as catastrophically successful as it has. Of course particular technologies and the ways in which we use them are not natural or inevitable, but the viability of any user interface design is dependent upon its ability to make use of a set of inescapable attributes of our way of engaging with the things around us. The many non-natural factors—be they cultural, commercial, legal and so on—that go into the design and adoption of particular ways of using technological artefacts are of course worthy of investigation also, but to consider them in isolation is to begin too far downstream from their point of origin. My dissatisfaction with most current analyses of user interfaces stems from the fact that they ask, 'Why did someone make it this way?' without ever wondering what field of possibilities that someone was operating within when they did so. For this reason, I am primarily concerned with trying to map out this field of possibilities, not as a project opposed to the investigation of user interface design as a cultural process, but rather as a necessary but to-date neglected precondition for its successful prosecution.

But there is also that second word: artificial. In addition to being completely natural, our relationships with technological artefacts are completely unnatural. The paradoxical nature of this claim is merely a reflection of the fact that our relationships with artefacts are paradoxical through and through. When I employ a technological artefact, the status of the artefact, that of my own body and that of the whole assemblage constituted by both things operating together becomes unclear. While our bodies and minds have evolved an intrinsic amenability to the incorporation of objects into our capacity for action and sensory experience, at the same time the experiences we have through objects are never simply an expansion or improvement of capacities we have without them. If an object has the qualities necessary to enable a close relationship with a human body, then on the first occasion of a human body taking it up and making use of it a new form of human action and perception springs into being, one that has never previously existed. Interfacing is therefore never simply determined by a pre-existing set of natural circumstances.

Interfacing results from a propensity of living bodies to attach themselves to objects in ways that produce new kinds of action and perception, and this propensity can be seen as a kind of glue that allows the creation of larger, distributed assemblages. Interfacing necessarily encourages a focus on synthesis or blending, rather than the interaction of more readily differentiable interacting parts; it also centres on the special status of living bodies (whether those of humans or other animals, vegetable, microbial, etc.) as entities that actively and continuously negotiate and reformulate relationships with their environments. As a result, bodily experience is central to my understanding of interfacing, even as that bodily experience is understood to arise from both the biological body and the material objects and environments with which it interacts. This centrality should not be taken to reflect a belief that material objects have no dynamism or reality beyond their relationships with living bodies, but does spring from a belief that interfacing as discussed here is a phenomenon unique to living bodies.

Throughout this book, I work to map the plane across which human body and technological artefact meet, seeking to understand the attributes and potentials that allow these two entities to become tightly integrated. At least some examples of this integration demonstrate our capacity to become part of human–machine assemblages that transform experience and leave only a vestigial sense of the boundary between body and artefact. At first blush, such a claim might seem to lead towards a worryingly dismissive attitude towards the material specificity of the body and embodied experience, towards the kind of abstracted and impoverished account of 'the body' prevalent late in the last century, or even the transhumanist disavowal of any distinction between flesh and the machines it is hoped will one day replace it. Certainly it is not difficult to find suggestions that new technologies such as prostheses and virtual reality demonstrate a fundamental interchangeability between our biological bodies and technological artefacts, one that could allow us to replace unsatisfactory biology and physicality with machinery and digital information in various ways. However, my claim need not lead in such a direction, and in fact I would argue that it should lead away from it. Central to the approach taken by this book is, not a discounting of the uniqueness and specificity of the human body, but rather a focus on it. It is the particularity of human embodiment that allows our close relationships with technological artefacts; rather than technological artefacts simply replacing human embodied capacities, they combine with them to create new capacities that exist in neither body nor artefact in isolation. A key part of our experience as physical, embodied entities is the creation of close and productive relationships with features of our environment, sometimes forging relationships so close as to make those features a part of our embodied experience itself.

On the other hand, it might alternatively be objected that my approach shares the limitations of the phenomenological accounts that have obviously influenced it: it universalises the body, treating the attributes and capacities of bodies as invariant across populations in its positing of unchanging principles underlying all relationships with technology. After all, it might be argued, if we compare the young, poor Chinese woman labouring on a production line to create a sleek new laptop with the wealthy, middle-aged American executive who will ultimately use that laptop, it is clear that these two different bodies have very different relationships with the same technological artefact. And yet, despite the very different contexts within which they work, these two different bodies do share fundamental attributes in their relationships with technology, attributes generated by a common set of human capacities for action and perception, and the potential modes of engagement with technological artefacts that are available to, or available to be inculcated in, them due to the nature of their physical embodiment. Technological artefacts, through the role they play in human society, are of course implicated in larger political, economic and other contexts, and an acknowledgement of and critical engagement with these things is of tremendous importance, as are the ways in which bodily differences such as race, gender, age and more inflect relationships with technology. But this does not change the fact that there is an underlying set of material qualities and human potentials that provide the mechanisms by which technological artefacts come to play a role in human society—for example in the various ways in which the Chinese factory worker's body can engage with artefacts in order to perform a valuable, if repetitive and fragmented, role in the creation of economically significant objects.

Part of the specificity of individual human bodies is the particularity of their relationships with material objects. The approach I take to human–technology relations is therefore different from some other frameworks that similarly highlight what might be described as material assemblages, while not antagonistic towards them. Approaches such as actor network theory (Latour, 2005) or object-oriented ontology (Bryant, 2010) and related forms of speculative realism share a desire to demonstrate the degree to which circumstances often described either in terms of or from the perspective of immaterial subjectivities or self-directing agents in fact function as interactions between and within material systems. However, this book is not an attempt to describe a set of non-human material interactions that take place *outside* human subjectivity, but rather to consider the degree to which non-human material interactions exist *inside* human subjectivity, in the sense that human capacities for perception and action are always to some degree produced by our bodily engagements with features of the environment.

The book comprises five chapters. The first, 'The Myth of the Myth of Transparency', provides an overview of existing conceptualisations of the relationship between human bodies and technology through a critique of research into 'the interface'. The popularisation of the term 'interface' is a result of the dissemination of digital devices in all aspects of everyday life, which itself has brought a greater awareness of the role of body–technology relationships; in this chapter I trace the evolution of the word 'interface' from specialised technical term to popular usage by way of computer science and the marketing of high-tech consumer goods. My central claim is that this process has led to a narrowing and shifting of the meaning of the word, which has in turn inflected the foundational assumptions of various attempts to critically discuss what interfaces are and how they work. It is in response to this that I favour the verb 'to interface' over the noun, as it maintains a processual and interactional focus that has been largely evacuated from the idea of 'the interface'.

In Chapter 2, 'Where Do Bodies End and Objects Begin?', I consider the kinds of relationships that can and have arisen through the coming together of bodies and artefacts, and from this extract some general principles that can be used to understand what further kinds of relationships might arise as the artefacts we use continue to change and develop. Using a combination of past analyses and new scientific research concerning the ways in which tools, machines and interfaces can and have changed our experiences of action and perception, I will highlight the degree to which our relationships with new digital technologies are a continuation of the ways in which our experience of who we are has been transformed by our incorporation of external objects throughout the entirety of human history. New digital technologies enable new modes of engagement, which are in turn able to further the ongoing development of our productive relationships with artefacts, but it is part of our evolved nature to seemingly effortlessly extend the boundaries of our bodies to capture them.

In the remaining three chapters, I shift to a more targeted analysis of the embodied experience of body–machine interfacing. In Chapter 3, 'Beside Ourselves', I take the experience of proprioception, or our sense of the location and disposition of our bodies, as a focus, considering the ways in which interfacing with technology can change our relationship with space in paradoxical ways. New digital user interfaces are increasingly reliant on the creation of an experience of space through 3D images, and yet this three-dimensional space is ultimately irreconcilable with the space of our embodied action and perception. As an attempt to create an experience of action and perception within a simulated space whose familiarity and commercial success establishes its effectiveness, the third-person video game provides an opportunity to pull apart and identify the components that together produce a new experience of space. The key insight generated by doing so is that, beneath a veneer of realistic simulation, the third-person video game actually relies on a complex integration of multiple and irreconcilable experiences of space, which are held together as much by the player's ability to effortlessly merge multiple, distributed sensory experiences as by the clever artifice of the game itself. The coming together of computer space and user space is never perfect, creating a layering of differing kinds of space, and a multiplication of the posited points of origin for our perceptions and actions, and yet the unity of the resulting experience demonstrates the role of the body in synthesising and reconciling different kinds of experience generated by its multiplex relationship with its environment.

Chapter 4, 'Aesthesiogenesis', moves from the perception of space to a broader consideration of the degree to which interfacing can produce perceptual experiences that are not easily accounted for using existing sensory schematisations. Our senses are much less discrete and independent of one another than we often assume, and the introduction of artefacts with their own distinct physical characteristics into our sensory experiences has the capacity to create further and more productive interactions between them. When these artefacts are imbued with an ability to encode sensory stimuli as digital data, work upon those digital data in various ways, and then convert them back into sensory stimuli, this capacity to transform sensory experience is greatly expanded. For example, vision can be converted to touch or sound, or even perhaps entirely novel forms of sensory experience with the potential to produce previously unknown relationships between human beings and their environments. This potential demonstrates the largely unrecognised degree to which human experience has always been dynamically generated through the specificity of our embodied relationships with objects, and the ways in which, as a result, it has changed dramatically throughout our history and possesses an ever-expanding capacity to continue changing in the future.

The final chapter, 'Real Time', investigates the centrality of chronoception, or the perception of time, to the ways in which bodies and artefacts can work together to produce sensory experience. The modern era of digital user interfaces has its origins in the appearance of interactive computing, which was a key development because it created a closer engagement between computer and user by reconfiguring the temporal relationship between machine and body. While existing accounts of technology's impact on the human sense of time have tended to portray machines as outstripping, or even annihilating, the human temporal scale, interactive computing originates with an explicit attempt to reconcile the inhuman speed of the computer with the human speed of its user.

This chapter provides a theorisation of time and user interfaces that reaches beyond digital technology in order to argue that our experience of time is crucial to our ability to act and perceive with and through any artefact. Human perception and recollection combine with material objects to produce the capacity for physical action, and this relationship between body and object is developed further by the principle of interactive computing as an increasing number of devices are designed to respond in a temporally significant way to our interactions with them, attempting to anticipate and respond to our behaviours and integrate themselves into our habits. The synchronisation of body and artefact is a key part of how artefacts can come to be experienced as part of our bodies more generally, and the new rhythms of synchronised action and perception made possible by digital technologies can strengthen and alter this process.

Throughout these chapters, the key focus is the ways in which the material qualities of objects and the material qualities of bodies come to be bound together. Numerous individual examples of this process will be discussed, but these examples nonetheless only scratch the surface of an immensely diverse realm of human experience.

Note

1. See 'The Mother of All Demos, presented by Douglas Engelbart (1968)', uploaded by MarcelVEVO. Available at: www.youtube.com/watch?v=yJDv-zdhzMY.

1   The Myth of the Myth of Transparency

If there has been an age of cinema, an age of radio or an age of television, then our current media era might be described as the age of the interface (Yonck, 2010). But the way in which the term is used is often hazy and contradictory. While definitions of older media technologies might not be beyond contestation, when asked what television is, for example, most people would confidently point to a specific physical artefact in answer; but where should we point when seeking to answer the question of what an interface is? Over the past two decades, work has already been done to place the human–computer interface within a wider media context, but this work can obscure the ways in which human–computer interfaces do not fit into existing frameworks for discussing media technologies.

When trying to answer the question of what an interface is, perhaps it is best to start by stating what an interface is not. Most importantly, and contrary to most existing accounts, the primary purpose of an interface is not representation. Certain kinds of interfaces might utilise forms of representation, but these representations are not themselves interfaces. In addition, we can also at least problematise the idea that interfaces are media. If it is appropriate at all to refer to an interface as a medium, then it must be understood that the term 'medium' in this context means something different from what it does when applied to other kinds of media technology: if a medium is generally understood to be a technology that mediates between the human and something 'beyond' that technology, an interface must be understood to mediate between the human and the technology itself.

In this first chapter, I want to spend some time looking at how the term 'interface' has come to be a part of our everyday understanding of human–technology relations, both reflecting and inflecting common-sense conceptions of the role of digital technologies in our lives, as well as informing the values and priorities that are applied to the development of new devices. This understanding has also had an important influence on scholarly investigations of digital technologies: while the values and priorities of technology makers have frequently been critiqued by scholars, these critiques nevertheless tend to share with the objects of their criticism a set of basic assumptions about what interfaces are and what they mean.

Debates over what an interface is—or should be—provide a good starting point when trying to characterise a dominant conception of our relationships with technological objects: cutting-edge research into new kinds of personal digital device is most often associated with new kinds of interface (e.g. direct brain interfaces; see Chapter 4); the marketing of current digital devices commonly focuses on interface features rather than the (largely invisible and incomprehensible) hardware; and 'the interface' has become the object of study presented as equivalent to media forms such as television or film in new media scholarship. Because it is, by definition, connected to our physical interactions with digital devices, discussing the interface will allow me to tease out a set of widespread assumptions concerning how we use technology, and the opportunities for interaction technology can provide—and show their failings. Having done so, I can then draw attention to important dimensions of technology use that an emphasis on the interface has obscured before turning to a more detailed and sustained investigation of these dimensions in Chapter 2.

The Evolution of the Word

The word 'interface' is a relatively new one—the first example of its use given by the *Oxford English Dictionary* comes from 1882—but today it tends to be used as if its history is a century shorter. This is not surprising given that it only began to enter common, everyday usage in the mid-1980s. It has entered the popular lexicon via a very specific route, a route that has importantly shaped common understandings of what an interface is and how it works.

Branden Hookway has already given a detailed prehistory of the term 'interface' prior to the spread of its current popular usage in the 1980s (Hookway, 2014, Chapter 2). Originating in Victorian research on fluid dynamics, the word's nineteenth-century meaning of 'a face of separation, plane or curved, between two contiguous portions of the same substance' was appropriate for specialised technical, rather than everyday, usage; however, it later became caught up in the post-WWII infiltration of everyday life by specialised technical concepts brought about by the rise of cybernetics and the spread of the digital computer. In a post-cybernetic moment that often saw the world as composed of systems in interaction with one another, it was necessary to talk about the regions where those systems came into contact, and those regions were, literally, interfaces. As new knowledges and technologies allowed new kinds of interactions between systems to be created artificially, the noun 'interface' even gave rise to the 'space-age verb'[1] 'to interface' (to which I will return later).

Cyberneticists saw systems all around them, but in the context of computers, interfaces might exist between computers, between different subsystems within computers, between computers and other machines, or between computers and the human beings who interacted with them. The spread of the personal computer brought the term into popular usage in the restricted sense in which it was used in computer science. In fact, it was introduced as a restricted subset of the restricted sense in which it was used in computer science: that is, while within computer science the word 'interface' could be used to refer to the meeting of computer hardware, computer software, and human user in any combination other than two human users, in everyday usage the term 'interface' has become simply an abbreviation for and thus synonymous with the human–computer interface. Technical or semi-technical references to other kinds of (usually hardware-to-hardware) interfaces can occur, but this is rare for the average computer user. In everyday discussion, the word 'interface' alone is understood to refer to the mode of interaction between human user and machine; for example, a computer will be described as having a 'graphical user interface', or a smartphone will be described as having a 'multi-touch interface'.

Probably the most important phase of this trajectory that took the word 'interface' from varied technical usage, through the restricted technical usage of information technology and then into common usage in the further restricted sense of the human–computer interface began with Doug Engelbart's famed 1968 demonstration of what would become the foundations of the modern graphical user interface, or GUI (Johnson, 1997, pp. 20–22). It was the GUI, typified by computer operating systems such as Microsoft Windows and Apple's Macintosh, that more or less single-handedly introduced the term into the popular lexicon, and made the interface a key concept in our understanding of what a computer or other digital device is. Speaking of Ridley Scott's famous '1984' television advertisement, which introduced the Apple Macintosh to the American public during that year's Super Bowl, Steven Johnson notes that 'it was the first mass-media promotion that devoted as much attention to an interface as to the underlying hardware itself' (1997, p. 50).

In 1989, John Walker, one of the founders of Autodesk, noted

> the extent to which the term *user interface* has emerged as a marketing and, more recently, legal battleground following the introduction and growing acceptance of [graphical user interfaces] . . . Many people would probably fail to identify anything before a fourth-generation menu system as a 'user interface' at all.
>
> (Walker, 1990, p. 443)

And in 1993, influential interface design expert Brenda Laurel commented that '"Interface" has become a trendy (and lucrative) concept over the last several years—a phenomenon that is largely attributable to the introduction of the Apple Macintosh' (1993, p. 2). During this period, the GUI was presented as the magic ingredient that could transform computers from something arcane and specialised, something only available to a dedicated technical élite, into a mass-market consumer appliance 'for the rest of us', as the famous Apple campaign claimed.

The term 'interface' was turned into a buzzword (Heim, 1993, pp. 75–76) primarily through its use in marketing the GUI. The ease with which a user might operate a complex digital device is crucial to its appeal, and so advertising seeks to instil a belief that the device's user interface is inviting— even 'intuitive', to repeat a common marketing expression. But this suggestion that a digital device 'has' a certain interface is out of keeping with the literal meaning of the term. After all, the word interface literally means the point at which the exteriors of two or more entities meet; strictly speaking, to talk about one entity independently possessing an interface makes no sense.

In fact, a fundamental transformation has taken place over the course of this word's evolution from specialised technical term to everyday marketing jargon: the meaning of the word did not simply become progressively more narrow and restricted, but also underwent a qualitative change. An interface came to be a thing. This change is not surprising, given that it accompanied the introduction of digital computers as consumer items, and consumerism deals in things. In the late 1980s, Alan Kay, a key figure in the development of the personal computer, quipped, 'User interface has certainly been a hot topic for discussion since the advent of the Macintosh. Everyone seems to want user interface but they are not sure whether they should order it by the yard or by the ton' (1990, p. 191).

To explore this change, let's consider an application of the word 'interface' that would have been unremarkable at the turn of the twentieth century, but is quite different from the dominant contemporary usage derived from computer engineering. The term 'interface' originated in the field of fluid dynamics (Hookway, 2014, pp. 59–67) to refer to the internal division created by the meeting of differing kinds of liquid, such as hot water and cold water, or still water and moving water. This interface is a kind of non-thing, a non-place. It is a two-dimensional plane defined not by *what* it is, but by *where* it is in relation to other things, and what those other things are doing. It is a place that occupies no space; it is simultaneously one entity, the other entity, both entities and neither entity—it's often unclear if there even *are* two entities, or if the interface is rather internal to a single entity. If the contours of one body of liquid change, the interface alters, and alters the contours of the other body, but it is not at all clear that we should say that it is the interface that changed the contours of that other body. The interface is both a product of the contours of the two liquids and the thing that shapes the contours of the two liquids. It maintains the perfect reciprocity and complementarity of the two liquids, and exists only while they are in contact. It is purely a phenomenon of the meeting of the two liquid bodies and will vanish at the moment they disengage from one another or merge. This is an interface, but it is hardly something that you could put in a box and sell in an Apple Store.

When the term 'interface' is used in computer science to describe the point of contact between two systems, the qualities of this contact are fundamentally different. As products of human engineering, each of the meeting systems is separate and distinct, separable and readily distinguishable. If two hardware interface ports are connected to one another, this inevitably creates a new phenomenon analogous to the interface between the two liquids—one that is equally a part of both systems and neither of them—but at the same time the engineering logic of computer hardware development understands the interface as primarily a piece of hardware, a physical structure built as part of one system that will allow a connection with another. Similarly, when software interfaces with either another layer of software, or hardware or a human user outside itself, this is understood in terms of the engineering of a specialised system.

In computer science, an interface becomes a point of articulation, of translation or exchange. It becomes a point of connection across which data moves. This is quite different from the interface between two fluid bodies: in that case, the interface is precisely that plane across which there *is* no exchange; there is no mixing of the two fluids, nor is there any exchange or translation between them. The interface of some liquids— such as oil and water—might be characterised precisely by the fact that they cannot mix or merge; other kinds of fluids might be able to mix with one another, but if they do so the interface collapses and disappears. The borders of the interface might shift—liquid that was still, for example, might begin to move, shifting the location of the interface between still and moving water—but in that case one entity has simply become part of the other entity, which is something different from translation or exchange. Where they create an interface, the two fluids remain distinct and separate from one another, stable and unchanged in their physical composition, and yet the exterior contours and disposition of each fluid *are* changed, determined by its contact with the other to produce a perfect complementarity that does not originate with either body or move from one to the other. Each liquid body is changed by its relationship with the other, but there is no clear point of origin for this change and it has no directionality. Their meeting creates a new phenomenon (the interface) that brings about a convergence and reciprocity between them as long as they are in contact, but vanishes when either their contact or their distinctness ceases.

The more general engineering logic of the computer interface is shifted further by the specificity of the human–computer interface. Where other kinds of computer interfaces seek to create a bridge between different kinds of hardware or software, the human–computer interface seeks to create a bridge between the computer and a human being, something fundamentally different from hardware or software, and ultimately alien to the principles of computer engineering. This creates the initial failing of HCI (human–computer interaction) research, which is that it tends to treat the human user as simply another piece of computer engineering, whose behaviour is fixed and predictable. The human being is treated as if it is simply another piece of hardware—a 'model human processor' (MHP; Card, Newell and Moran, 1983; see Turner, 2009, p. 6)—to be plugged in to the larger system, and the behaviour of the user is largely treated as a product of the design of that system.

An awareness of this problem developed during the broader turn-of-the-millennium critique of disembodied information (e.g. Hayles, 1999; Hansen, 2000; Dourish, 2004 [2001]), which took issue with a late twentieth-century discourse of 'cyberspace' as 'the new home of Mind', where '[o]ur identities have no bodies', in the words of John Perry Barlow (Electronic Frontier Foundation, 1996; see introduction, this volume). Today, the designers of digital technologies are trying to move from a model of the user as a collection of inputs and outputs towards one that understands interactions with technology as embodied, affective and frequently non-rational (Turner, 2009). User experience, or UX, in particular seeks to adequately acknowledge the importance and complexity of the role played by embodied human users in the utilisation of technological artefacts, and self-consciously grounds itself in criticisms of traditional cognitivism, which have arisen from areas such as phenomenology (van Dijk, 2009) and the extended cognition thesis of Andy Clark and David Chalmers (1998; see Chapter 2).

While this shift has been important, acknowledging that embodiment is a part of our relationships with technology is not the same as understanding *how* embodiment is a part of those relationships, and the UX approach arguably still struggles to build a clear and consistent conceptual framework that can meaningfully inform design practices. A belief in technologies as disembodied perhaps has been more effectively discredited by changes in technology itself: mobile devices, virtual and augmented reality and wearables are self-evidently dependent on the bodies of their users (see introduction, this volume).[2] At the same time, however, developers of new technological devices all too often treat these new user interface technologies as necessarily and innately progressive in their engagement of users' bodies, even as they merely reproduce an existing set of assumptions about what bodies are and what they can do. Furthermore, while the critique of disembodied technology originated in the humanities, UX's attempts to account for the user stand in contrast to the complete absence of users in many influential theorisations of digital user interfaces from the humanities and social sciences.

Transparency and Opacity

Florian Cramer has noted the way in which '[h]umanities media studies have simultaneously restrained and inflated the notion of interface' (2011, p. 120). Of the variety of possible applications of the term, Cramer argues,

> media studies have historically privileged one, the human-to-software user interface, using it often enough as a synonym of the term 'interface' . . . Interface, in that definition, becomes a synonym of a perceptive 'medium', much like optical devices in Renaissance philosophy, only that the former is specific to computing technology. Interface aesthetics then is simply how humans—respectively computer users—perceive the world via the organisational and sensory structures programmed into the device.
>
> (2011, pp. 119–120)

There is a great deal of consistency in humanities and social sciences accounts of the supposed attributes of interfaces, and there is perhaps no more frequently recurring theme than the dichotomy of transparency and opacity. The idea that interfaces are characterised by a tension between a kind of experiential presence and experiential absence is put forward repeatedly, sometimes in slightly different terms, but usually in very similar language. In *Windows and Mirrors* (2005), Jay David Bolter and Diane Gromala present transparency and opacity as two extremes in a fundamental ideological conflict over what interfaces are and how they should be designed and operated, and mount a partisan attack on those (typified by influential design expert Donald Norman) who believe 'the myth of transparency':

> HCI specialists and some designers speak as if that were the only goal of interface design: to fashion a transparent window onto a world of information.
>   There are times, however, when the user should be looking at the interface, not through it, in order to make it function . . . At such moments, the interface is no longer a window, but a mirror, reflecting the user and her relationship to the computer . . . If we only look *through* the interface, we cannot appreciate the ways in which it shapes our experience.
>
> (Bolter and Gromala, 2005, pp. 26–27)

More recently, Lori Emerson repeats Bolter and Gromala's argument regarding transparency and opacity in *Reading Writing Interfaces* (2014, ch. 1), although the iPad, having appeared in the intervening years, is substituted for Norman's hypothetical 'invisible computers' and 'information appliances' (1999) as indicative of a misguided attempt to make interfaces transparent. Anne Friedberg similarly describes the computer screen as 'both a "page" and a "window", at once opaque and transparent' (2006, p. 19), while Alexander R. Galloway describes the recurring theme of transparency versus opacity in terms of a surface versus a doorway, window or threshold (2009, pp. 936–937), initiating his discussion of the 'unworkability' of interfaces (2009, 2012, Chapter 1): an interface, like any technology of realistic representation, seeks to reproduce the object of its representation as closely as possible, but to actually attain perfect verisimilitude would render the representation redundant as a result of its complete interchangeability with the real thing.

> [F]or every moment of virtuosic immersion and connectivity, for every moment of volumetric delivery, of inopacity, the threshold becomes one notch more invisible, one notch more inoperable. As technology, the more a dioptric device erases the traces of its own functioning (in actually delivering the thing represented beyond), the more it succeeds in its functional mandate; yet this very achievement undercuts the ultimate goal: the more intuitive a device becomes, the more it risks falling out of media altogether, becoming as naturalized as air or as common as dirt. To succeed, then, is at best self-deception and at worst self-annihilation.
>
> (Galloway, 2012, p. 25)

It might be argued that the matter of the transparency and/or opacity of interfaces is of great importance, given that our interactions with one another and the world around us seem to be conducted more and more through interfaces of various kinds. On the other hand, it might also be argued that questions about the relationship between transparency and opacity in digital interfaces are simply banal, given that a tension between experiential presence and experiential absence is a seemingly inevitable feature of human action and perception using any external feature of the environment. Rather than being thrown up by digital user interfaces specifically, the same kinds of questions could be asked about a hammer (if you are Martin Heidegger), a telephone or a pair of chopsticks.

Which is not to suggest that Bolter and Gromala or others do not place the theme of transparency versus opacity within a wider historical context. Bolter and Gromala, for instance, argue that the 'myth of transparency' originates in ancient Greece and Rome, and like many others they highlight the magic window of Renaissance perspective as a formative influence on the representational strategies of the computer screen (Bolter and Gromala, 2005, p. 36; see also Bolter and Grusin, 1999, pp. 31ff.). In a slightly different but related way, Lev Manovich has noted a hybridisation of two representational conventions in the computer interface: a window to be looked through, originating from the conventions of realistic pictorial representation,[3] and a surface to be looked at originating in the instrument panels of the military command and control technology that is the computer's most direct hardware ancestor:

> As a result, the computer screen becomes a battlefield for a number of incompatible definitions—depth and surface, opaqueness and transparency, image as illusionary space and image as instrument for action.
>
> (Manovich, 2001, p. 90)

What I find most striking about these examples is that they are all tied to the matter of representation, and visual representation specifically. While Manovich quite explicitly suggests 'that software interfaces—both those of operating systems and of software applications—. . . act as representations' (2001, pp. 15–16), all of the claims about the transparency or opacity of interfaces made previously to some degree rely on an assumption that interfaces function as systems of (visual) representation.

An interface *can* look like something, but it needn't do so. It is not the purpose of an interface to look like something in the way that it's the purpose of a photograph to look like something. While the representational language of linear perspective might have informed the development of computer graphics, the fact remains that an interface is not a form of visual representation. Unlike a painting, film, music recording or book, a digital user interface is presented to us, not as a more or less self-justifying representation, but as a tool enabling certain kinds of action. And if we recast the tension between transparency and opacity in terms of *acting on* the world rather than *representing* the world, the discussion is transformed in significant ways, most importantly because this recasting shifts the central focus away from the relationship between the interface and some object of representation *beyond it* to the relationship between the interface and the body of a user who is *part of it*.

Representation

It has already been argued that, at a certain point in its history, the computer became a medium (e.g. Bolter and Grusin, 1999, p. 99; Bolter and Gromala, 2005, pp. 15–17; Kay, 1990, p. 193). If the computer is a medium, it seems reasonable to talk about computer interfaces in terms of representation. But what exactly does a digital interface represent?

According to Bolter and Gromala,

> For our current culture . . . the term *appliance* doesn't describe computers very well. Computers don't feel like toasters; they feel much more like books, photograph albums, or television sets. For us today—and it's a realization that our culture has made gradually over the past thirty years—the computer feels like a medium.
>
> (2005, p. 4)

However, if the computer has come to feel like a television set, it should be noted that a television set is both a medium *and* an appliance. And the human–computer interface does not perform a task analogous to the programme on the television screen—as the window of a Web browser, for example, might be said to do in at least some ways—but rather one analogous to the remote control in the television viewer's hand.

Arjun Mulder differentiates between a general and a specific meaning for the term 'medium' (2006, p. 189). If we take the more general sense of a medium as something that 'extends or amplifies some organ or faculty of the user' (McLuhan and McLuhan, 1988, p. viii; see also Bryant, 2014, pp. 30–31), then both human–computer interface and remote control might be considered media; but in the more restricted sense of extending only the senses rather than any bodily faculty, their use as tools to perform actions raises problems. Certainly one cannot use a television to act upon the people and places represented on its screen. The computer interface is designed to effect changes in what it mediates, and potentially even changes in the nature of the medium of the interface itself. If a computer interface *seems* more unproblematically a medium than the television remote control, it is presumably because the interface is partly manifested on the screen as images, rather than entirely outside the screen as a physical object, and so confuses divisions familiar to us from older technologies. But it should also be borne in mind that the computer interface does not exist *wholly* on the screen: material components such as keyboard, mouse—or even the glass of the screen itself in the case of capacitive touch screens—are integral to the interface. Like the television remote control, if the interface is a medium, it mediates between human body and machine, not between human body and something beyond the machine.

Perhaps an interface is a representation in that it represents to us processes interior to the machine, rather than representing some larger external reality. Perhaps its purpose is to represent the workings of the machine in a humanly comprehensible way. One manifestation of the underlying logic of the interface as representation is its explanation in terms of *translation*, through claims that interfaces are all 'about translating between computer-readable code and human-readable language' (Chun, 2011, p. 91). That is, the human–computer interface is understood to be a place where two systems that presumably are otherwise incompatible are brought together through the conversion of each system's inputs and outputs into a format that the other can understand. An important conceptual ramification of this idea is that, while in a larger sense an interface suggests a direct engagement between two systems, the theme of translation characterises the computer and user as discrete, separate, and to some degree isolated and self-sufficient entities only able to interact indirectly through and with representations of one another. Rather than the interface being about the joining of these two systems, it becomes a discrete locus of mediation.

And yet something about this explanation also doesn't ring true. Donald Norman noted some time ago that the computer's user interface doesn't make the operation of the device itself comprehensible, rather it provides a 'conceptual model': a model of how the user's actions impact on the operation of the device.

> What does it mean to understand how something works? Do I really have to understand automobile mechanics to drive my car, or to understand solid state physics and computer programming to use my computer? Of course not. But what I do need is a good conceptual grasp of what is going on, an understanding of the different controls and alternative actions I can take and what their impact is on the device. I need a story that puts together the behavior and appearance of a device in a sensible, comprehensible pattern.
>
> (Norman, 1999, p. 177)

In other words, the purpose of the interface is not to represent the workings of a computer to us; rather it is to make such a representation unnecessary by constructing a logic of interaction that can be independent of them. When using a word processor, my goal is not to activate switches inside my computer or instruct my computer to display the shapes of certain letters on its screen; my goal is simply to write. I understand myself to be acting *with* the computer, not *on* the computer, and I certainly don't understand myself to be engaged in an ongoing process of translation between me *and* the computer.

It might be objected that this is only a manifestation of my naïve relationship with the computer, that this is simply another result of the privileging of transparency in interfaces about which Bolter and Gromala complain. However much I might understand my computer to be like a typewriter, this doesn't change the fact that it is a complex engine of representation, which uses its representational powers to merely simulate the operation of a typewriter. However, this objection doesn't get us very far. After all, what's going on 'under the hood' of a television set isn't really important for its status as a representational medium; this status is dependent upon the television viewer's sensory experience of the television, not the processes that produce that sensory experience. And my experience of writing on my computer is one of pressing a key labelled with a particular letter and seeing that letter appear on the screen. Despite claims that 'HCI's version of direct manipulation is never "direct", only simulated' (Chun, 2011, p. 64), I am *really* pressing on a physical key and this is *really* causing a genuine event to take place; it is not a simulation of writing, any more than a blind person feeling a road surface at the end of a cane is experiencing a simulation of sensing (see Chapter 4).

What happens outside the reach of my senses between the pressing of the key and the appearance of the letter doesn't have any bearing on my relationship with the computer. Furthermore, rather than being a manifestation of a lack of sophistication in my relationship with the computer, this lack of awareness is what makes the computer useful. In order to write, I need to feel that I am acting *with* the computer rather than *on* the computer, and this requires an experience of direct, synchronous action.

In fact, if the digital user interface is a technology of representation, the human user is more the object of that representation than its subject. Human–computer interfaces seek to present the machine with a representation of the user more than they seek to provide the user with a representation of the workings of the machine. After all, the explicit aim of the user interface is to make the machine responsive to the intentions of the user rather than vice versa; much of how the machine goes about achieving its outcomes can remain hidden from the human user, but the machine should ideally be highly attuned to small details of human action and perception.

And this representation of the user is not a visual one, despite the fact that existing accounts of interfaces as representational systems are primarily either literally or metaphorically visual in nature.[4] The sonic attributes of interfaces are more difficult to fit neatly into a conventional representational framework, but, in any case, interfaces are primarily neither visual nor auditory, but kinaesthetic in nature. If they represent anything, they primarily represent the actions of a user. To quote Brenda Laurel, writing in 1993:

Q: What is being represented by the Macintosh interface?

1. A desktop.
2. Something that's kind of like a desktop.
3. Someone doing something in an environment that's kind of like a desktop.

Number three is the only answer that comes close. The human is an indispensable ingredient of the representation, since it is only through a person's actions that all dimensions of the representation can be manifest.

(Laurel, 1993, p. 2)

If user interfaces work to represent the user to the machine, this is a representation of the user's *movements*. While we have become accustomed to elaborate visual components to interfaces, the capturing of the user's actions is the one crucial component of the interface, for which visual imagery can only function as a support, as a cue for or feedback concerning action.

For example, with an old rotary dial telephone, once we have matched the abstract numbers on its face to the system of telephone numbers, the user interface is intended to invite the insertion of fingertip into numbered hole and the spinning of the dialling wheel; in other words, the visual appearance of the telephone is a manifestation of the kinaesthetic performance its interface is designed to represent as a series of numbers. Similarly, if a mouse cursor is shaped like an arrow, it is in the expectation that this shape will encourage the user to move the mouse in a way intended to make the mouse cursor indicate on-screen objects, and the movements of the cursor are simply a representation of the movements of a user's arm, the capturing of which is the mouse's reason for existence.

A visual and representational bias has had a very real impact on the arguments made about interfaces. In the vast majority of cases, the theorisations of 'the interface' that have been presented to date are in actual fact theorisations of digital visual media texts (something readily verifiable by the fact that there is little in these theorisations that could not be applied to almost any digital media text, regardless of whether it is understood to have anything to do with interfaces or not). Furthermore, in addition to focusing almost entirely on those aspects of individual interfaces that appear as screen-based representations, they also largely ignore the user. This is inevitable given that discussing a user interface in this way requires that it be treated as a static text, looking *through* the user to treat the images on the screen as a set of self-determining representations rather than more properly as only a by-product of the user's interaction with the device. This approach ignores the interface proper in favour of what the interface leaves behind in terms of imagery—studying the interface pinned to a board rather than on the wing as it responds to the turbulence of a living body's activity.

The distorted view produced by attempts to impose theoretical frameworks intended for visual media texts onto interfaces is itself presumably responsible for the widespread obsession with the issue of transparency, and explains the vociferous ideological opposition to it. If an interface is understood to be primarily something that we see, then an invisible interface is one that we will be unable to investigate or understand. In fact, claims regarding an ideology of transparency in interfaces are often unclear or contradictory regarding what, exactly, it is that is supposed to *be* transparent. They tend to conflate the transparency/opacity of the device's workings, screen, and the user experience, and the very subordination of these different areas under the title of transparency itself reflects the imposition of a visual framework of understanding; after all, the experience of using a device can only be described as transparent by applying a visual metaphor to those dimensions of interface-use that are not visual—most obviously the kinaesthetic.

If interfaces are primarily media of kinaesthetic representation, this imposition of a visual framework cannot help but distort our understanding; in fact, the rhetorical opposition between ideologies of transparency and opacity typified by Bolter and Gromala can be explained by a mismatching of these two kinds of representation: those (most often designers and engineers) who privilege transparency are actually talking about the desirability of a kinaesthetic transparency exemplified by skilled tool use,[5] while those (most often critics of visual media) who find the privileging of transparency naïve or ideologically odious are interpreting the pronouncements of the former group as referring to a kind of visual transparency that provokes their opposition to any belief that media can provide a transparent window on reality, which in turn suggests an obscuring of the ideological mechanisms at work in the medium itself:

> While in everyday usage 'transparency' stands for simplicity, clarity and controllability through viewability (for example in the name of Transparency International, an organisation combating corruption worldwide), in computer science the term means the very opposite, namely invisibility and information concealment. A 'transparent' interface is one that the user can neither detect nor notice. While this concealment of (superfluous, excessive) information is often expedient in terms of reducing complexity, it can also lull the user into a false sense of security: the invisibility of the interface suggests a direct view of something, an unimpaired transparency in which it would be foolish, of course, to believe.
>
> (Arns, 2011, p. 256)

This idea most directly arises from Bolter and Grusin's arguments about transparency in new media more generally in the book *Remediation* (1999), in which they claim that

> Virtual reality, three-dimensional graphics, and graphical interface design are all seeking to make digital technology 'transparent'. In this sense, a transparent interface would be one that erases itself, so that the user is no longer aware of confronting a medium, but instead stands in an immediate relationship to the contents of that medium.
>
> The transparent interface is one more manifestation of the need to deny the mediated character of digital technology altogether.
>
> (1999, pp. 23–24)

But again this treats a user interface as just another medium of visual representation. The latest television technology might be presented to us as the next step towards creating a transparent window on reality with its high pixel count and colour reproduction that supposedly makes it indistinguishable from the real thing, but what exactly is it that a user interface is trying to transparently represent to us? Once again, if it can be said to aim to transparently represent anything, it is seeking to transparently represent the human body to the computer. After all, those new user interface technologies most often claimed to herald a future of transparent human–computer interaction tend to be related to things like gesture and motion recognition rather than high-fidelity visual representation—in other words, they are technologies intended to provide devices with more responsiveness to bodily movement while obviating the need to present human users with representations.

The prioritisation of what a human–computer interface looks like arises from the strong focus on visual design in screen interfaces, which in turn arises from the relatively nondescript physical shapes of the devices that carry them; the interface of a rotary telephone, car, or hammer doesn't look like something else, and the very idea seems nonsensical in their context. This presumably explains the pull towards skeuomorphism[6] in graphical user interfaces: a traditional telephone's physical shape aims to explain its interface and thus its mode of use, while a smartphone's physical shape should be sufficiently nondescript to facilitate a variety of different uses. Thus, when a smartphone's screen interface signifies the action of making a telephone call, it presents a visual representation of a traditional telephone.

Icons and Indices

But an icon in a graphical user interface generally no more functions as a representation than a stop sign functions as a representation of stopping. The purpose of a folder icon is not to communicate something; it is something intended for interaction, for acting on or with. It might be objected that the folder icon is also a representation, telling the user that it functions like a physical manila folder, but this is largely inconsequential. First, the folder metaphor in itself tells the user very little: for example, thinking that the folder icon is like a manila folder does not tell the user that it can be interacted with by double-clicking on it; the metaphor does not extend beyond 'something that can hold something inside itself'. The shape of the icon is primarily a mnemonic device; it was originally designed for business users, for whom a manila folder was a familiar office tool that would make them feel more comfortable and at home with the computer desktop, and the very broad association with 'something that you can put something else inside' could help the business user to remember what the folder icon was for. Of course, GUIs are used much more broadly now than was imagined at Xerox PARC in the 1970s and 1980s, and many of those who now interact with folder icons have never even seen an actual manila folder (see Manovich, 2013, p. 101). For those who have long been familiar with GUIs, the original need for the folder iconography to be familiar and have a metaphorical logic no longer exists, as the icon itself and its operation are familiar, and so could have any shape and work just as well. We now primarily use the terms 'desktop' and 'folder' to refer to GUI elements, not because we associate them with physical desks and folders through a metaphorical relationship, but rather because we now dominantly understand these terms to be referring to GUI elements.

We can see this also in the fact that the generally accepted icon design for the 'save' command is an image of a 3.5″ floppy diskette: no one today has regular interactions with this physical artefact, and many computer users will have never even seen one, but it doesn't matter because there is now no need to acclimatise users to the save command through physical analogies, and a shape that corresponds to nothing the user has ever seen or interacted with outside the computer desktop is just as serviceable as anything else. This is presumably a key part of the unfashionability of skeuomorphism in user interface design today: icons that look like features of the physical world based on an analogy regarding use are widely considered twee and ugly, and surely this is to a large degree because they are associated with the naïve user of yesteryear, whose lack of familiarity with computers supposedly made such analogies necessary.

It might be argued that the very use of the term 'icon' in graphical user interfaces reflects its foundation in a model of visual representation; that is, a GUI icon is called an icon in the understanding that its purpose is to serve as a representation of something. The fact that the significance of a 'save' or 'folder' icon has less and less connection with its appearance already throws this idea into doubt, but is only a relatively recent addition to a much more fundamental set of problems with the idea of the GUI 'icon' as an icon in the broader semiotic sense of the word.

While the computer icon has become a key part of our understanding of how a personal computer works—for most people, I suspect, the icon is considered the most important part of the 'graphical' character of the graphical user interface—it was not a part of the foundational model of personal computing developed by Doug Engelbart's Augmentation Research Centre at Stanford University in the 1960s and famously demonstrated in San Francisco in 1968 at all. It was actually quite a late addition in the evolution of the GUI concept, being introduced to the user interface of the Xerox Star (the first consumer device to feature a GUI)[7] in the lead-up to its release in 1981, thirteen years later.

When comparing the Star user interface with contemporary graphical user interfaces, it is clear that this initial deployment of the concept was more limited than we are accustomed to today. For example, the idea of a 'save' icon does not fit the logic of icons as they existed in the Star; rather, its icons served as virtual objects that the user could manipulate with the mouse, not representations of actions. The icons of the Xerox Star were divided into two categories, data icons and function icons, and a function was performed by dropping a data icon (for example, a document) onto a function icon (for example, a printer);[8] the logic was therefore that of using one object to act on another, which is fundamentally different from the later logic of simply clicking on an icon that is an abstract representation of an action such as saving. In fact, actions such as 'save' were performed with physical keyboard buttons, and, in contrast to the superabundance of visual representations inside contemporary applications like Microsoft Word, open Star windows only featured a small number of text buttons to click on.

David Canfield Smith, who introduced icons to the Xerox Star user interface, first developed the concept for his PhD project, the PYGMA-LION programming environment (Smith, 1975). Smith's PhD thesis is notable for its explicit attempt to introduce a framework of visual representation into the operation of computers; in fact, in the thesis, Smith (perhaps somewhat self-importantly) states that

> PYGMALION brings art into computer science. Rather than providing a computer resource which artists can use to create (paint, compose music, etc.), PYGMALION is a first attempt to provide an artistic resource which computer scientists can use to create.
>
> (1975, p. 59)

Smith makes an explicit appeal to art theory and art history to argue for the value of this approach. Citing the likes of Ernst Gombrich and Rudolph Arnheim, as well as psychological theories claiming a visual nature for thought and memory influential at the time, Smith's foundational argument is that the manipulation of visual representations is more natural and suited to creativity than the more abstract systems developed previously.

> PYGMALION is a visual metaphor for computing. Instead of symbols and abstract concepts, the programmer uses concrete display images, called '*icons*'. The system maps the visual characteristics of icons into corresponding machine semantics.
>
> (Smith, 1975, p. 69)

The logic of icons as virtual objects to be manipulated is clearer and more far-reaching in PYGMALION than the Star interface, following the broader trajectory that took computers from being tools for programming to being tools for non-programmers. PYGMALION was a tool for a programmer—or rather 'iconographer' (Smith, 1975, p. 72)—who created icons that served as tokens to be manipulated in the creation of programs. These icons were therefore more open-ended than the icons of the Star interface in that they could represent a wide range of things including functions, computer processes and so on, but at the same time they were more 'hands-on', being defined and created by the programmer as things that could be manipulated, moved around and built into larger structures. Although these icons could cause things to happen themselves, the larger logic was that they were things that the programmer acted with. Smith therefore understood icons as visual representations, but they were representations intended to concretise the operations of the computer in a way that made them more amenable to a model of human physical action.[9]

The icon concept seems much looser today than it did at its origins, obscuring its foundation in efforts to bring a model of concrete human action into computer use. But to what extent have GUI icons ever functioned primarily as part of a system of visual representation? David Canfield Smith seems to have gone no further than a Webster's dictionary for his understanding of the meaning of the term 'icon' (Smith, 1975, p. 71), and perhaps he would have adopted a different word if he had had access to terms more appropriate to his attempt to create virtual objects that invited human manipulation.

The precise nature of icons, and their relationship with other kinds of symbols, is defined much more carefully within the semiotics of Charles Sanders Peirce. According to Peirce's definition,

> An *Icon* is a sign which refers to the Object that it denotes merely by virtue of characters of its own, and which it possesses, just the same, whether any such Object actually exists or not.
>
> (Peirce, 1955, pp. 102–103)

The applicability of this definition to GUIs clearly arises from an understanding of these 'icons' as most importantly visual representations of actions (or, rather, of objects that can in turn represent actions, such as floppy diskettes). The GUI icon is an icon by virtue of the fact that it possesses visual qualities that call to mind the action it represents. But there is a fundamental conceptual problem with this idea, and the fact that many GUI icons continue to function perfectly well despite a withering of their ability to denote anything by virtue of their visual qualities is ultimately only a symptom of this problem.

Compare the following two examples. First, I visit a country whose inhabitants do not use the familiar icons that represent male/female/disabled toilet facilities. Looking for a public toilet, I find a doorway that looks to be a likely candidate, on the wall beside which is a blue plastic shape, which I speculate fulfils an equivalent function to those icons. The shape seems similar to a human figure, but I do not associate the implied shape of its clothing with a particular gender because I am unfamiliar with the conventions of dress in this country, and in any event it might just as easily signify that only blue-uniformed security staff are permitted beyond that point or some other meaning. I have no way of determining if this shape is the icon that represents 'male', or even if it is really an icon at all (it might only be a decoration, for example). In the second example, I find myself using an unfamiliar word processor application, whose creators did not use the familiar convention to denote options for bold/italic/underline text. Needing to bold a piece of text but not knowing which icon on the application's tool bar to use, I identify three unfamiliar icons whose appearance seem evocative of bold text. I then simply click on each icon in turn until the selected text becomes bold. In this second example, in a sense, the right icon 'told me' its function because my interaction with it produced an observable outcome. The blue plastic shape in the first example could never 'tell me' its significance in the same way because it has a fundamentally different nature to the GUI icon in the second example, and this fundamental difference arises from the fact that, in Peirce's terms, the word processor icon is actually not an icon at all.

As Peirce states, an icon is an icon by virtue of its character, a character that has some manner of equivalence to its object. If I am unable to *characterise* an icon (e.g. I don't know that in a given culture only women wear skirts, and thus that the shape of a skirt makes a figure look like a woman), I cannot make sense of the icon. By contrast, even if a GUI button on a word processor displayed no 'icon' at all, then—as long as I understood that the button shape itself identified something that could be clicked on, and the action triggered by the button was perceptible—I could discover what the 'icon' meant simply by clicking on it. The reason for this is that these GUI components are not *icons*, defined by their ability to communicate meaning through their visual similarity to something else; rather, they are a form of digital *index*, defined by their direct, specific relationship with physical objects and actions.

According to Peirce's definition,

> An *Index* is a sign which refers to the Object that it denotes by virtue of being really affected by that Object . . . In so far as the Index is affected by the Object, it necessarily has some Quality in common with the Object, and it is in respect to these that it refers to the Object. It does, therefore, involve a sort of Icon, although an Icon of a peculiar kind; and it is not the mere resemblance of its Object, even in these respects which makes it a sign, but it is the actual modification of it by the Object.
>
> (Peirce, 1955, p. 102)

An index can, therefore, *also* be an icon, but this is not its defining attribute. Instead, it is defined by the fact that, rather than simply having some resemblance to its object, it has a real physical connection to its object. Understandably given the kinds of examples available in his time, Peirce tends to present this in terms of the object's capacity to affect the index, but the fact that clicking on an index with a mouse pointer can affect its object (e.g. by causing a computer to perform some action) does not change the nature of Peirce's account. To quote Peirce again,

> An *icon* is a sign which would possess the character which renders it significant, even though its object had no existence; such as a

lead-pencil streak as representing a geometrical line. An *index* is a sign which would, at once, lose the character which makes it a sign if its object were removed, but would not lose that character if there were no interpretant.

(Peirce, 1955, p. 104)

In other words, an index has a real, direct relationship with something. A GUI 'icon' is not defined by the fact that it represents the idea of making text bold through some kind of visual representation (although it might do so); rather, it is defined by the fact that, if you interact with that icon, you will cause an *actual, specific* event as a result of which an *actual, specific* piece of text is made bold. No icon can be said to create a real connection with an object, as an icon cannot have a direct, individual relationship with a singular event. An index, on the other hand, is defined by such a relationship.

The GUI 'icon' is actually an index because it is intended to put the user in a real, specific physical relationship with something—it is meant to generate contextually specific action. A GUI 'icon' is not meant to represent the general activity of starting an application or saving a document; it is intended to have a direct relationship with specific instances of these things happening.

Someone still wedded to the idea of interface as representation might maintain that the GUI 'icon' is still importantly different from Peirce's concept *because* it is a representation. That is, the 'bold' GUI icon does not actually make text bold; rather, both the icon and even the bold text itself are simply visual representations created by the computer to provide human beings with a simple way of understanding what the computer is doing and how to interact with it—there is no physical connection between the GUI icon and the behaviour of the computer, because GUI icons are not physical things, only visual representations. But this objection is untenable.

First, indices can incorporate visual representations, and even function as icons. No one would dispute that a save icon *is also* a visual representation of a 3.5" floppy diskette; the important question is, does the primary value of the save icon lie in its ability to visually evoke an association with a 3.5" floppy diskette, or even the act of saving itself? The answer is no. A thermometer can be described as a representation of the temperature, but its defining characteristic is not that it represents the temperature (if it were, then a photograph of a thermometer would be just as good as the real thing). Rather, what makes a thermometer a thermometer—and an index—is the fact that it changes in response to the temperature of the air around it. Similarly, what defines the save icon is not that it looks like a floppy diskette, or anything else, but that clicking on the save icon causes the computer to do something. Even if the save icon is only a computer visualisation, the act of clicking on the save icon results from the physical movement of the user, and causes a change in the physical state of the computer itself. While David Canfield Smith can be understood to have been trying to create such a sense of direct connection through physical action when he developed the computer icon, he seemingly fell into an account founded on a model of visual representation rather than action for want of a more appropriate conceptual framework.

Conclusion

While the GUI was considered a breakthrough in human–computer interaction in the 1980s, familiarity has perhaps bred some degree of contempt, and today it's not unusual to hear either predictions of or calls for its demise. Given that the GUI's narrow reliance on the visual is often prominent amongst the complaints made about it, it might be argued that the historical account I've given of the recurrence of visual representation as a model of human–computer interaction is unnecessary. It might be argued that this problem has already been acknowledged, or at least swept aside by the march of technological development, with the GUI model of an immobilised user sitting at a desk and staring at a computer screen already on its last legs, soon to be replaced entirely by new input technologies (like voice or gesture) and new ways of presenting information (like haptic feedback or augmented reality). But to respond in this way would be to miss the point that I have been trying to make.

This chapter is not intended to be taken as a critique of ocularcentrism in user interface design. In fact, I believe that there is a tendency to artificially separate vision from supposedly more direct or embodied modes of interaction that is not justified. This tendency leads to a common assumption that appeals to other senses such as touch inevitably entail an increase in our bodily engagement with technology and promise an escape from older paradigms typified by the GUI, one that is readily discernible in proposed post-GUI approaches such as the natural user interface (see Chapter 2). While adding to the number of sensory modalities engaged with can enrich a user interface, there is no reason to believe that replacing one sensory modality with another will itself create a new model of interaction.

In highlighting the recurrent theme of transparency and opacity in accounts of interfaces, my criticism has not been that this reflects a focus on the visual; it has been that it takes (visual) representation as a model for how we engage with technological devices. This model could (and, as we will see, can) be applied to non-visual components of human–computer interaction just as well as visual. A digital device can be understood as attempting to transparently represent its operation to a user through the medium of sound or touch; while the informing metaphor is visual representation, a literal visual component, while invariably present in the examples I've cited, need not be.

My aim in this chapter has not been to problematise the visual, but to problematise a belief that interfaces engage our senses through representation. In order to develop a clearer understanding of how we develop intimate engagements with technological devices, we must abandon a tendency to see user and device as isolated, separate entities that send instructions and information back and forth as discrete representations of the workings of body or machine. If certain kinds of action with artefacts can be described as transparent, it is not because we are tricked by a slick interface into forgetting that we are dealing with a system of representation, or that the nature of the machine itself is rendered invisible. Rather, it's because we move beyond the experience of an interface of artefact and body to the experience of an interface of body–artefact assemblage with the world beyond.

Central to my account of the spread of the term 'interface' into popular use is the claim that its understanding has been restricted and distorted by its association with particular kinds of technology. Rather than being a fluid, dynamic, unstable phenomenon generated by the particularity of individualised interactions between a living user and an artefact, an interface has come to be understood as a fixed, predetermined, constrained and self-contained system mass-produced by technology companies in order to generate certain kinds of exchange between a user and a digital device, one largely dependent upon screens and visual cues. This change has brought an important conceptual shift, away from the interface as a two-dimensional entity—a plane that not only joins but is produced by two systems—to the interface as something more separate, a kind of bridge between two systems that remain, at a fundamental level, disconnected and autonomous from one another. This claim might be greeted with an observation that language is constantly changing, and that this is hardly the first time advertising has warped the meaning of words, and left at that, but I would like to argue for a contestation of this development. I am not arguing for a contestation of this usage on the grounds that the alternative sense is truer to the original definition and logic of the word— attempts to wind back the evolution of language are counterproductive and doomed to failure—but rather on the grounds that the alternative sense is a richer definition that helps us to understand our contemporary relationships with technology, while the dominant one impedes understanding. It impedes understanding because it restricts the meaning and applicability of the term interface such that it is removed from the wider context of human relationships with technological artefacts, cutting off possibilities for a broader understanding of our contemporary experience. I am not trying to purge the term 'interface' of the popular associations it has developed—these associations are at least in part a result of changes in the technological landscape to which it refers—but I am trying to reverse the process by which other, broader significances for the term have been shut out of both its popular and scholarly understanding by its very focused, goal-directed propagation by technology companies and their marketers.

But of course my personal dissatisfaction with this usage of the term can hardly be expected to result in its wholesale re-evaluation and a shift in the evolution of the English language. So where does this leave the term 'interface'? For the remainder of this book, I have made a decision to shift my focus away from the term as it has been applied to technology as a freestanding noun. Where the noun 'interface' is employed alone in this book,[10] after this chapter it will only be in the original, literal and general sense that predates its use and abuse at the hands of cybernetics, computer science, software design and advertising, a sense explained by the *Oxford English Dictionary* as 'A surface lying between two portions of matter or space, and forming their common boundary.'

Which brings us finally to an explanation of the title of this book. When I began writing, my title was the more straightforward *The Interface*. However, as I progressed, I came to consider this title untenable precisely because the noun 'interface' carried so much baggage of conflicting and incompatible meanings, and had to a significant degree come to represent the very antithesis of the themes I wished to explore. Finally I decided to replace the noun 'the interface' with the verb 'interfacing', which—despite ironically having its origins in the era of cybernetics and information technology but inevitably by virtue of being a verb rather than a noun—has not come to signify the same themes of fixity, isolatability and enduring physical situatedness. Also, perhaps because of its lack of amenability to this shift in the associations of the term interface, it has never been adopted widely into popular discourse, which might have shielded it from some of the conceptual torture meted out to the noun. While *an* interface has been stripped of its literal status as something that exists only in relation to other things, *to* interface, as a transitive verb, must always acknowledge the other things it exists in relation to.

Certainly, the ever-growing capacity for autonomy in the operation of digital devices suggests that this attribution of separate agency dividing machine from user is natural and inevitable. But, at the same time, human beings seemingly have a natural and inevitable capacity to develop intimate and productive relationships with artefacts, and the history of digital devices shows a movement towards ever-closer physical engagements with them, in which they come to seem less and less like interlocutors or autonomous agents and more and more like extensions of our own bodies and an integrated part of our capacity to act and experience the world around us.

The addition of screens to computers, and then the appearance of the graphical user interface, were key developments in the propagation of digital devices throughout society. But the impact of these developments has led to an untenable dependence on analogies between user interfaces and older technologies of visual representation in how they have been explained and theorised. Even where attempts are made to engage with emerging frameworks that seek to replace or supplement the visual with other senses (such as gesture, for example), frameworks derived from visual representation—opacity and transparency being chief amongst them—generally continue to shape the resulting analysis. But what if we believe that 'the interface' isn't any material component of a machine or a representation of its workings, but is rather the plane of interaction where the machine and human body meet? What if we see it as a field of potentiality that hovers over certain surfaces of the machine, which is activated by the human body only to vanish when it withdraws? Rather than seeing user and computer as separate agents in dialogue with one another, what if we understand the computer to be an integrated part of the human capacity for action and sensory experience as long as the interface exists? Rather than user behaviour arising independently of the computer and then being translated for it, what if that behaviour arises from user and machine together? What if we move away from thinking about 'the interface' as a thing and a place, and towards thinking about 'interfacing' as an experience and a process?

As interest in understanding interfaces has grown, there has been a tendency to pay lip service to the idea that an interface is crucially about the interaction of device and user while remaining wedded to accounts that either ignore the user completely or treat the user as a fixed entity that either constrains or is constrained by the operation of the system. Focusing on the verb 'to interface' counteracts this tendency; rather than becoming bogged down in unproductive arguments concerning whether this thing called an interface is transparent or opaque, for example, it leads us rather to ask questions about how our pre-conscious incorporation of material artefacts can lead to a transformation of our capacity for action and perception.

An interface is not a discrete entity that mediates between a body and an object. Rather, it is a phenomenon generated by the coming together of two entities to produce capacities not seen in either. Interfacing, as the process that calls this phenomenon into being, alters our mode of engagement with the world by inflecting human experiences with these new capacities. It arises from the real physical attributes of bodies and artefacts, and is therefore never simply a system for representing or instantiating things external to it. The purpose of interfacing is to maintain a particular productive relationship with the environment beyond both the user and the artefact, meaning that it is defined primarily by how a particular body—machine combination engages with the world, rather than how a particular body engages with a particular machine. Our interactions with technological artefacts are always some combination of acting *on* them and acting *through* them, but our closest engagements seemingly transcend such divisions. Looked at from this perspective, to become 'as naturalized as air or as common as dirt' (Galloway, 2006, p. 25) would not be considered an unworkable failure of the interface; in fact, to consider such an experience a 'self-annihilation' (2006, p. 25) is to ignore the fact that a user interface that falls below the threshold of conscious awareness and does not function as a representation nonetheless continues to have an effect on our capacities for sensation and action and so loses none of its importance (cf. Ihde, 1983, p. 52).

When I use my hand to perform a task, the material qualities of my hand have a fundamental role in determining the nature of my actions and perceptions as I do so; however, arguing about whether a hand is experientially transparent or opaque does not get us very far—largely because it is always to some degree both, and the nature of its supposed transparency and opacity changes constantly. (Even less useful would be a discussion of what 'code' or 'language' I use to tell my hand what to do, or how my 'thoughts' are translated into my hand's 'instructions'.) The more productive question concerns what it means to act using a hand; how the nature of my engagement with my environment is shaped and determined by the physical qualities that my hand has. Of course, my hand is not a technological artefact; however, at the same time, it is a fundamental part of the nature of embodiment that hard divisions between the biological body and the world around it are impossible to draw, as we will see in the next chapter.

Notes

1. As described when applied to the marriage of astronaut and spacecraft systems in a 1969 *New Yorker* article, which the OED cites as an early use of the verb.
2. Although even virtual reality, during the first attempt at its commercialisation in the 1990s, was still described as disembodied (Ihde, 2010).
3. The relationship between computer graphics and western traditions of pictorial realism will be discussed in more detail in Chapter 3.
4. In line with the long-standing bias towards the visual in aesthetics more generally (Paterson, 2007, pp. 83–84; see Boothroyd, 2009).
5. For example, former Xerox PARC chief scientist Mark Weiser has said 'A good tool is an invisible tool. By invisible, I mean that the tool does not intrude on your consciousness; you focus on the task, not the tool' (1994, p. 7). Weiser's employment of the term 'invisible' is clearly visual in only a metaphorical sense.
6. The term 'skeuomorphism' refers to the design practice of incorporating into GUI elements (usually visual) features of the physical objects that they have replaced (for example, making a calendar application look like a physical paper calendar, or a 'trashcan' icon look like a physical wastepaper bin).
7. The Star had a predecessor, the Alto, which was never put into mass production.
8. David Canfield Smith himself can be seen explaining this scheme in this video: www.youtube.com/watch?v=_OwG_rQ_Hqw.
9. It is with this original conception of the computer user as programmer that the larger idea of the user interface as system for representing the workings of the computer arises, and it is appropriate to this relationship while

being inappropriate to the relationship between the computer and a non-programmer, for whom changes in the workings of the computer are merely a by-product of her efforts to perform a task, rather than the object of the task itself (see Utterson, 2013, p. 67).

10. By 'alone' I mean not as part of some more clearly defined term, such as 'natural user interface' or 'user interface'.

2   Where Do Bodies End and Objects Begin?

During his development of the phonograph, Thomas Edison toyed with the idea of providing the machine with a voice chamber modelled on the human mouth, complete with teeth and tongue (Wood, 2002, p. 128). While there is something grotesque and disturbing about the idea of a machine with a tongue and teeth,[1] given that Edison initially conceived of the phonograph as a machine that would be primarily concerned with reproduction of the voice (e.g. by recording telephone conversations; Johnson, 1997, pp. 145–146) rather than music or other sounds, the idea was presumably born merely of an attempt to impart the resonance of the human body to the words emerging from the device. Still, there remains a sense of redundancy: the phonograph should capture the resonance of the human speaker's body and reproduce it on command, not attempt to add resonance of its own. A phonograph with its own mouth would take the speech of a living body and subtly alter it, adding the resonance of another, fictitious body, perhaps blurring the line between reproduction and mimicry in the process. Common sense dictates that the human body does the work of imbuing the voice with the resonances of the mouth, provides the hardware of lungs and tissue, bone and cartilage; the machine merely captures and reproduces these things without editorialising or enrichment.

But the phonograph is not the only machine to have produced an initial confusion regarding how much of the human body it should replace. Friedrich von Knauss, the inventor of the first typewriter, came to the device through a series of evolutionary steps: the first four writing machines created by Knauss, between 1753 and 1760, were actually androids, reproductions of the entire human body, which did their writing with hands and arms like a living writer (Bedini, 1964, p. 39).[2] The typewriter, like the phonograph, was an attempt to replace human activity, and, as with the phonograph, there is the suggestion of an initial vagueness regarding how directly to recreate the human bodily actions upon which it was modelled, and thus how much of the human body should be replaced by the machine.

These cases might be dismissed as resulting from a past naivety regarding technology; evidence that, prior to our present intimacy with machines, people were less adept at identifying the point where machines should end and bodies begin. On the other hand, however, it might just as easily be argued that our contemporary intimacy with machines makes identifying this point more difficult than ever.

Take the following example. The spread of multi-touch user interfaces, through digital devices such as the iPhone, has resulted in numerous research projects aimed at developing haptic feedback. The great limitation of touch interfaces is that, while they free us from separate hardware inputs by allowing the user to simply touch the screen, they provide no tactile feedback, such as that which allows a touch-typist to find the correct keys with fingertips alone. Ironically, touch interfaces do not engage the user's sense of touch; but haptic feedback would allow machines to produce the missing sensory cues in response to the user's physical interactions.

Most attempts to create haptic feedback have employed methods such as vibrations or electrical or sonic fields to create sensory stimulation, but not so in the case of a haptic feedback system developed by Haruhisa Kawasaki and his colleagues at the Kawasaki and Mouri Laboratory at Gifu University. What is striking about the approach taken by this research is that it seeks to create the experience of actually exploring the shape of a solid object in space with the hand, rather than simply feeling a bump or buzz when pressing a virtual button, and to do this it employs a robotic hand, called HIRO III (Endo et al., 2011; Endo and Kawasaki, 2015; Figure 2.1). The user looks at virtual objects on a computer screen while, hidden from view, her fingertips are locked to those of the robot with magnetic thimbles. Because the robot can realistically reproduce the movement of a human hand and fingers, it can expertly shepherd the fingers of the human operator so that they move in any anatomically possible way. By miming the inverse of a human hand's movement over a specific set of contours, the robot can enforce the manual movements that would accompany contact with a physical example of the virtual object on the screen.

So just as Edison's mouthed phonograph would have reproduced the mouth of the speaker, the robot hand reproduces the hand of the toucher. Whereas robots are usually understood to be surrogate bodies, acting upon the world in place of a human being, HIRO III reverses this, acting on a human body in place of the world. It is a mirror image of the hand, which creates the sensation of interacting with illusory objects situated on the other side of the mirror.[3]

All the machines with which we interact serve—to a greater or lesser extent—to replace human action or respond to human expression or sensation. Rather than being anomalies born of a misidentification of the boundary separating body from machine, these examples can be taken to indicate the impossibility of ever fixing such a boundary. The automatism of the machine brings a sense of duplicating or replacing some of the

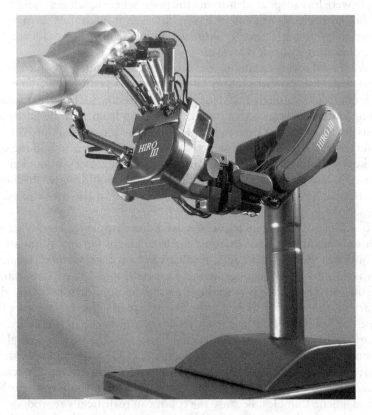

Figure 2.1 The HIRO III robotic hand
Source: Image courtesy of Professor Haruhisa Kawasaki

activity of the user's body, and hence uncertainty regarding how much duplication is appropriate. This duplication brought about by automatism is widely understood to create a sense of alienation or redundancy for the user, and yet perhaps a high degree of automatism can produce an artefact whose capacity to autonomously sense and respond to a human body instead creates intimacy and integration.

In order for the HIRO III robot to create tactile and proprioceptive sensory experiences for a human operator, the robot must itself sense the movement and resistance of the human fingers it shepherds through space. Even the humble manual typewriter creates marks that reflect the arrangement and kinetic force of human fingers—Friedrich Kittler argues that the key change that accompanies the shift from handwriting to typewriter is a move from dependence on vision to patterns of touch (1990, pp. 194–195). The intersection of body and artefact creates a plane where both are blended into a unity, where each senses and responds to the other. A human–machine interface is, by its very nature, the location of a doubling of perception and action, where these things seem to occur both at the outer limits of the body and the outer limits of the artefact. This chapter will seek to clarify the nature of our embodied relationships with technological artefacts, and make some suggestions regarding the ways in which the development of ever-more complex technological artefacts has—and might in future—alter the nature of those relationships.

Existing periodisations of an evolutionary movement towards increasingly autonomous technological artefacts tend towards a lapsarian narrative, in which our natural self-sufficiency and direct manipulation of the environment is taken away from us by our machines, and more recently it has been suggested that new digital technologies can return us to an Eden of spontaneous and direct interaction through the 'natural user interface' (NUI). If we want to understand how a certain digital user interface manifests a particular logic of action or changes our experience of the world, we need to start, not with digital technology, but by thinking about how a digital user interface fits within a larger context of interactions with technology that has been around for so long prior to digital devices that its origins predate the human species. What does this larger context tell us about the kinds of relationships it is possible for us to have with artefacts, and the ways in which it is and is not possible for our actions and perceptions to be altered by those relationships? Do digital devices possess unique qualities that can transform such relationships, or are they simply a new means of changing our experience of the world in ways as old as human history itself? Is it possible to act or perceive 'through' an artefact, and if so, how does this differ from acting and perceiving using only the bodies we were born with?

The central argument of this chapter is that, rather than being a new kind of experience produced by the Information Age—or even the Industrial Age before it—interfacing is and has always been a part of human experience. Rather than something that comes between our bodies and the other people and things around us, cutting us off from a direct experience of perception of or interaction with our environment, interfacing transforms our capacity for action and perception to produce experiences that, while they might be new or different, cannot be said to be any less direct or natural than any other. The reason for this is simply that such transformations of action and perception are themselves a foundational part of the experience of being human.[4]

Accounting for Artefacts

The understanding of the modern citizen that was formulated during the European Renaissance and Enlightenment periods is of a figure distinct and separate from both the people and objects around him; he is a free, self-determining agent and a rational mind whose body is merely a tightly controlled instrument for imposing his will upon the world (Synnott, 1992; Black, 2014, Chapter 2; Menary, 2009, pp. 31–32). There is a long tradition of seeing human beings as separate and independent from their environment, and human thoughts and experiences as insulated within the brain. From the vantage point of this tradition, the interfacing of body and artefact is a matter of little concern because there is no real possibility of it generating or influencing human experience. If human beings are seen as rational and self-contained, then artefacts are simply picked up and utilised to prosecute actions or service motivations that have already arisen inside the mind and then put down again afterwards; they are just a means to an end with no capacity to shape or influence the human user. If artefacts were credited with a capacity to shape the human user—if a man might see the world differently depending on whether he held a hammer, as suggested by the epigraph at the beginning of this book—then this would threaten the whole idea of that man as a self-determining, independent being who made free and rational decisions (concerning how to vote or what to buy, for example) that is the founding myth of our society. It would mean that how we perceive the world, how we think and act, is to some degree a product of the things around us, rather than our free, rational minds alone. As a result of this, when machines *are* credited with influence over us, this influence is often understood to erode our humanity, or rob us of our status as free, separate, self-determining citizens. Close relationships with machines are often understood to make us more machine-like.

But our embodied relationships with artefacts cannot be explained adequately by drawing a hard boundary between the body proper and the environmental features with which it interacts, or sharp contrasts between how we sense and act with objects and without. At the same time, they cannot be explained adequately by discussing the body as if it were just one more object interacting with other objects, and seeing our embodiment as simply (re)constituted by the technologies that surround it. Is there a way of talking about living bodies and technological artefacts that is sensitive to both the specificity of the human body as an organism and the specificity of the particular kinds of objects that it comes into contact with? Is it possible to give an account of the area of overlap and reversibility between bodies and machines that does not either essentialise the body and naturalise its modes of sensation and action, on one hand, or lose the specificity of the body and embodied experience, on the other?

The Natural and the Unnatural

We have been left with a legacy of thinking about human–technology relations that largely revolves around the problem of what's natural. Are relationships with technological objects unnatural, disconnecting us from an Edenic pre-technical state as self-sufficient biological organisms? Or are they rather natural, the very things that make us human? According to some accounts, the dehumanising influence of automated machinery can be contrasted with an older relationship with tools, even to the point where tools have been put forward as definitional to humanity, a part of our natural essence. However, while ostensibly opposed to one another, these two positions (technology as natural and technology as unnatural) nevertheless share an underlying logic dependent upon a common conceptualisation of both nature and the human.

The opposition between these two positions is partly illusory, a result of differing definitions of nature as much as differing understandings of the human–technology relationship. In both cases, tools and technological objects are separate from and opposed to nature, and thus disconnect human beings from nature; it's just that, in the first case, 'nature' refers to the larger nature from which humans become disconnected through technics, while in the second case, 'nature' refers to human nature, of which the employment of technics is considered a key part. However, this human nature is implicitly opposed to the larger nature referred to in the first position and thus still presented as something that sets the human species apart as radically different to and disconnected from it; as a result, the two positions are not so different after all. They both see technological objects and the human beings who use them as separate from and opposed to nature, broadly conceived; they only disagree on when and how technological objects came to bring about this separation.

André Leroi-Gourhan's account of the tool as '"exuded" by humans in the course of their evolution' (1993, p. 239) puts forward probably the best-known case for artefacts as 'natural'. In the first volume of *Technics and Time* (1998), Bernard Stiegler draws on Leroi-Gourhan to repudiate Rousseau's pre-lapsarian account of 'savage man', whose 'body is the only instrument he knows' (Rousseau, 2007, p. 23). According to Rousseau, the use of tools and machines has led to a degeneration of human physical capacities:

> The body being the only instrument that savage man is acquainted with, he employs it to different uses, of which ours, for want of practice, are incapable; and we may thank our industry for the loss of that strength and agility, which necessity obliges him to acquire . . . Give civilized man but time to gather about him all his machines, and no doubt he will be an overmatch for the savage: but if you have a mind to see a contest still more unequal, place them naked and unarmed one opposite to the other; and you will soon discover the advantage there is in perpetually having all our forces at our disposal, in being constantly prepared against all events, and in always carrying ourselves, as it were, whole and entire about us.
>
> (Rousseau, 2007, p. 23)

However, according to Leroi-Gourhan, human beings have never experienced such an Edenic existence innocent of technology, as the tool is a criterion for humanity: 'the human and the tool invent each other' (Stiegler, 1998, p. 175).

But, on closer inspection, Leroi-Gourhan's account can be seen to rely on an opposition between technological objects and 'nature' just as Rousseau's does. First, while the adoption of technics is presented as the continuation of a process of anatomical 'liberation', it is nonetheless understood to represent a break with evolution and the rest of nature that sets humanity apart. In addition, Leroi-Gourhan sees the move from tools to automated machinery as a further break, one that alienates the human being from a natural state of tool use, and the later appearance of information storage and processing as a still further alienation of the human from its natural state—this time in the cognitive or mnemonic realm rather than the manual.[5] In the words of Vilem Flusser, 'first the hand-man, then the tool-man, then the machine-man, and finally the robot-man' (Flusser, 1999, pp. 44–45).

So although Leroi-Gourhan argues that tool use is natural for human beings, he understands this fact to separate human beings from the rest of nature; and furthermore, 'natural' tools can be contrasted with automated machines, which run counter to a natural human relationship with arte-facts. According to Leroi-Gourhan, once the process of 'liberation' shifts to the use of machines, it renders the body progressively more marginal as increasingly sophisticated artefacts come to replace more and more of its powers; industrialisation fundamentally shifts our relationship with arte-facts through the introduction of objects whose autonomy from human action means that they are no longer tools. If anything, human bodies are now tools utilised by these machines.

By replacing the fine manipulations of the skilled worker with auto-mated machinery, the Industrial Age produced 'crowds of workers requir-ing no more than a five-fingered claw to feed in the material or simply an index finger to push the buttons' (Leroi-Gourhan, 1993, p. 255). Leroi-Gourhan's vision of humanity being progressively freed from the physical particularities of our bodies through 'the pursuit of life by means other than life' (Stiegler, 1998, p. 17) leads him to invoke science fiction imagery of our postindustrial descendants as foetus-like blobs, supinely poking at computer screens (Leroi-Gourhan, 1993, p. 129).

As with Rousseau, then, Leroi-Gourhan's account includes a fall from grace. Where Rousseau's Fall casts humanity from a technology-free self-sufficiency into a world where the powers of the individual are supplanted by tools and so atrophy, for Leroi-Gourhan the atrophy that turns hand back into claw occurs later and more slowly, as machines gradually render more and more of our manual skills redundant and demote us to a sup-porting role in automated industry.

This theme is hardly an invention of Leroi-Gourhan, of course. It had already been set out by Adam Smith in *The Wealth of Nations* in 1776. In fact, Smith describes the changed relationship between working body and tools under the division of labour in terms strongly reminiscent of Rousseau, complete with a contrasting characterisation of the self-sufficiency of the 'barbarous' individual, although the decline is cognitive rather than physical: the worker 'generally becomes as stupid and ignorant as it is possible for a human creature to become' (Smith, 2009, p. 461).

For Karl Marx (who quotes this passage in *Capital*, 1976, p. 483), the changes wrought by the division of labour in manufacturing are carried further by industrialisation: where the division of labour creates 'a productive mechanism whose organs are human beings' (Marx, 1976, p. 457), with industrialisation the factory is colonised by a 'mechanical monster' whose 'countless working organs' are not human beings but individual machines acting in concert (Marx, 1976, p. 503). Where for Leroi-Gourhan the tool is definitional to the human being, for Marx the tool is definitional to the machine: Marx defines the industrial machine as a device that appropriates the human worker's tools and wields them in his stead (Marx, 1976, pp. 494–495).

These various accounts of industrialisation's impoverishment of the human being's physical and intellectual powers make perfect sense from a perspective focused upon tools: Leroi-Gourhan's human being is brought into existence by her use of tools, but the creation of ever-more complex tools results in the appearance of Marx's machine, which then plucks the tool from the human being's hands and continues to labour without her, leaving the human being looking on, empty-handed and dejected, from the sidelines, literally de-humanised. In the words of Marx, 'In handicrafts and manufacture, the worker makes use of a tool; in the factory, the machine makes use of him' (Marx, 1976, p. 548).

In the original biblical narrative of the Fall, technics is a result of the Fall itself: no longer living in a state of grace, Adam and Eve and their descendants must create tools to wrest sustenance and shelter from the environment. However, as explained by Jonathan Sawday, during the Renaissance, at the dawn of modernity and mechanisation, this association between technics and the Fall could produce both a negative view of the machine as 'fundamentally at variance with the ideal of "nature", or even of God', something that 'epitomized the moment of transgression, exile and loss . . . a mark of shame' (Sawday, 2007, p. 4), and a positive view of the machine as 'a partial compensation, through God's grace, for that original punishment by which humanity was exiled from its place of origin', by which 'a partial replica of the lost paradise might be confected' (Sawday, 2007, p. 3). In the secular accounts of technology's influence on the natural human state, there can be a similar ambivalence, but in the absence of God, the machine itself tends to be the agent of humanity's downfall. To struggle against nature is itself the natural, pre-lapsarian state of humanity rather than its successor, and the arrival of the machine precipitates our descent from this into an indolent state of weakness, dehumanisation and evolutionary decline. For Rousseau, to struggle with his bare hands is the natural state of Man, and by making this unnecessary the machine robs him of his self-sufficiency and physical powers. For Marx, to wield a tool is the natural state of the autonomous worker, and the machine takes the tool from him and wields it in his place, leaving the worker as 'a mere living accessory of the machine' (1980, p. 134). For Leroi-Gourhan, to use the hands with or without a tool is humanity's natural state, and the machine renders both obsolete, putting an end to the very activities that made us human in the first place.

Tools as Human

For Leroi-Gourhan, relationships with tools can be 'natural'. But even in the case of the tool, by making it definitional to humanity, he—and, by extension, Stiegler—retain for it a status as something special, outside nature broadly conceived. The tool is part of *human* nature, but in an important sense this removes both the tool and the human from nature as a whole. While the appearance of the tool is presented as part of a larger evolutionary process of 'freeing' (dependent upon and following other physical changes such as the freeing of the hands by bipedalism), the use of tools, understood to be exclusively and quintessentially human, nevertheless represents a qualitative change in this process, a moment of rupture (Stiegler, 1998, pp. 141–142). The very language of freeing, with its suggestion of the human animal progressively liberating itself from the limitations of inherited physicality—first by reshaping its body and then by moving into the realm of culture through language and technics—suggests an underlying opposition between the natural world of biology and the development of tools and technology.

However, as with that other cherished myth of human exceptionalism, our monopoly on language, increased knowledge of other species has forced a series of retreats from the claim that our relationship with tools sets us apart. Since Jane Goodall first documented chimpanzee tool use (Goodall, 1968),[6] new examples of animal tool use have been turned up regularly, not only amongst our nearest primate relatives but amongst birds and crabs, octopi and insects; a table of documented cases compiled in 2010 runs to nearly thirty pages (Bentley-Condit and Smith, 2010, appx. A).[7] From 'man the tool user' to 'man the tool maker', and from there to a rueful acknowledgement that many other species can fabricate as well as use tools of their own, we are now in a position where tool use is no more able to mark an absolute difference between human and animal than any other criterion.

Indeed, it might be argued that any privileging of tool use, regardless of the ends it is intended to serve, will always be tainted by anthropocentric, lapsarian baggage. The categorisation of some kinds of behaviour as tool use (or tool making) originates in attempts to isolate a certain sphere of action as uniquely and exclusively human, leaving the very category under suspicion of being simply an artificial and arbitrary grouping designed to flatter and elevate human beings. While Leroi-Gourhan and Stiegler might reject the idea that human beings were ever on the non-tool-using side of the fence, they still subscribe to a belief in the fence itself, and thus maintain an implicit division between the technical world of the human and the natural world of non-human animals, who supposedly are, evolutionarily speaking, 'no more than spray from the central jet that gushes human-ward' (Leroi-Gourhan, 1993, p. 58).[8]

The widespread use of tools amongst animals is now indisputable, although amongst experts on animal behaviour there remains no universally accepted definition of what precisely constitutes tool use. While Benjamin Beck's 1980 definition of animal tool use as

> the external employment of an unattached environmental object to alter more efficiently the form, position, or condition of another object, another organism, or the user itself when the user holds or carries the tool during or just prior to use and is responsible for the proper and effective orientation of the tool
>
> (1980, p. 10)

has been influential, Beck acknowledges contentious 'borderline cases' (1980, pp. 124–133) that blur the boundaries of the category, and even amongst those who broadly agree with this definition there are often attempts to modify or improve it so that it will better map onto particular examples.[9] Can water be a tool? (Seed and Byrne, 2010, p. R1032). Would a tool really stop being a tool if you attached it to a feature of the environment with a piece of string? (St Amant and Horton, 2008, p. 1201).

The difficulty of clearly differentiating tool use from other kinds of animal behaviour generates a suspicion that it is a largely arbitrary category, produced more to serve the assumptions of human researchers than account for gathered data. In 2008, Mike Hansell and Graeme D. Ruxton presented an effective critique of the focus on tool use from the perspective of researchers of animal construction behaviour. Excluding the building of structures such as nests tends to be a key criterion for success in definitions of tool use, and yet Hansell and Ruxton highlight the distortion of values this creates. For example, much was made of the first observation of tool use amongst wild gorillas (Breuer, Ndoundou-Hockemba and Fishlock, 2005), and yet for some time previously gorillas had been known to construct sophisticated nest structures every day and to culturally transmit the skills necessary to do so. The documented tool use, which consisted of using a stick to test the depth of a stretch of water, would seem to be much less sophisticated behaviour, and yet it was understood to challenge existing beliefs concerning gorillas' cognitive abilities (Hansell and Ruxton, 2008, p. 75). More absurd, Hansell and Ruxton point to claims of beaver tool use following the observation of one animal cutting a step into a tree in order make a cut higher up its trunk. Whether or not this behaviour qualifies as tool use, the significance attributed to its discovery when beavers are already known to engage in the vastly more complex and impressive material undertaking of building dams highlights the exaggerated value placed on certain types of animal–environment interaction (Hansell and Ruxton, 2008, p. 75).

It would not be difficult to hypothesise about the cause of this privileging of more 'masculine', outwardly directed tool use associated with hunting, pounding, fighting and exploring as a marker of cognitive sophistication, and its resultant devaluing of equally (or more) complex material interactions associated with shelter and nesting, but whatever its cause, it again highlights the arbitrariness of hiving off certain kinds of interaction with the material environment from a much larger and more varied totality and treating them as the gold standard of cognitive sophistication. Clearly, when Leroi-Gourhan and Stiegler argue that the human appears with the tool, they are not simply placing tool use back into nature but are perpetuating the idea that tool use is something special, something qualitatively different from other ways of existing in the material environment, and reasserting the human exceptionalism that gave rise to a focus on tool use in the first place. The use of tools might therefore better be understood as simply one way in which living organisms interact with their environments, something that is quite widespread and part of a much larger continuum of material interaction. Human beings certainly do not have a monopoly on this kind of action, and it therefore cannot be said to define the human condition or set it apart.

According to Bentley-Condit and Smith, '[t]he definition of "tool use" is problematic, often arbitrary or subjective, sometimes anthropocentric, and open to interpretation' (2010, p. 186). Where does tool use end and a more general engagement with the world begin? If Beck's definition accepts an elephant spraying water on itself to cool off as tool use (which it does), then perhaps air can be understood as a tool animals use to gather oxygen and track prey by scent, or to manufacture the vibrations used in communication. Assuming a special relationship between humanity and tools as he does, Stiegler states that '[t]he being of humankind is to be outside itself' (1998, p. 193); however, all living organisms are to some degree outside themselves—constant exchange and interaction with the environment is a precondition for all life.

Brains and Tools

Brain research suggests that, not only do many different kinds of animals employ tools, but brains that have evolved to specialise in the employment of tools exist beyond the human—at least amongst other primates. Mirror neurons, initially identified in the brains of macaques but since shown to exist in the human brain, are neurons associated with movement, but which are activated not only by an individual's own movement but by the observed movements of others.

> In humans, as in monkeys, the sight of acts performed by others produces an immediate activation of the motor areas deputed to the organization and execution of those acts, and through this activation it is possible to decipher the meaning of the 'motor events' observed, i.e. to *understand* them in *terms of goal-centred movements*. This understanding is completely devoid of any reflexive, conceptual, and/ or linguistic mediation as it is based exclusively on the *vocabulary of acts* and the *motor knowledge* on which our capacity to act depends.
> (Rizzolatti, Sinigaglia and Anderson, 2008, p. 125)

This ability to understand the actions of others by, at a very basic level, sharing the experience of those actions, importantly comes into play in the manipulation of objects. Furthermore, just looking at an object involves a kind of perception that situates that object in the context of this 'language' of action, so that 'evoked potential motor acts categorize the "seen" object as *graspable in this* or *that manner*, with *this or that grip*, etc., endowing it with a "meaning" that it otherwise would not have had' (Rizzolatti, Sinigaglia and Anderson, 2008, p. 50).

Giacomo Rizzolatti, who led the research team that discovered the mirror neuron system, suggests that this capacity to model, understand and mimic the actions of others played a key role in human evolution (Rizzolatti, Sinigaglia and Anderson, 2008, pp. 162–163), and its likely role as a facilitator in the development of language and transmission of skills such as the use of tools is self-evident. Our very perceptual system has an evolved specialisation in acquiring, understanding and carrying out interactions with external objects that lies prior to consciousness, culture and language (although it is mediated by these things).

Clinical research also suggests that spatial perception is dependent upon an awareness of the location of different parts of our bodies and their position relative to objects in the environment, meaning that relationships with objects can alter the nature of human perception itself. The clearest example of this is the way in which perception changes depending on whether an object is 'near' or 'far' in relation to the body of the perceiver.

The division between far ('extrapersonal') space and near ('peripersonal' or 'cutaneous') space, discovered through primate brain research, is marked by the sphere of possible physical interaction (Gallese and Lakoff, 2005, p. 460; Rizzolatti, Sinigaglia and Anderson, 2008, p. 64). That is to say, peripersonal space is 'the area of space reachable by body parts' (Gallese and Lakoff, 2005, p. 459), which is perceived differently precisely because it is understood in terms of the possible movements and interactions that might take place within it. This establishes that

> space takes its form initially from the objects and the numerous coordinated acts that allow us to reach out to them. It follows that objects are simply *hypotheses of action* and therefore places in space cannot be interpreted as 'objective positions' in relation to an equally alleged objective position of the body, but must be understood, as Merleau-Ponty pointed out, in their 'marking, in our vicinity, the varying range of our aims and our gestures'. This range dictates our possibility of distinguishing between peripersonal as opposed to extrapersonal space and of understanding the dynamic nature of the boundary that separates one from the other.
>
> (Rizzolatti, Sinigaglia and Anderson, 2008, p. 77)

How we interact with our environment is therefore foundational to our perception, and other research has demonstrated that the use of tools is itself a component of this perception of space.

The brain activity of Japanese macaques trained to reach for objects with small rakes demonstrates that, when using a tool for reaching, the limits of peripersonal space are extended to account for the increased reach allowed by the tool. In other words, the tool is incorporated into the body schema of the monkey, changing basic perceptions of distance and environmental relations.

This influence is fundamental enough that individuals with brain lesions that interfere with one or other kind of spatial perception will gain or lose the capacity to spatially process an object as it moves nearer to them or farther away. An experiment by Anna Berti and Francesca Frassinetti centred on a subject who, following a stroke, had an impaired perception of peripersonal space, meaning that she could not process spatial information about locations within reaching distance of her body. While she was able to indicate a location a certain distance away from herself as being the answer to a question using a light pen, she was unable to do the same thing with a stick. The reason for this would seem to be that her peripersonal space expanded to encompass the stick, encroaching into the area in question and thus impairing her ability to perceive it.

> Based on . . . the assumption that the human brain is equipped in a similar way as the monkey brain, our data can be explained as follows. When the patient used the stick to reach for the object of interest in far space, the tool was coded as part of the patient's hand,

as in monkeys, causing an expansion of the representation of the body schema. This affected the spatial relation between far space and the body. The structure of peripersonal space was then altered and peripersonal space was expanded to include the far space reachable by the tool.

(Berti and Frassinetti, 2000, p. 418)

What these examples from brain research suggest is that our relationship with objects and artefacts arises from having innate, evolved abilities that facilitate the understanding, learning and execution of interactions with objects, and our very sense of our own bodily boundaries and sphere of action can gather tools into itself in order to facilitate their use in a direct, unreflective manner. At the same time, however, these abilities are not exclusively human, and probably not a prerequisite for the use of tools; they have been shown to be present in apes and monkeys, but it seems highly unlikely that a digger wasp employs them when it uses a pebble to work the earth around its burrow. Nonetheless, these innate abilities, highly developed in human beings, must at least be a factor in our more extensive and intimate relationships with artefacts, allowing objects to temporarily function as if they were part of our bodies. When we take them into account, the difficulty of identifying a point where body ends and object begins becomes even greater, as it shows that our facility with tools arises from an ability to dynamically shift this boundary.

Tools and Machines

Tools do not mark a point of rupture with non-human nature any more than they do with Rousseau's human nature; but the physical properties of those objects with which humans interact have changed dramatically over time, from stone tools to the tools of the master craftsman to automated machinery and digital user interfaces. The differing modes of interaction facilitated by these various artefacts must have produced important changes in our embodied relationships with them, and thus our field of action and perception when using them. We have already seen that Leroi-Gourhan's account of the development of technics differentiates tools from machines, and non-human animals do not build machines, nor presumably have human beings evolved specialised machine-using capacities.

I have already thrown the specificity of the tool into some doubt; but what about this implicit further differentiation between a tool and a machine? Although most people probably have an instinctive sense of what falls into which category, the key definitional qualities of each—an artefact directly employed by the hand, for the former, and an artefact designed to achieve a particular purpose, for the latter[10]—are not mutually exclusive, and as machines have become smaller and more tightly integrated into various kinds of work and interaction, the amount of overlap between the two has increased. Certainly a machine can be a tool, and our everyday sense of which term to apply to a given artefact (e.g. most people would identify a hammer as a tool and a smartphone as a machine) would seem to result from evaluating it against several sets of opposing terms and plumping for the side the answers fall on most often. The key oppositions would seem to be human-powered–self-powered, non-autonomous–autonomous, and simple–complex.

However, attempts to draw more final and significant distinctions between tools and machines suggest a larger, phenomenological difference between the two. A clear differentiation of tool and machine is crucial to both Leroi-Gourhan's and Marx's accounts of human action, and their drawing of this harder distinction suggests that the reason why no clear and final differentiation can be drawn based on the physical properties of a given artefact is that the difference lies in the experience of *using* the artefact, rather than the artefact itself. Therefore, qualities like complexity or autonomy can change the experience of use in ways that contribute to a more tool-like or machine-like experience, but the ultimate difference lies in the net experience produced by these various factors in combination rather than any single one in isolation.[11] By implication, therefore, there can be more tool-like machines and more machine-like tools depending on the balance of these factors, as suggested by Martin Heidegger's description of the typewriter as 'an "intermediate" thing, between a tool and a machine' (in Kittler, 1999, p. 200).

The key phenomenological quality of the tool is, of course, its Heideggerian 'handiness' (Heidegger, 1996, p. 65). For both Leroi-Gourhan and Marx, the machine refuses this kind of direct engagement with the artefact and, through it, with the world. The machine operator's actions might be more or less harmoniously integrated with the industrial machine, but the machine nonetheless remains the object of the operator's attention and actions; the tool user contrastingly experiences the tool as simply extending her range of actions towards something beyond it.

> Handiness is not grasped theoretically at all, nor is it itself initially a theme for circumspection. What is peculiar to what is initially at hand is that it withdraws, so to speak, in its character of handiness in order to be really handy.
>
> (Heidegger, 1996, p. 65)

In this context, at least, the term 'handy' is better than 'ready-to-hand'[12] because the latter explicitly sets out a relationship between the artefact and the hand (which it makes itself available to). 'Handy' blurs the distinction between the two terms by taking the name of one as the root of the adjective used to describe the other. This is appropriate because what Heidegger is describing is the quality of *being like a hand*. This becomes immediately apparent if we alter the previous quote to make the hand its subject:

> [The hand] is not grasped theoretically at all, nor is it itself initially a theme for circumspection. What is peculiar to . . . [the] hand is that it withdraws, so to speak, in its character of handiness in order to be really handy.

This special quality of withdrawal is most notably present not in tools but in our own bodies. The title of Drew Leder's book *The Absent Body* (1990) derives from this principle whereby '[t]he body conceals itself precisely in the act of revealing what is Other' (1990, p. 22), and this aspect of embodiment is central to Merleau-Ponty's phenomenology:

> In so far as it sees or touches the world, my body can therefore be neither seen nor touched. What prevents its ever being an object, ever being 'completely constituted' is that it is that by which there are objects. It is neither tangible nor visible in so far as it is that which sees and touches.
>
> (Merleau-Ponty, 2002, p. 105)

Of course, neither body nor tool can simply disappear from our experience, but they are both still characterised by their ability to recede from our experience while remaining constitutive of that experience. Insofar as this quality can be discerned in tools, then, it is there simply as a consequence of our using tools as if they were themselves part of our own bodies.

This relationship with the body can serve to bring tools back into focus as a discrete category of things. And the capacity to unreflectively employ tool-like objects is most crucially a result of a seamless sensory connection with the object. While most obviously 'the stick is no longer an object perceived by the blind man, but an instrument *with* which he perceives' (Merleau-Ponty, 2002, p. 175), the handiness of the hammer arises from a similar sensory relationship. This sensory connection need not function simply as a conduit for perception of the external world, but can also function as a mechanism to facilitate the body–artefact assemblage's action in the world. The knowledge of how much force a hammer blow requires arises from a sensing, through the body of the hammer, of the nail's resistance; the ability to focus attention on the nail, unconcerned by questions regarding the hammer's position in space, results from the hammer sharing in the unconscious awareness of spatial positioning we have with regard to our hands and feet. This sensory relationship with the tool can be explained as the tool's incorporation into the body schema, but the specificity of the sensory basis of this relationship must be explained in terms of proprioception.

The extension of our sensory reach through a tool can potentially engage any of our senses, but the extension of any sense through the tool and out into the environment requires the primary engagement of a proprioceptive relationship with the tool itself. Proprioception, our sense of the position of our own body in space (Gallagher, 2005, pp. 43–47), is what allows our bodies to recede from conscious awareness while we are focused on the goals of our actions; I can catch a ball because I can direct all of my attention at the ball rather than having to simultaneously worry about where my hand is and how it will intercept the ball. Similarly, a blind person using a cane can sensorially engage with the world through the cane because she does not need to concentrate on where the cane is—she has an immediate and pre-conscious understanding of her distance from an obstacle struck by the end of the cane because the qualities of the cane itself require no consideration or calculation.

So tool use can be understood, not as demonstrating the uniqueness of either human beings or certain kinds of objects, but rather as part of a larger context of how living things engage with their physical environments. Rather than focusing on tools' physical properties, we can take them as exemplary of a certain kind of bodily engagement with objects.[13] Ironically, while tool use has traditionally been seen as a marker of humanity's greater cognitive prowess and capacity for conscious planning and reflection, this mode of bodily engagement is actually differentiated by its independence from conscious reflection. While a gorilla's shelter might be more sophisticated and require more thought and planning than its use of a stick to test water depth, the gorilla does not have a direct sensory relationship with the shelter equivalent to its experience of using the stick. The stick is incorporated into the sensorium, and for it to be useful the gorilla must have a direct sense of a relationship of scale between the extension of the stick and the dimensions of its own body.

While breathing and talking; spraying water on oneself to keep cool and building a shelter; or using a rock as an artificial fist and operating a smartphone, are clearly different activities in important ways, the differences do not ultimately arise from whether they utilise features of the environment or innate features of the living body. Rather they depend most importantly on the degrees of agency and attention associated with their productive occurrence. Breathing occurs without conscious direction or intention; speaking and pounding with a rock occur with intention but little or no conscious direction (I [and presumably an ape] do not plot the trajectory of rock to nut, but simply harbour an intention to smash the nut and leave it to non-conscious processes to bring this about); building a shelter, operating a smartphone and spraying water (at least for me; I do not know how intuitive it is for an elephant) require both intention and a substantial degree of conscious direction. In other words, these various activities are defined more by the modes of engagement with one's body or environment they entail than by whether they employ features of the environment, or the physical properties of those features.

Automatism and Autonomy

A tool is therefore an object that can be absorbed into the body schema of its user. As exemplified by Heidegger's hammer (1996, pp. 64–65) and Merleau-Ponty's cane as utilised by the blind (2002, pp. 165–166, 175–176), certain objects can be gathered into our sense of the limits and capacities of our bodies so effectively that they become a part of the direct, unreflective capacity for action usually associated with our own limbs. As pointed out by Lewis Mumford in the 1930s, this quality can in some ways, and ironically, make tool use more automatic than automatic machinery:

> The difference between tools and machines lies primarily in the degree of automatism they have reached: the skilled tool-user becomes more accurate and more automatic, in short, more mechanical, as his originally voluntary motions settle down into reflexes, and on the other hand, even in the most completely automatic machine, there must intervene somewhere . . . the conscious participation of a human agent.
>
> (1963, p. 10)

But what of the machines that Leroi-Gourhan, Marx and others contrast with tools? This contrast between the direct, embodied relationship with the tool and the awkward, servile and disjointed relationship with the machine is implicit in their accounts, but to what degree do machines really refuse the close relationships described previously, and resist the cognitive and perceptual capacities human beings and other animals have evolved to make use of artefacts in a tightly articulated way? I would argue that the nature of automated machinery—and consequently our relationship with it—has changed in important ways since the times in which these authors were writing.

There is a difference between the rigidity of the machines of the Industrial Age and the flexibility of those machines considered most representative of contemporary technology, machines that are more ubiquitous and seek to insinuate themselves more comprehensively into human habits. While the machines of the factory, according to Marx or Leroi-Gourhan, marginalise the human user, demoting her to an onlooker or helper at the margins of an automated system, the consumer electronics of the Information Age seek to integrate both their form and their function into the everyday habits of a human user. These devices still change the nature of work and the bodily habits of their operators, but they do so at a finer grain, and, because they are no longer tied to the specialised environment of the factory or office, the user is never (or almost never) free of them. Rather than the worker being required to operate in a factory that is a space tailored to the function of machines, the information-processing device has been tailored to the functioning of the human user, and tends to breach divisions between spaces of work, recreation and social interaction.

While human–machine interfaces have existed for centuries, it is no accident that the term 'interface' only became a household word on the heels of the introduction of the personal computer. While the autonomy of personal digital devices is even greater than that of the industrial machine, this greater autonomy allows them more flexibility and experiential transparency; where the industrial machine's autonomy made it an intractable, inhuman entity that left little room for human bodily actions or habits, the information-processing device's autonomy allows it to pre-empt the needs and mimic the habits of its user while hiding its functioning away behind a readily manipulable exterior. These devices call for a user with more than Leroi-Gourhan's 'five-fingered claw'; their autonomy is employed to give the appearance of responding directly and transparently to the fine manipulation of a human body—in other words, to seem more like tools.

It seems clear that this development was not foreseen by writers on technology working in the mid-twentieth century. At that time, automation was coming to the factory, raising 'the specter of joblessness and propertylessness in the electric age' (McLuhan, 1964, p. 357) as an army of blue-collar workers became redundant.[14] Certainly, Leroi-Gourhan's account of automation contains within it an assumption that it necessarily leads to the redundancy of the human body, which is progressively excised from the world of work as machines become more self-sufficient. What he and others at the time could not have foreseen was the arrival of interactive computing (see Chapter 5).

In 1960, Joseph Licklider called for a shift in the goals of human–computer interaction research, away from automation towards 'man–computer symbiosis' (2003). His justification was simple: while it might one day be possible to create computer systems that could operate independently of human workers as effectively as many industrial machines did on the factory floor, that day was clearly a long way off; until it arrived, the aim should be to create the most productive possible interactions between computer and worker rather than replacing one with the other.

> Computing machines can do readily, well, and rapidly many things that are difficult or impossible for man, and men can do readily and well, though not rapidly, many things that are difficult or impossible for computers. That suggests that a symbiotic cooperation, if successful in integrating the positive characteristics of men and computers, would be of great value.
>
> (Licklider, 2003, p. 77)

The resulting shift in thinking led, not to the abandonment of automation, but rather to the development of machines whose automation is directed towards, not doing the work once done by human bodies, but rather making the human body itself the object of their work. Matching the contours of the human body or fitting snugly into a pocket; sensing the touch of a human finger or responding to a human voice; or perhaps even recognising the expressions of a human face or following the focus of a human gaze—their automated systems, rather than rendering the human body meaningless, are meaningless without it.

At the opening of this chapter, I presented the example of the HIRO III robot, which is notable precisely because it reinterprets the idea of the robot, reversing the traditional understanding of the robot as something that moves independently of a human body with the result that its movements become meaningless *without* a human body. Robotics' project of studying and simulating the movement of human anatomy is here not directed towards replacing the human hand, but rather towards integrating seamlessly *with* the human hand, creating a kind of mechanical shadow whose shape and movements only become meaningful and useful when twinned to its living model. This neatly illustrates the two sides of autonomous technology: the autonomy of the artefact can either draw it away from the body of a human user or draw it into greater intimacy.

The very success of the process that automated the factory and rendered many of its workers redundant has meant that the role of industrial machines is now largely invisible to us. The emblematic contemporary technology user is not the worker enslaved by a factory machine, or even Jean Baudrillard's media consumer sealed inside her home like an astronaut in a space capsule, tethered to the television set (1988); rather, it's a highly mobile figure, accompanied by attentive digital devices as she strides through multifarious spaces without restriction.

The Eden of the Interface

The design of contemporary digital user interfaces can be seen as motivated precisely by a desire to return us to a more 'natural' and intuitive mode of interaction with technological artefacts that the machines of the Industrial Age took away. Periodisations of the history of HCI move from the command line interface, in which commands are typed into the machine, to the graphical user interface, and place us at the threshold of the era of the NUI, or 'natural user interface', which is expected to replace the outmoded and restrictive conventions of the GUI.

NUI was popularised in the first decade of the twenty-first century as a term drawing together a variety of new input technologies (such as speech, gesture and touch) under a broad philosophy of intuitive control free from a need for specialised skills. The following quote is indicative of a widespread belief in the desirability and inevitability of the NUI amongst those involved in interface design:

> A natural user interface or 'NUI' seeks to harness the power of a much wider breadth of communication modalities which leverage skills people gain through traditional physical interaction.
>
> Much in the same way the graphical user interface (GUI) was a leap forward for computer users from command line interfaces, natural user interfaces in all of their various forms will become a common way we interact with computers. The ability for computers and human beings to interact in diverse and robust ways, tailored to the abilities and needs of an individual user, will release us from the current constraints of computing allowing for complex interaction with digital objects in our physical world.
>
> (Liu, 2010, p. 204)

NUI has become a technological buzzword, although it is certainly not without its critics (e.g. Norman, 2010), and even amongst its supporters it remains unclear precisely what attributes might qualify as natural in an NUI (George and Blake, 2010, p. 2). In general terms, however, there is a belief that natural user interfaces should 'build upon users' pre-existing knowledge of the everyday, non-digital world and hence lead to a more natural and reality-based interaction' (König, Rädle and Reiterer, 2009, p. 4562); even where the term 'NUI' is not used, a belief that the design of new user interfaces should be informed by such aims is pervasive.

Terms such as 'invisible', 'spontaneous' and 'innate' are often utilised in descriptions of the NUI. The user interface's characterisation as 'natural' suggests that control of the machine should 'come naturally' to the user; rather than the user conforming to a set of conventions and principles produced by the machine, the machine is expected to conform to conventions and principles already familiar to the user from other forms of interaction.

The most obvious means of realising this goal is to make the operation of the interface mimic interaction with other features of the user's environment; as a result, the digital representations produced by the machine should behave as if they were physical features of the world upon which the user might act. This would seem to fit with the suggestion from the neuroscience research cited earlier that we have a 'natural' way of engaging with the objects around us.

> The interface is seen only as a *simulacrum of reality*, seamlessly integrated into surrounding reality . . . The objective of the framework is to let people spontaneously interact with digital objects as they do with real ones; to achieve this, *digital objects must appear and behave like real ones*.
>
> (Valli, 2007, p. 6)

Where the industrial machine as characterised by Marx and Leroi-Gourhan takes away our humanity through its requirement that we change to accommodate it and the larger systems to which it belongs, then, the NUI promises to reinstate the 'natural' mode of action machines have previously taken away from us. We will interact with our environment using our natural faculties of manipulation, gesture and speech, for example, although this 'natural' mode of action will rely upon an environment that is itself a technological fabrication, a digital Eden composed of complex technological artefacts able to mimic the properties of 'natural', non-technological, physicality.

However, the idea of making interaction more natural by mimicking physical objects and the existing gestures and movements of the user introduces the possibility of a closed circularity. Many of the physical objects with which we currently interact, and which shape the range of movements that are familiar to us, are themselves machines, which have their own human–machine interfaces. Therefore, the 'natural' modes of interaction appealed to by the NUI will in many cases simply be older forms of human–machine interaction; furthermore, the older kinds of machines responsible for those kinds of interaction are likely to have been far more rigid and constrained in the range of human interaction made possible by them, as they lacked the flexibility and simulationary abilities of recent digital technologies. The 'natural' way of interacting bodily with technology a NUI seeks to complement might actually have developed in response to the physical particularities of some older technological device, which will be superseded by the NUI and thus fall from use; ironically, once this has happened, the feeling of this interaction being natural would be entirely a result of the user's familiarity with the NUI itself. As with other kinds of technology, the user's sense of what is natural or intuitive would be created by the interaction of body and machine, rather than arising from the user's body independently of the machine.

The natural user interface, then, seeks to replace the alienated, machine-centric world of the Industrial Age with a new state of nature, in which we can act in a natural, spontaneous way rather than having to work within the constraints and conventions of machines. However, it would do this by creating a new nature out of machines. Rather than some romantic escape from technology, it means creating new machines that can naturalise themselves by virtue of having user interfaces that seem wholly determined by our existing habits. It might therefore be considered a conservative movement rather than a progressive one. The reason why we interact with old-fashioned telephones in the way we do is that the unavoidable physical properties of the machine give us no other option; the reason why one might open an avenue for verbal communication using a NUI by making the 'hang loose' sign, with a pinkie finger at one's mouth and a thumb at one's ear, or activate an 'invoked computing' telecommunication system by putting a banana to the side of one's head (Price, 2012),[15] is simply because these gestures are reminiscent of using an old-fashioned telephone. Such gestural interfaces seem destined to become a trash heap for actions once mandated by obsolete machines, compelling us to continue miming our interactions with the machines of the Industrial Age long after they have disapppeared.

The NUI therefore results from the mischaracterisation of user interfaces discussed in the previous chapter. Rather than being something that appears spontaneously through interaction between machine and body, the NUI becomes something 'given' by the machine to a body that is understood to be a fixed externality, an intractable set of external variables that the machine must accommodate. Ironically, this reverses Marx's characterisation of the relationship between human body and machine: the human body becomes the rigid system that the machine must modify its behaviour to complement.

Of course, all the natural user interface really can aspire to is 'feeling natural', rather than 'being natural'. But to what extent can our interactions with technological artefacts feel natural? Even when looking at the research into our perceptual relationship with tools discussed previously, it would be a mistake to see this as establishing the existence of some set, innate, natural mode of interaction with tools to which a natural user interface can be tailored. Rather, such research highlights the flexibility and adaptability of our evolved relationship with objects, not their predictability and quantifiability.

An attempt to create a mode of interaction that is 'transparent' while ignoring both the degree to which our current baseline motor skills are not given, but are themselves created through previous interactions with artefacts and objects, and precludes the development of a more skilled, acquired capacity to use new artefacts, could only impoverish our future opportunities for interaction with our material environment. The idea of creating an interface that uses 'natural' gestures, or even gestures that at least feel natural, is highly problematic. After all, the 'handiness' of Heidegger's hammer does not arise from the fact that hammering nails is a 'natural' human activity. A violin player does not produce music from her instrument using natural gestures transplanted from some other sphere of action; nor do these gestures feel natural when a violin student first begins to play, or quickly and easily come to seem so. The gestures required to play the violin are highly unnatural, dictated largely by the physical properties of the instrument rather than the player's existing habits of movement, and yet the final level of habituated, naturalised interaction between expert player and instrument is very high. But for this to happen, the brains of violin players must actually change, increasing the cortical representation of those digits used for fingering (Elbert et al., 1995). While it might not be considered reasonable to create new user interfaces that require users' brains to change before they can be effectively used, user interfaces currently in use already must require this to some extent, given that the basic motor capacities applied to them are presumably developed through the learning of other skills such as writing.

In fact, any mode of interaction that employs the fingers individually, such as playing musical instruments or typing, is an 'unnatural' movement that can be learnt only through slow habituation. The human hand has evolved for grasping using all its fingers simultaneously; when we move one finger individually, we do so not by willing that one finger to move, but rather by willing the hand to grasp while simultaneously willing the other four fingers of that hand to stay still.[16] Clearly, a digital user interface that did not make use of individual finger movements would be much less sophisticated than one that did; however, we only know that complex movements of individual fingers can become part of our habituated repertoire of gestures because they have been necessitated by our use of older tools and devices, objects whose physical characteristics required human operators to modify their bodily habits and abilities to accommodate them. A 'natural' user interface would be one that sought to reflect only the movements of a hypothetical 'natural' human body, rather than being produced by a negotiation between the potentials of both body and artefact. If the NUI approach had informed the design of technology throughout history, presumably orchestras would contain only percussion instruments that can be played with a gripped stick, and car horns that can be played by squeezing a rubber bulb, rather than sophisticated instruments that require their players to alter the capacities of their own bodies in order to operate them.

The touch-typist's relationship with the keyboard, the blind person's relationship with the cane or the pianist's relationship with the piano keys are not natural; the only thing that is natural is the human capacity to incorporate objects and artefacts in new ways. In each case, the human is presented with an artefact that must be absorbed into the body schema. This process of absorption might be more or less easy, more or less time-consuming, but ultimately the absorption can be almost complete, leaving almost no phenomenological seam where the two entities have been joined. Such a process obviously cannot take place for every kind of artefact—an object's physical properties must fall within the field of habituated gestures possible for a human body—but the human body is highly adaptable, and there is a dizzying array of such novel gestures that have arisen throughout the performance of music, the playing of sports, the piloting of vehicles, expert craftsmanship and more. The natural user interface seeks to end this evolution of human habit and gesture, freezing it in time by utilising only those gestures already available. At most, new gestures that can be quickly and easily mastered would be added, but no new equivalent to typing or playing a violin or even writing could arise. Doug Engelbart's approach to human–computer interaction, which contributed more than anything else to the establishment of the digital user interface as we know it today, was fundamentally informed by a desire to produce new capacities for the user through an expert relationship with the system, rather than simply appropriating habits from elsewhere. However, it was for this very reason that his influence waned, as PARC and later commercial interests wanted something unintimidating that could be picked up straight away by an unskilled user (Moggridge, 2007, pp. 35–37), and it is this 'user-friendly' tradition that has provided the underlying assumptions of natural user interface development.

Thinking Outside the Skin

To fully understand our relationships with technological objects, then, it's not enough just to have a framework of understanding that reflects the foundation of these relationships in innate, evolved capacities. We also need to account for the degree to which human bodily habits and the physical properties of artefacts work to shape one another, and how our relationships with technological artefacts consequently shift over time in response to technological change.

Probably the most influential attempt to explain the complexity of our relationships with and dependence on technological objects to date has been the extended cognition thesis, introduced by Andy Clark and David Chalmers in the late twentieth century (Clark and Chalmers, 1998). This approach argues that cognition should not be understood as something that simply happens 'inside the head', but rather incorporates external resources. A classic example is how we play Scrabble: rather than expending mental resources on holding mental representations of the letters in our heads while we compare them to a mental list of words they might create, we simply move our letter tiles around in front of our eyes and see if any of the resulting combinations are useful (Clark, 2001, pp. 36–39, 63–67).

> Our brains make the world smart so that we can be dumb in peace! Or, to look at it another way, it is the human brain plus these chunks of external scaffolding that finally constitutes the smart, rational inference engine we call mind. Looked at that way, we are smart after all—but our boundaries extend further out into the real world than we might have initially supposed.
>
> (Clark, 1997, p. 180)

Abaci, notepads and pens, smartphones—once you start looking, it is easy to find examples of how external artefacts come to be, not simply implements that we pick up in order to execute plans wholly developed in our heads, but part of the process of planning and problem-solving itself. Even a humble umbrella can become integrated into human memory and planning if it is left by the front door as a reminder to take it out with you in case it rains.

Rather than being something abstract and stable, the extended cognition thesis suggests that our capacity for thought can change its character and capacities as material culture itself changes over time, and Clark notes the significance this has for the continuing development of intimate relationships between human beings and automated and personalised technological artefacts:

> New waves of user-sensitive technology will bring this age-old process to a climax, as our minds and identities become ever more deeply enmeshed in a non-biological matrix of machines, tools, props, codes, and semi-intelligent daily objects. We humans have always been adept at dovetailing our minds and skills to the shape of our current tools and aids. But when those tools and aids start dovetailing back—when our technologies actively, automatically, and continually tailor themselves to us just as we do to them—then the line between tool and user becomes flimsy indeed . . . As our worlds become smarter and get to know us better and better, it becomes harder and harder to say where the world stops and the person begins.
>
> (Clark, 2003, p. 7)

However, talk of a 'climax' suggests a teleological development towards ever-greater human–object integration that can reach some ultimate endpoint of perfect and harmonious union. To what degree is it actually the case that, not only have artefacts always been a part of who we are, but it's actually getting harder to say where the world stops and the person begins? What specific attributes of specific technologies are enabling this, and how will we change as we approach and then attain this 'climax'?

Such work on extended cognition, I would argue, has little to say in answer to such specific or speculative questions. The reason for this is that, while the extended cognition thesis hinges on a belief in a human capacity to integrate external resources into cognition, it doesn't have much to say about *how* or *why* this integration works. An explanation for this lies in the very name extended *cognition*. While this approach might reject a traditional Cartesian belief in cognition as something that happens in a realm of thought disconnected from the physical environment, the fact remains that the term cognition itself has an abstractness and immateriality about it. That is, when I shuffle Scrabble tiles around, I am not converting the tiles into cognition, nor is cognition reaching out of my head to absorb the tiles. Cognition can't literally reach out into the world along the lines of the figurative language utilised by Clark and others. If I want to reach out into the world I need to use my hand.

In fact, as a loosely allied set of ideas that fall under the broad heading of embodied or extended cognition have taken root, internal divisions have become more apparent amongst them (see Kiverstein and Clark, 2009), and more recently Clark has sought to distance himself from those who see his work as supporting a strong focus on the role of embodiment (Clark, 2008a, 2008b, Chapter 9). For example, he explicitly rejects 'cognitive body-centrism' (Kiverstein and Clark, 2009, p. 2), arguing that, for extended cognition, the capacities of the extended assemblage of body and environment are what matter, not the physical attributes of the individual bodies that go into them.

In support of this, he has presented the case of three hypothetical characters, Adder, Ada and Odder, who are engaged in 'complex accounting' (Clark, 2008a, 2008b, p. 203). Adder is a snakelike creature who performs its calculations by wriggling over 'an advanced touch-screenlike environment' and receiving feedback via a Braille-like tactile system; Ada is a regular human accountant who performs her calculations using a pen and paper; and Odder is a being who can simply perform all the necessary mental calculations without external resources. In each case, Clark feels himself able 'to assert that the very same cognitive routines are being implemented, with nothing distinguishing the cases apart from some nonessential matters of location' (2008b, p. 203). Clark is therefore not only arguing that the specificity of embodiment itself has no necessary significance, but also that interfacing has no necessary significance: Adder's 'wriggling' haptic user interface, Ada's interfacing with pen and paper and Odder's lack of interfacing all equate to the same thing.

It seems significant to me that Clark's thought experiment takes mathematical calculation as the 'problem' being solved by these three entities. Clark is taking mathematics as something with an invariant, objective relationship to external reality; if the activities of Adder, Ada and Odder all result in the conclusion that two plus two equals four, then for Clark this establishes the equivalence of their various cognitive assemblages, even if their bodies, brains and equipment are different. But even amongst those happy to accept that mathematics is a purely abstract, contextless form of objective information independent of the specificity of embodied perception and experience, it must still be accepted that this makes it importantly different from the vast majority of what occupies human thought, rather than representative of it. The understanding of cognition underlying Clark's account of cognitive extension can be contrasted with N. Katherine Hayles's account of the 'cognitive nonconscious' (2017, pp. 47–49), a term that captures those parts of cognition that exist beyond the kind of planned, abstract reasoning or symbol processing that Clark universalises through his accountancy example, but can similarly spread across assemblages of biological bodies and technological artefacts.

Even in the case of mathematics, of course, the conclusion that two plus two equals four does not capture the entirety of what is happening, and Clark's account is worryingly free from any acknowledgement of the external, material influences on cognition that the extended cognition thesis purports to focus on. For example, what exactly is the format of the mathematics being done? Europeans replaced Roman numerals with Arabic numerals because Arabic numbers aided calculation when arranged on the page in the columnar layout presumably used by Ada the accountant with her pen and paper. If her ability to perform the required calculations would change depending on whether Ada was using Roman numerals or Arabic, is it really plausible to claim that there would be no significant difference between writing Arabic numerals and limblessly wriggling on a touchscreen? (cf. Bryant, 2014, pp. 86–87).[17]

Don Ihde and others have remarked on the ways in which different writing technologies change the nature of writing itself: handwriting encourages the writer to formulate expression before committing it to the page, and to proceed at a deliberate, careful pace, for example, while a word processor encourages the writer to rapidly commit words and ideas as they arise, then edit and modify them later (Ihde, 1990, pp. 141–142). Friedrich Nietzsche, the first philosopher to use a typewriter, believed that 'Our writing tools are also working on our thoughts' (cited in Kittler, 1999, p. 200). Comparing this to Clark's example, we can first see that writing cannot be reduced to invariant right and wrong answers like mathematics, and the pieces of writing produced through these different body–artefact articulations are likely to be different from one another because they have caused the writer to develop and explore ideas in different ways. But we can also extrapolate back to the different kinds (or lack) of interfacing in Clark's account and suggest that for Odder, who can presumably perform calculations in a seemingly effortless way as a result of his innate mathematical abilities, accounting has a status very different from its status for Adder, for whom calculations require a laborious exertion of his entire body. For Odder, the practice of mathematics is perhaps similar to speech for us: it requires no external tools or conscious effort, and so is casual, playful and constant; Odder perhaps likes to toy with 'risky' speculative and untried ways of doing accounting because the investment of effort and punishment for failure are low. For Adder, on the other hand, while it can shift cognitive load onto a machine, the time and physical effort required to enter information into that machine would encourage it to nonetheless do some of the preliminary calculation and problem-solving in its head rather than proceeding through an exhausting process of experimentation and trial and error. Adder is likely to be tentative, cautious and conservative in its accounting practices, making Adder's style of mathematics very different to Odder's. Mathematics is a practice, not a piece of information, and it is manifested as different practices in each case, even if the same result is arrived at.

The extended cognition account implicitly requires a human interfacing with external objects and resources, but it doesn't account for that interfacing. Clark's approach, which he has called 'extended functionalism' (Kiverstein and Clark, 2009), explicitly rejects the idea that the material qualities of the human body affect cognition, but it also implicitly rejects the idea that the material qualities of objects utilised in cognition can affect it into the bargain. An abacus or smartphone can only play a role in human problem-solving if it has been integrated into a human capacity for action and perception through a productive relationship with the human body. The examples given by Clark are dependent on artefacts interacting productively with the operation of human senses, or the physical specificity of the human body and its movements, rather than being directly integrated into some immaterial 'cognitive routine', but Clark's approach presents objects and bodies as no more than functions that can be combined interchangeably to produce correct outputs.

Without some framework for understanding the underlying physical relationships, it's possible to list many examples of extended cognition—with beads, sticky notes, buildings, knots in handkerchiefs and who knows what else—but it isn't really possible to give a detailed account of how one artefact or practice brings cognitive extension about and another doesn't, or how one case might be more successful than or produce different results from another (cf. Ihde, 2011b, p. 376). It is also not really possible to imagine a future technology and evaluate its amenability to these kinds of relationships—I think this inability to analyse the material specificity of different instances explains Clark's suggestion of a 'climax' in this development: a greater appreciation for the diversity of such relationships would produce an understanding that this development will never end, as it is not dependent upon a single set of capacities in either the human or the artefact that might one day be so effectively exploited that there are no further opportunities for its evolution.

Making the Cut

A car, a hearing aid, an electric drill, a radio telescope and an automatic loom are all machines, but clearly a user's mode of engagement with each is importantly different. A phenomenological approach to our interactions with technological artefacts provides a framework for understanding these relationships, not in terms of immaterial 'cognitive routines', but rather as physical interactions between bodies and objects with specific material attributes. Heidegger's account of tool use is an obvious starting point, but Don Ihde's phenomenology of technology has added nuance to Heidegger's description by looking in more detail at different human–technology relationships and their differing advantages and costs. For example, where, for Heidegger, handiness represents a productive human–technology relationship, and obversely an awareness of the technological device itself is associated with a breakdown or failure in that relationship, Ihde argues for a spectrum of awareness of the technological artefact, the further end of which is not necessarily unproductive (see Ihde, 1979, p. 28, 1990, p. 88).

Ihde presents four kinds of human–technology relationships (embodiment, hermeneutic, alterity and background), although only the first two of these apply to the kinds of close and direct interactions I'm describing as interfacing.[18] Embodiment relations correlate to Heideggerian handiness, but hermeneutic relations, where the artefact becomes the focus of attention and requires the user's interpretation rather than functioning as simply an extension of the user's body, can also be an appropriate and productive mode of engagement (Ihde, 1979, p. 13). If we take driving a car as an example, working the pedals and turning the steering wheel should create successful embodiment relations; rather than requiring reflection on the principles by which the car works or the development of plans concerning how far to depress the brake or accelerator, or at what angle to turn the steering wheel, the car should feel like an extension of my body, allowing the appropriate movements to arise as a natural response to what is happening around me. However, my mode of engagement with the speedometer is quite different. The speedometer is there because my embodiment relation with the car does not produce an objective sense of the car's speed. I do feel the speed of the car and can understand the significance of its speed within the context of the car's operation—for example, I have a sense of how much I need to decelerate in order to safely take a corner—but this sense is a sense of the relationship between the car and its environment (the shifting of its weight, its turning circle, and the play of forces through its body), while legal speed limits are based on objective, 'scientific' measurements of speed that are alien to the human sensorium. As a result, while looking at the speedometer might not be of much value when decelerating to take a corner, I still need to check it regularly to make sure I am not in danger of receiving a speeding fine. My relationship with the speedometer is a hermeneutic one in Ihde's terminology because, rather than my attention passing 'through' the artefact to gain a direct sense of the world beyond it (as is the case when I glance in the rear-view mirror), the gauge is itself a focus of attention, whose significance requires interpretation. My awareness of the speedometer, rather than signifying its failure, is a result of its usefulness as a device that facilitates a relationship with my environment that cannot be rendered in direct, embodied sensory terms.

The distinction between embodiment relations and hermeneutic relations might therefore seem to return us to the theme of transparency versus opacity seen in the previous chapter, and, indeed, Ihde employs the terms transparency and opacity to describe them. However, just as I noted a mismatch between the employment of these terms by designers and media theorists, there is an important difference between Ihde's analysis and those seen in media studies. In the analyses critiqued in the previous chapter, I noted a vagueness concerning what, precisely, was supposed to be transparent or opaque, but Ihde's claims wholly reference the experience of the world facilitated by the technological artefact. The accounts discussed previously, by treating 'the interface' as simply a kind of cultural product or text, generally ignore both the user and the object of the user's work or attention, while Ihde's phenomenological account understands the technological artefact in terms of the ways in which it functions as a point of articulation between these two components.

While both Ihde's opacity and Bolter and Gromala's opacity can refer to the user's level of awareness of the computer screen as a planar representation of information that requires interpretation, in Bolter and Gromala's account the computer is both the subject and object of representation (rather than providing the user with information about something beyond the computer, as in Ihde's account of useful opacity, it is telling the user about itself) but the primary purpose of a computer's visual display is not to tell us about the workings of the computer. Ihde's account always seeks to understand technological artefacts as part of relationships between human beings and their lifeworld, rather than as isolated, closed representational loops. As a result, in addition to rejecting the privileging of experiential transparency over experiential opacity seen in Heidegger's account, Ihde's account also implicitly rejects the valuing of opacity over transparency in many accounts of digital user interfaces; when technological artefacts are understood to be devices *for* something, primarily a means of engaging with something *beyond* them, transparency and opacity become simply different modes of engagement aimed at the same general goal, their value varying according to their appropriateness for conveying particular kinds of information.

While Ihde's account is therefore more sophisticated and valuable for understanding our relationships with technological devices than any of those discussed in the previous chapter, there are still two areas where I believe it requires modification or elaboration. The first problem arises from the previously noted fact that exemplary contemporary relationships between user and machine possess a character that was largely unknown when Ihde developed his approach in the 1970s. It is not simply that we now have more technological devices, that we are more dependent upon them or that they are smaller and more ubiquitous—although these things are part of it. It is that they are more closely integrated with our bodies than was previously the case for artefacts with such a high level of complexity and autonomy.

Take, for example, Ihde's illustration of a hermeneutic relationship with technology using the heating system of university, whose basement contains 'a room filled with dials, gauges, rheostats and switches watched intently by a heating engineer' (Ihde, 1979, pp. 11–12). While I am not trying to suggest that such machinery no longer exists, I do think there is a parallel between Ihde using such machinery as indicative of a certain relationship with technology and Marx's use of the factory machine to a similar end. Like any investigation of technology, they are of their times, and there have been important changes in the exemplary technologies and technologised experiences since. Large, immobile, static machines that users must make themselves physically compatible with are not indicative of most technologised experiences today.

Take the example of navigation. Ihde utilises this example because, like Edwin Hutchins, author of the influential study of environmentally dependant problem-solving *Cognition in the Wild* (1995), he is a sailor and sees maritime navigation as a productive example of how humans use material systems to function in the world. Both Ihde and Hutchins see the central problem of navigation to be the establishment of some correspondence between the navigator and the map (Ihde, 1990, pp. 66–68); that is, while the map may be a perfect representation of the environment, it is of no value to me if I don't know which location on the map corresponds to my current location, and the map cannot tell me this crucial piece of information. I need some procedure for connecting what I see on the map to the reality of where my body is in space.

But if we put aside the paper maps referenced by Ihde and Hutchins last century and take the example of navigating using a map on your smartphone, things change. Obviously, the matching of physical location to map is no longer necessary because the map identifies and centres itself on my location, but the shift is more significant than the simple fact that the process of identifying your location on the map has been automated. It is not just that the navigation app tells me where I am on the map; connected to that is the fact that the map responds directly to the movement of my body. If I walk to the end of the street, the map shifts to put my new location at its centre, but I don't even need to change location: if I turn 180°, the map will swing 180° in the opposite direction to match itself to my orientation. The problem of representation and visualisation investigated by Ihde and Hutchins—that there is no physical connection between the world as captured by the map and the world as captured by my sensorium—no longer holds wholly true because a smartphone is able to capture and represent information about its user's body as well as the world around it. The map has been transformed from an icon into an index (see Chapter 1). Again, this change is more significant than simply the automation of a task; it is more significant because it means that walking or turning around are now part of the map's user interface. And, although the map has traditionally been an exemplary hermeneutic technology (it has no real value without the employment of an interpretive schema), this new part of the map's user interface is clearly not hermeneutic. It is so closely integrated to my unreflective embodied capacity for action that I don't even need to formulate an intention to turn the map around to match my orientation; it just occurs as a by-product of the bodily movement that would lead to such an intention arising so that the need and its satisfaction occur simultaneously.

The second area where Ihde's account requires modification is more fundamental, and relates to the narrowness of his conceptualisation of technologically mediated engagement with the environment. Ihde's account implicitly understands technological artefacts as a way of *knowing* the world, and this means creating certain ways of sensing and understanding our environment. Ihde's examples of technology use therefore revolve around instruments that enable technologically mediated sensing; while looking through a telescope and looking at a temperature gauge might be very different in terms of the distinction between embodied and hermeneutic relations, they are still both examples of visually interrogating some phenomenon beyond the artefact. On the rare occasions when Ihde strays from such examples, he stumbles; a notable example is his account of musical instruments as technological devices:

> If scientific or knowledge-developing praxis is constrained by the need to have a referential terminus within the world, the musical praxis is not so constrained. Indeed, if there is a terminus, it is a reference not so much to some thing or region of the environment as to the production of a musical event within that environment. The 'musical object' is whatever sound phenomenon occurs through the performance upon the instrument. Musical sounds are produced, created.
>
> (Ihde, 1990, pp. 94–95)

Because Ihde understands technological artefacts to be producing certain ways of knowing the world, he must conjure up a 'musical object' to occupy the last position in the equation (Human–machine) → World (cf. Ihde, 2010, pp. 20–22). But to me this seems unconvincing, simply an awkward attempt to deal with a case that resists his framework of analysis. Of course the musical instrument is not used to know or sense something about the world as Ihde's other examples are, but even if we shift to the use of a technological artefact to create something *in* the world (which is obviously a common purpose of technological artefacts, even though Ihde's account tends to shy away from this in favour of instrumentation meant to provide sensory data), the idea that a musical instrument is a machine for manufacturing musical objects doesn't seem very satisfactory. Perhaps we could say that a musical performance creates a musical object intended to provide entertainment, or even that ringing a bell creates a musical object intended to tell people that it's time for dinner or a building is on fire. But give a small child a bell and she is likely to ring it until you have a headache and beyond, but this ringing has no object and is no object. The sound of the bell is obviously satisfying for the child, but the sound is part of a non-decomposable whole with the physical movement of the child's body. The act of ringing the bell, the fact of the child–bell assemblage's movement and noise, is the source of pleasure. For all Ihde's highlighting of artefacts' place within relationships between body and environment, his focus on knowing the world weakens the sense of integration between these components by requiring a division between the human subject and the world that is out there to know. The child ringing the bell is not a human being operating a machine in order to produce a 'musical object' that then has an existence separate from her out in the world—rather her joy comes from the jumbling together of movement, artefact and noise in raucous unity.

Central to Ihde's account is an awareness of the ways in which our relationships with artefacts can cause shifts in the boundary between body and world. At the same time, however, his analysis is schematic and limited: we must choose between the hermeneutic: Human → (machine–World); and the embodied: (Human–machine) → World (Ihde, 1979, pp. 7–11).[19] In the former case, we are primarily aware of the boundary between the body and the machine, while in the latter our sense of the boundary separating body from machine fades so that the distinction between body and world is foregrounded. But I would argue that the child ringing the bell does not have any clear sense of a boundary anywhere; the bell is experienced as a part of the arm, its weight inflecting the arm's swings and manifesting the vigour of the child's movements as sound, but the bell is also experienced as an integrated part of the environment, an environment that, at that time, exists primarily as a bubble of sound with the bell at its core. It is this very experience of action, sensation, body, object and world blending together that produces the pleasure of the experience (and the absence of this pleasure for anyone not physically engaged in the ringing of the bell, who, due to the absence of this integration, will have a contrasting experience of being trapped in a hostile environment).

Even though Ihde highlights the lack of stable divisions between human, machine and (the) world, these terms are still understood to refer to given, predetermined entities that can produce a limited number of stable relationships. In the words of Peter-Paul Verbeek,

> By saying that mediation is located 'between' humans and world (as in the schema I—technology—world), Ihde seems to put subject and object over against one another, instead of starting from the idea that they mutually constitute each other. His analysis appears to suggest that he takes as a point of departure humans already given as such and a world already given as such, in between which one can find artifacts.
>
> (Verbeek, 2005, p. 129)

This aspect of Ihde's account can be contrasted with another that also has its origins in a consideration of the use of scientific instruments. Karen Barad's 'agential realism' begins with Niels Bohr's writings, in which he seeks to develop a framework for resolving the conflict between the principles of quantum physics, in whose explication he played a key part, and a traditional understanding of scientific investigation. From there she develops a far more wide-ranging framework for understanding how all entities appear as distinct configurations within a shifting, dynamic whole.

> Bohr constructs his post-Newtonian framework on the basis of 'quantum wholeness' or inseparability, that is, the lack of an inherent distinction between the object and the agencies of observation. He uses the term 'phenomenon', in a very specific sense, to designate particular instances of 'wholeness' . . . The physical apparatus marks the conceptual subject–object distinction: the physical and conceptual apparatuses form a nondualistic whole. That is, descriptive concepts obtain their meaning by reference to a particular physical apparatus, which in turn marks the placement of a constructed cut between the object and the agencies of observation.
>
> (Barad, 2007, p. 196)

According to this view, the classical conception of the scientist, scientific apparatus and object of study as discrete, independently constituted entities, in which the apparatus mediates between a scientist and an object of enquiry that exert no influence on one another, must be abandoned in the face of quantum indeterminacy. However, abandoning this idea need not lead inevitably to a loss of faith in objectivity; instead, our understanding of the world needs to focus on the processes by which these categories of things emerge as distinct entities out of a whole that does not independently or inevitably generate such divisions.

While the conceptual ramifications of this approach extend beyond the kinds of cases discussed by Ihde, it does also provide an alternative to the schematism of Ihde's approach. Human, machine and world, according to this view, would cease to be pre-given categories and would instead be understood as products of 'constructed cuts' into an interconnected whole where no division is natural or inevitable.

If we apply Barad's approach to Ihde's analyses, we can make the same points about the same examples (e.g. the steering wheel feels like part of the 'me' who feels the road passing beneath the car, while the speedometer appears as a separate entity by means of which I can make a determination about the speed at which the car is moving); but rather than establishing the existence of two categories of relationships with artefacts into which we can then sort other cases we might come across subsequently, these become simply two amongst a potentially infinite set of possibilities.

> Matter is a dynamic intra-active becoming that never sits still—an ongoing reconfiguring that exceeds any linear conception of dynamics in which effect follows cause end-on-end, and in which the global is a straightforward emanation outward of the local. Matter's dynamism is generative not merely in the sense of bringing new things into the world but in the sense of bringing forth new worlds, of

engaging in an ongoing reconfiguring of the world. Bodies do not simply take their places in the world. They are not simply situated in, or located in, particular environments. Rather, 'environments' and 'bodies' are intra-actively co-constituted. Bodies ('human', 'environmental', or otherwise) are integral 'parts' of, or dynamic reconfigurings of, what is.

(Barad, 2007, p. 170)

Ihde's hermeneutic and embodied relationships are two examples of the way in which an 'inexhaustible, exuberant, and prolific' (Barad, 2007, p. 179) plenum is carved up into distinct entities: in the first case, the most important cut is made between the human body and the artefact, while in the second case the most important cut is made between the artefact and the world. In fact, Barad notes that Bohr even employs the Merleau-Pontian illustration of the way in which a stick can be both an object, and part of an agent, of sensory exploration:

The mutual exclusivity of these two different practices is evident. The stick cannot usefully serve as an instrument of observation if one is intent on observing it. The line between subject and object is not fixed, but once a cut is made (i.e., a particular practice is being enacted), the identification is not arbitrary but in fact materially specified and determinate for a given practice. It is important to keep in mind that Bohr is making a point about the inherent ambiguity of bodily boundaries and the resolution of those boundaries through particular complementary cuts/practices.

(Barad, 2007, pp. 154–155)

What makes Ihde's account of the musical instrument unconvincing is the fact that his hermeneutic and embodied schematisations share a requirement that either human or machine be separated out from 'the world', and our relationships with artefacts must therefore serve a need to gain access to this world. But Barad's approach throws such relationships open to a broader range of possibilities; we can understand the child with the bell as experiencing a different and more complex relationship with the things around her, one that might even produce an experience (however fleeting) of there being no cuts at all into the plenum of reality.

And this draws attention to the fact that the agential realist approach goes further than simply acknowledging the possibility of different relationships between human, machine and world. These three terms themselves result from a prior carving up of a continuity. Where Ihde's account provides alternatives for arranging three pre-extant entities—the human being, the world 'out there', and the machine the human being uses to gain access to that world—Barad's approach requires an answer to the question of how and why these three things came to be the entities that are arranged. And the nature of the entities that come to be produced in this way affects the kinds of relationships that arise between them: where we understand there to be discontinuities between entities, and the nature of those discontinuities, is likely to determine which kinds of connections we consider possible. As Barad says about our bodies:

> human bodies, like all other bodies, are not entities with inherent boundaries and properties but phenomena that acquire specific boundaries and properties through the open-ended dynamics of intra-activity. Humans are part of the world–body space in its dynamic structuration.
>
> (Barad, 2007, pp. 171–172)

The lived body that informs the tradition of existential phenomenology from which Ihde's work arises is itself created by this process, its boundaries delineated by chiselling it out of a larger continuum of material connections. What it means to have a body—what our bodies can do and how it feels to be a body in the world—is always to some degree a result of where the cut is made between the body and the world, and the location of that cut is not simply—or perhaps even predominantly—dictated by the boundary of our skins.

Conclusion

The productive coming together of body and technological artefact always problematises the integrity of these two entities, creating an area of overlap, multiplication or fluidly shifting boundaries. This productiveness is not reducible to the utilitarian employment of external objects by the mind, nor can it be reduced to immaterial functions of information processing, cognition, or problem-solving. It is a foundationally material phenomenon whose properties arise from the material specificity of both body and artefact.

While human beings have never existed in a pre-lapsarian state of nature prior to the use of tools, this is only because the use of such objects is just one part of all animals' extensive engagement with the material environment around them. This engagement is produced by an ability to actively sense and sensitively act upon the things around us, and our capacity to seamlessly incorporate tools into our body schemata is one of the most impressive examples of the way in which human perception is geared to facilitate this. The 'handiness' of a tool arises from a direct, pre-conscious sensory relationship with it, one in which the tool is absorbed into our sense of the capacities of our own bodies. This transforms not only our capacity to act, but also our perception of the world.

Where figures such as Leroi-Gourhan and Marx have contrasted the tool with the industrial machine, this contrast has hinged on a characterisation of the machine as something that precludes such a relationship. The machine, as something that can operate to some degree independently of a human body and whose operation is highly constrained by the physical particularities and limitations of its mechanism, cannot function as a seamless extension of the human body, acting in perfect concert with it; rather, the human worker must struggle to act in a way tailored to the inhuman habits of the machine.

However, automatism does not necessarily militate against the absorption of machines into our schemata of perception and action. The automatism of many, more recent digital devices is directed towards giving them a capacity to sense our bodies or sense our sensing of them. Rather than being directed towards industrial manufacturing and therefore being organised around the attributes of the products being produced, for example, these devices are organised around the experiences and behaviours of human users. This holds out the possibility of seamlessly incorporating machines into our sense of bodily action and perception in new ways.

Generating new ways of interfacing with objects is natural to human beings. At the same time, though, we need to be careful about what we understand the term 'natural' to mean. For example, attempts to create 'natural user interfaces' are founded upon a misunderstanding of how the word 'natural' can be applied in this context, and thus misconstrue our relationship with tools and other material resources. The user interface is understood as something separable from body and machine, each of which can be addressed in isolation from the other: where human–machine interfaces were once 'all about the machine', according to champions of the NUI, they must become 'all about the user'; in reality, the embodied relationships with technology that the NUI seeks to produce make any clear differentiation between machine and user impossible.

The NUI is an attempt to create a technological simulation of a pre-technological Eden where our repertoire of gestures and habits arise from the body alone, unconstrained by the material limitations of specific physical artefacts. However, our gestures, habits and perceptions are produced by the interaction between our bodies and material features of our environment; there is no natural, originary dimension to these things that arises purely from within human bodies in isolation. Our capacities for action and perceptual experience develop through interaction, taking different shapes and producing different kinds of experience depending upon the material objects with which we engage. My argument for the naturalness of human–machine interfacing thus should not be taken as a conservative or essentialising position. In fact, in contrast to the concept of the NUI, it moves us in exactly the opposite direction. What is natural about human–machine interfacing is its artificiality—its capacity to dynamically redefine our experiences of embodied action and perception through the forging of new and intimate relationships with objects that lie outside the boundaries of our skin. The fact that they are produced through natural human capacities does not mean that they have a stable, fixed set of possibilities or reference points; their naturalness is a natural capacity to adapt to new circumstances and generate new kinds of engagement.

We naturally shift the boundaries of embodied experience constantly and fluidly—as we move from riding a bicycle to typing a letter to buttering toast. And our potential for action and perception shifts along with the location of the cut between our bodies and the things around them. Rather than trying to create new user interfaces that cater to assumptions about what human action and perception already are, we should exploit the potential of new technologies to produce new ways of acting on and with our material environment, and new kinds of sensory experience through which it can be explored.

Notes

1. More grotesquely, an important ancestor of the phonograph, Alexander Graham Bell and Clarence Blake's 'ear phonautograph', was equipped with an actual excised human ear (Sterne, 2001).
2. Friedrich Kittler gives a different origin story for the typewriter, but also other examples of the reproduction of anatomy in early sound machines (1999, Chapter 1).
3. This approach is now also being taken with exoskeleton feedback gloves for VR and AR (see Dexta Robotics, 2018).
4. Some of the material in this chapter has previously been published in Black, D. (2014). Where Bodies End and Artefacts Begin: Tools, Machines and Interfaces. *Body & Society*, 20(1), pp. 31–60.
5. And Stiegler carries this last theme further with his pessimistic account of the effects of representational media on human subjectivity (see Chapter 5).
6. Goodall's groundbreaking research was published several years after Leroi-Gourhan treated tool use as definitional to the human in *Le Geste et la Parole*, but many years before Stiegler did the same in *La technique et le temps: La faute d'Epiméthée*.
7. Exactly how many animals are credited with tool use will depend upon the definition of tool use employed (a point to which I will return).
8. This problem with Leroi-Gourhan's account is discussed in more detail in Ingold (1999, p. 422).
9. See, for example, St Amant and Horton (2008); Bentley-Condit and Smith (2010). Beck's 1980 work has also been revised in Shumaker, Walkup and Beck (2011).
10. Here I am liberally paraphrasing from the relevant *OED* definitions.
11. Compare this with the more schematic and 'mechanistic' differentiation between tool and machine of Tim Ingold (2000).
12. To favour Joan Stambaugh's translation of the term *Zuhandenheit*.
13. Which is not, of course, to say that physical properties are irrelevant. Obviously certain kinds of bodily engagement are only possible with objects that possess certain kinds of physical properties (a mountain, for example, will never be used as a hammer).

14. Although Marshall McLuhan did accurately predict that this would cause a breakdown in divisions between different areas of life and different kinds of knowledge (McLuhan, 1964, Chapter 3).
15. For a demonstration, see www.youtube.com/watch?v=ZA6m2fxpxZk.
16. And we often can manage this only imperfectly: it's extremely difficult to move one's ring finger with no accompanying movement of the fingers to either side of it.
17. Paul Dourish's book *The Stuff of Bits* (2017) is devoted to examples of the ways in which even supposedly 'immaterial' digital technologies actually constitute material contexts that inflect human thought and action.
18. And Marco Nørskov (2015) has argued that the latter two categories can be collapsed into the first two in any event.
19. As noted previously, there are two more options in Ihde's schema, but for the sake of clarity and simplicity I am confining the discussion here to the two I have already explained.

3 Beside Ourselves

In Chapter 2 I made reference to research into how tools transform the experience of space. Our perception of space is seemingly divided between far ('extrapersonal') space and near ('peripersonal' or 'cutaneous') space, whose boundary is defined by the limits of possible physical interaction with our environment. At the most basic level, this suggests that—at least within a certain distance—we do not perceive space as neutral or empty, but rather as a sphere of potential action given meaning by our capacity for bodily engagement with its features. Furthermore, the fact that peripersonal space seemingly expands when we extend this capacity by wielding a tool suggests that this perception is dynamically influenced by our intimate relationships with artefacts. But this dynamic integration of tools into our sense of the location and limits of our own bodies raises some interesting questions about where we understand ourselves to be when interfacing with technological artefacts.

We have already seen that, when making tool-like use of artefacts, the locus of action and perception can seem to be at the point of contact between artefact and environment, rather than body and artefact. And yet the interfacing of body and artefact remains a part of perceptual experience. Don Ihde has used the example of writing with a piece of chalk; there is what he calls an 'echo focus' at the meeting of fingers and chalk, even as the meeting of chalk and chalkboard takes precedence (1979, pp. 7–9). For the blind person using a cane, the locus of perception is importantly situated in the ball at the end of the cane, but at the same time her arm is sensing the cane that it holds.

It may seem that I am undermining the arguments I have made so far by highlighting such considerations; having sought to establish our capacity to perceive and act through artefacts as if they were part of our own bodies, I now seem to be highlighting the separateness of the body proper, and locating perception on its surface rather than that of the artefacts that might be in contact with it. However, it is important to maintain an awareness of the fact that artefacts do not perceive; only bodies perceive, and when we perceive through an artefact we are always also perceiving that artefact even when the perceiving *through* is more experientially vivid for us than the perceiving *of*. To lose sight of the sensory relationship between artefact and body is to lose sight of the experience of interfacing itself, because it is this melding of two different sensory experiences—perception through the artefact and perception of the artefact—that makes it possible.

Nonetheless, no matter how seamless this melding might be, the fact remains that the two loci of sensory experience are separated from one another in space. The blind person's locus of perception is situated both in her arm *and* at the end of the cane some distance from her arm. Being situated in a kind of non-space that is both between body and artefact and encompasses the entirety of both of them, interfacing produces a paradoxical relationship with space by its very nature—to take but one commonly remarked upon example, where in space does a telephone conversation take place?—but the most interesting and instructive cases are those in which the sensing of space itself is implicated in these sensory transformations. Returning to the example of the blind person using a cane, the cane is being used to sense space, and this is being done primarily for the purposes of navigating the blind person's body through space. There would seem to be something more deeply paradoxical about this, given that sensory stimuli about the space being negotiated is being gathered from a place some distance from the blind person's body, and yet it can effortlessly be utilised to understand the spatial disposition of the body itself. Of course, at one level this simply demonstrates once again the naturalness of incorporating artefacts into our embodied experience, but in this context I want to draw attention to the fact that this incorporation comes about through the superimposition of two loci of perception (the arm and the tip of the cane), two kinds of movement (the movement of the arm and the movement of the cane, which, while directly tied to it, is also amplified by the cane's shape) and two different understandings of where these things are taking place in space (both at the location of the body and the location of the tip of the cane). The integration of artefacts into our experience of action and perception necessarily distributes the apparent locus of experience across space. Questions about where we are in space, and the limits of our bodily boundaries and reach of perception and action, become difficult to answer definitively; the only reason why we are not confused or disorientated by such experiences multiple times every day as we drive our cars or talk on our telephones is again because we have an evolved capacity to integrate such multiplex and distributed experiences into a single, seamless whole.

But what then happens with the appearance of digital user interfaces that present simulated spaces as sites of action and perception? If the interfacing of my body with a simple tool like a hammer creates an experience of projecting my body out into my environment with an altered capacity to act upon it, what happens when a human–computer interface creates an experience of projecting my body into a simulated space 'on the other side of the screen', and having a capacity to act upon that?

Given that interfacing always complicates and multiplies our relationship with space, what happens when digital user interfaces begin to present us with sensory experiences of fictitious spaces, and our sense of where we are and the limits of our bodily boundaries and reach of perception and action come to be distributed, not just across physical space, but simulated space as well?[1]

Adjacent to Reality

Digital media's concern with the simulation of space might be thought to pose a problem for my account of interfacing as it has been explained so far. Where in Chapter 1 I sought to replace an understanding of the user interface as a representation of what was happening inside the machine with one in which it is understood to enable the engagement of the user–machine assemblage with something beyond the machine, it might be claimed that a computer-generated simulation of space is clearly something that does not exist anywhere *but* 'inside' the machine. However, computer-generated simulations of space do, in fact, exist outside the machine because they reside in a user, not a computer; clearly, there is no space 'inside' the computer, but rather the computer produces certain kinds of sensory stimuli that seek to create an experience of space in the user. This is implicit in research into virtual environments, which evaluates an environment's success according to its ability to create a sense of 'presence' as measured by instruments such as participant questionnaires or even physiological measurements (see Steuer, 2006): researchers look for evidence of the virtual environment's success, not in the computer hardware, but rather in human bodies.

At the time when I'm writing this, virtual reality is getting a lot of attention. Competing virtual reality hardware products have been introduced into the market by companies such as Google, the Facebook-owned Oculus, Sony, Samsung and video game giant Valve (in partnership with mobile device manufacturer HTC), and still more products from still more companies are promised to be on the way. A striking aspect of the marketing surrounding these products is that, while virtual reality is now being presented as an exciting new technology, it could be argued that, ironically, virtual reality's golden age as a feature of popular discourse came and went some time ago. Following from its origins in the research of Ivan Sutherland and art projects of Myron Krueger in the 1960s (Sutherland, 1968; Krueger, 1977),[2] by the late 1980s/early 1990s, excitement over the imminent arrival of virtual reality seemed at fever pitch: books—both fiction and non-fiction, popular and scholarly—were being written about it; films were being made about it;[3] and people pontificated about the dangers of simulator sickness, VR addiction, or crashing your car due to the sensory disorganisation of returning from VR to the real world. And, above all, promises were being made for it.

Arguably, the very fact that few people had experienced VR at the time was key to its power. It existed primarily as a discursive trope, an idea that was attached, not to any clunky machine in the present, but to a future promise of escapism, transcendence and mastery over the nature of reality. When people did have an opportunity to experience virtual reality, for example by playing on a Nintendo Virtual Boy ('Virtual Boy', n.d.), Sega VR ('Sega VR', n.d.), or $60,000 *Dactyl Nightmare* (Gaming History, n.d.) machine at a video arcade, the result was usually disappointment mixed with headaches and nausea, and the virtual reality hype was later washed away by a wave of disillusionment (see Laurel, 1993, pp. 199–202). The consumer virtual reality devices of the time failed and disappeared from the market (or, in the case of the Sega VR, were killed before release), and it has taken some time for VR to be resurrected as a marketable entertainment technology.

This history is important because the term 'virtual reality' has experienced a drift in meaning between its first and second comings, one that perhaps forms a minor counterpoint to that of the term interface as discussed in Chapter 1. The term 'virtual' can be understood in various ways (most notably as the plenum from which the actual arises in the works of Henri Bergson and Gilles Deleuze [see Chapters 4 and 5]), but in this context the intended meaning is clearly one of almost, but not quite. It is related to terms such as 'artificial' or 'simulated', but we can imagine a spectrum of terms lying between 'real' and 'not real', with 'virtual' lying as far from the 'not real' limit as possible, directly adjacent to the real. That is, the environments presented by VR are supposed to be 'virtually real'; in the words of Rob Shields, '"virtually so" is very close to being really so' (2005, p. 22). Virtual reality technology is foundationally an attempt to create a place that comes close to attaining the status of physical reality; as a result, while it is commonly understood to be most importantly dependent upon visual representation, it is more importantly an attempt to realistically engage spatial perception than visual perception per se.

Jaron Lanier, who popularised the term virtual reality in the 1980s, used it to refer most importantly to a simulated environment that functioned as a social space (Lanier, 2017, pp. 237–239). Lanier saw VR as promising a liberation from the restrictions of physical reality, which would allow a new kind of 'post-symbolic communication' (Lanier and Biocca, 1992, pp. 159–161) between people, in which the ability to express oneself directly through a mutable environment would make signs and representations unnecessary, and it would be possible to experiment with drastic reconfigurations of embodiment.

What if your eyes were on your fingers? What if you were crawling around inside the mouth of another person? What if you took all the

measurements and the movements of your physical body and somehow put them through a mathematical function that allowed you to
learn to control six arms at once with practice?

(Lanier and Biocca, 1992, p. 162)

While some figures associated with the second coming of virtual reality
might still privately hold to Lanier's utopian vision, the new generation of
hardware is presented more pragmatically as primarily a kind of gaming
peripheral, and secondarily perhaps as a way of watching movies, rather
than the agent of a new phase in the history of human communication and
social interaction. While the term 'virtual reality' has come to mean any
enveloping virtual environment, in the marketing of the new generation of
systems the reality part of the name has come to imply realism more than
reality, being attached more to the idea of realistic representation than
the creation of a genuinely new reality. Given the ultimate sense of disap-
pointment and disillusionment that rendered virtual reality unfashionable
at the end of the twentieth century, this more modest characterisation
is unsurprising. However, it has also meant that, just as interfaces were
transformed from experiences to products, the term virtual reality is now
popularly considered synonymous with the head-mounted displays that
are currently being marketed as 'virtual reality' delivery systems.

Stereoscopic head-mounted displays have a history that predates virtual reality discourse. While they can be seen as descendants of Victorian optical toys, their association with VR draws most directly on their
investigation by famous technologist Ivan Sutherland during the heyday
of digital interface innovation in the 1960s. However, the head-mounted
display itself isn't the virtual reality, nor does it 'create' virtual reality in
any straightforward way. An analogy with Doug Engelbart's work on the
graphical user interface during the same era is perhaps appropriate: the
head-mounted display no more 'is' the virtual reality than Engelbart's
mouse 'is' the graphical user interface. Both of these things are simply
pieces of hardware, computer peripherals that were considered necessary
to the viability of the system. The mouse enables the graphical user interface because it allows the user's body to move in certain ways that are a
meaningful part of the system, but it is not, itself, the system. This is why
these headsets, now popularly referred to as 'virtual reality headsets', are
more properly called 'head-mounted displays' (HMDs): there is actually
no direct or inevitable connection between them and virtual reality—it is
simply one of their possible applications. In fact, when creating the first
'artificial realities' in the 1970s, Myron Krueger considered but rejected
the use of HMDs in favour of less physically encumbering external projection (Turner, 1992), and developers of the first generation of HMD virtual
reality systems in the 1980s placed as much importance on another, now
largely forgotten, piece of hardware: the 'dataglove' that allowed a user to
interact with a virtual environment using the hand (Heim, 1993, p. 127).

The shift towards understanding VR purely as a creation of computer graphics is starkly illustrated by the fact that, when the Oculus Rift revived the idea of virtual reality in the twenty-first century, HMD and VR were seen as synonymous to such an extent that, not only was no attempt made to reproduce the dataglove previously seen as a key hardware component, but initially no attempt was made to develop any input peripheral at all, such that the first Oculus Rift systems had to be shipped with no VR-appropriate controller. In contrast, VPL, the first virtual reality start-up, developed the dataglove before its first HMD, and Jaron Lanier has lamented the fact that the ability to 'reach out' into virtual worlds is not given the centrality it deserves in current VR systems (Lanier, 2017, pp. 127–129).

Stereoscopic 3D graphics are not, themselves, virtual reality; the HMD is an important point of articulation between the user's body and the technology, but only has significance as part of a larger system. The HMD does not 'create' or 'deliver' virtual reality; this should be obvious given that VR's aim is to create a sense of 'presence', or of being in a believable simulated space. The aim is to create a certain kind of experience, meaning that 'virtual reality' is created 'in the user' rather than 'in the hardware'.

This distinction might seem like quibbling, but it does lead to important shifts in how some key VR-related concepts are discussed. Even if virtual reality is equated simply to an HMD, what often seems to be missed is that the HMD seeks to improve representational technology not by introducing a new mode of visual representation, but rather a new mode of representing bodily movement. The technology of visual representation employed by the HMD—which relies on the creation of two-dimensional moving images on screens—has, in broad terms at least, been familiar for well over a century. While attention tends to be focused on the HMD's stereoscopic representation, this, like the moving image, is an invention of the Victorian era and so nothing particularly new or noteworthy.

It is true that Mark Hansen has argued that stereoscopic images are a special case of visual representation because the merging of differing images presented to each eye to create a single, spatialised scene is a 'body–brain achievement' while other technologies of visual representation are simply 'instrument[s] contiguous with the eye' (2004, pp. 170–171)—in other words, the perception of space in the stereoscopic image is actually produced by the brain working to reconcile the two images, rather than simply being directly read off the technologically produced image itself. However, the problem with this claim is that it relies on an implicit opposition between stereoscopic representations as something produced by our perceptual apparatus, and monocular, planar images as something our eyes simply receive as the camera or other technology presents them. Hansen's account of stereoscopic representation as 'body–brain achievement' implies a belief that there is some part of vision that can be differentiated from a 'worked-up' finished product in which visual aspects that aren't reducible to a photographic model (like depth perception) have been 'added in' by the brain. However, all visual experience—like all perception in general—is a 'body–brain achievement', and so stereoscopic vision does not constitute a special case.[4] In any event, given the ambivalent reception audiences gave yet another attempt to introduce stereoscopic images to cinemas in the early twenty-first century, the argument that such representations are a breakthrough that fundamentally alters the nature of visual representation is probably more difficult to sell than it was previously.

More generally, the technology of visual representation that goes into current HMDs is unimpressive. They use 3D-rendered computer graphics, but these tend to be of a lower quality than users are accustomed to from other media, and their screens, being small and placed very close to the eyes, also tend to have lower clarity and picture quality. In fact, what allows the HMD to put 'reality' into virtual reality—inasmuch as it does—is not any new technology of visual representation, but rather the introduction of technologies that register the movement of the wearer's body: what supposedly creates an unprecedented level of realism is that the visual representations are bolstered by having the represented perspective respond to the movement of at least the wearer's head and perhaps the rest of the user's body too.

Our visual perception of space fundamentally relies on bodily movement: the shifts in visual perspective produced by bodily movements both large and small are important to our understanding of the spatial distribution of the objects around us (Noë, 2004). While the stereoscopic film or television image reproduces only one of the several kinds of perceptual information that generate a visual experience of space (binocular vision), the HMD adds to this a second: shifts in perspective created by the movement of the head or entire body. This is effected by tracking technology that plots movement of the head as a minimum, and software that reactively shifts the perspective of the images displayed on the headset's screens. Amongst all of the technology deployed in the headset, the only aspect that is truly novel for most users is this plotting of bodily movement.

In fact, the first head-mounted display, developed by Ivan Sutherland, did not feature stereoscopic 3D images at all, despite having a separate display for each eye (Rheingold, 1991, pp. 104–105). Even when stereoscopic 3D was introduced, Sutherland maintained that 'Although stereo presentation is important to the three-dimensional illusion, it is less important than the change that takes place in the image when the observer moves his head' (Sutherland, 1968, p. 757).[5] So, once again, a user interface technology must be understood as most importantly kinaesthetic, rather than visual, in nature; there is, of course, an important visual component to the head-mounted display, but vision is just the sensory modality addressed by its representation of bodily movement. The sensation of 'being there' is an embodied experience generated by proprioception (understood in its most expansive sense): our sense of where our bodies are in space.

The long-term impact or even viability of VR technology is still unclear at the time of writing. However, the creation of an experience of being 'inside' a computer-generated space was successfully commercialised well before the re-introduction of VR. When the iD software game *Doom* was released in 1993, it made the first-person shooter, or FPS, arguably the most recognisable video game genre by giving the player an experience of 'being' the protagonist of the game, seemingly situated at the same co-ordinates in the game space as the game character's body and seeing and hearing the game world through the character's eyes and ears. The FPS promised to, at least to some degree, give the game player an experience of being 'inside' a simulated space, and a stream of successful FPS games has continued to the present day.

Games are no more able to subordinate or replace the embodied experience of their audience than any other media form. In fact, like other media forms, they could not function as media if they did. At the same time, however, the player has the experience of acting through a simulated body on a simulated space—some kind of direct, pre-conscious engagement with simulated body and space is necessary in order to play the game, and without it games would presumably not be as viscerally enjoyable as their sales figures suggest they are. Consequently, the 3D video game requires a very particular experience of interfacing with digital technology: the player must be oriented in a fictitious space, and understand her actions and perceptions to originate at a particular set of co-ordinates within that fictitious space, even when those co-ordinates are presented as being some distance away from the player's viewing position (see Martin, 2012).

When I am controlling a vehicle or wielding a tool in the real world, these artefacts can produce new kinds of sensation for me and can even perhaps alter the boundaries of my experiential self, but 3D virtual environments seek to create an experience of a fabricated, simulated, three-dimensional space, and to do this they must produce a sense that the boundaries of our experiential selves extend into that fabricated space (see Calleja, 2007, pp. 254–255). To do this, they most importantly seek to create a viewpoint situated inside the simulated space, and this viewpoint is in most cases attached to the body of a game character. But how can player and character have any spatial relationship to one another at all, given that they exist in two fundamentally incompatible sets of spatial co-ordinates: the real-world space of the player's body and the simulated space of the game?

Perspective, Viewpoint and Point of View;
Ideal, Actual and Avatar Viewpoints

Any attempt to create a realistic visual simulation of space is complex and contradictory, whether it be in a Renaissance painting, a Victorian optical toy or a virtual environment. In order to be a success, however, such a simulation must seem, on the surface, to simply recreate our everyday visual experience, and this can obscure the complexity and inconsistency of its operation. As a result, we need to spend some time considering the strategies used by video games to simulate space visually, and the process by which they have appropriated and adapted these strategies from older representational technologies.

In order to do this, it is important to initially differentiate my use of the terms *perspective, point of view* and *viewpoint*. The general usage of these terms often overlaps or doubles up, but for the purposes of the following discussion it is necessary to draw hard distinctions between them in order to avoid confusion.

I will use the terms *perspective* and *linear perspective* interchangeably to refer to the arrangement of features within a two-dimensional image or images in order to simulate depth. In other words, whether it be in a Renaissance painting or a video game, it is the creation of an illusion that the viewer can see 'into' a simulated space beyond the flat plane of the image. In the words of Erwin Panofsky:

> The material surface upon which the individual figures or objects are drawn or painted or carved is . . . negated, and instead reinterpreted as a mere 'picture plane'. Upon this picture plane is projected the spatial continuum which is seen through it and which is understood to contain all the various individual objects.
>
> (1991, p. 27)

My distinction between point of view and viewpoint takes as its starting point Herbert Zettl's differentiation:

> Technically, there is a distinction between camera viewpoint and point of view. Viewpoint simply refers to what the camera is looking at and from where. Point of view, on the other hand, means that the camera takes on a bias of looking: it no longer describes (looks at) but comments on the event (looks into and interprets). Point of view refers to the camera's narrative involvement.
>
> (2014, p. 228)

However, for the purposes of the current discussion, I wish to use a more restrictive definition of point of view: while viewpoint simply refers to the camera's position within a space, point of view will be used to refer to the coincidence of camera viewpoint and a game character's (simulated) viewing position. So, in an FPS, the player is presented with the game protagonist's point of view, an effect created by situating the viewpoint in the protagonist's head.

It may be objected that Zettl's definitions are based on the conventions of cinematography, and games do not involve the use of a camera. However, camera position is fundamentally important to the depiction of any computer-simulated 3D space such that, while no actual camera is used to produce such representations, they all feature a 'virtual camera'. With no camera (actual or virtual) there would be no viewpoint, and without a viewpoint there would be no perspective. Without perspective there can be no visual simulation of space. While point of view is far more common in games than film, it remains an optional component of the representation; viewpoint, on the other hand, is necessary for any perspectival representational to be intelligible to a viewer.

Perspectival representations work by confusing the distinction between these different components in order to produce an illusion of sharing the location of the camera or character within the represented space, and thus of being within the representational space ourselves. By pulling apart these three different components and looking at the functions they serve in creating the game player's sense of moving around 'inside' a simulated space, we can develop an account of how, and to what extent, the visual components of the video game can produce an experience of being embodied in the game world. I will begin with a discussion of how perspective operates within the 3D video game.

Since Brunelleschi 'invented' linear perspective in the fifteenth century (Kemp, 2006, p. 15), realistic visual representations of space have been understood to be most importantly produced through the mechanism of a fixed, ideal viewing position outside the image. Linear perspective creates the illusion of space in realist painting, film and the 3D computer graphics of video games (see Manovich, 2001, p. 184). However, while the development of rendered 3D graphics is clearly part of a long history of technically simulating perspective—a descendent of technologies like the drafting frames used to produce early perspectival representations—this does not mean that they represent nothing more than a continuation or refinement of an existing mode of representing and looking. The relationship between user and computer-generated perspectival image is different from its pre-digital progenitors in important ways.

Linear perspective depends on the creation of a point of convergence inside the image, which produces the effect of a monocular viewpoint situated in a singular spatial position relative to the simulated space of the image. It therefore creates twinned points at either end of a line of sight, both of which seem to float outside the two-dimensional plane of the image: the convergence point that is *through* the image, terminating the line of perspective inside its illusionary space, and the viewpoint that is *outside* the image, the point at which the field of vision of the viewer should originate. This latter point has only an abstract, mathematical reality until photography, when it comes to originate with the actual physical presence of the camera (although of course it remains attached to the image after the camera has gone). When these two invisible points are lined up—in other words, when the viewer places herself at the viewpoint outside the image so that the lines of the painting converge in a way that conforms to the visual effect generated by three-dimensional space—the viewer experiences an illusion of depth. If the viewer is placed somewhere else—if, for example, she positions her eyes very close to the canvas near its bottom left corner—the illusion cannot be generated. When a painting is created, an invisible, phantasmal viewer is created with it, hovering directly in front of the painting a certain distance from its surface, and it is only by 'becoming' that viewer, positioning ourselves so that we are inhabiting the same point in space as the phantasmal viewer, that we experience the effect of perspectival realism. We therefore need to differentiate between two kinds of viewpoint: the *actual viewpoint*—that is, that of the living body engaged in the act of looking from a particular physical location, and the *ideal viewpoint*, a purely theoretical viewing position created as a by-product of linear perspective with which the actual viewpoint must coincide in order for the simulation of space to succeed.

This technique is initially developed in painting and drawing, but subsequent technologies that mechanically reproduce perspective work in the same way: the movie camera in effect records the trajectories of the various beams of light hitting its lens, immortalising a fixed perspectival position in space; when we sit in a movie theatre (ideally at its exact centre) we are positioning ourselves so that we are sharing a viewpoint with the ghost of that camera, which is projected off the screen. The key development with film is that this ideal viewpoint becomes mobile. The camera is able to record shifts in its viewpoint over time, creating a sense in the viewer that she is moving around inside the representational space of the film. Of course, the viewer is not moving at all, and neither is her viewpoint—she remains immobile inside a movie theatre. But as long as her actual viewpoint is piggybacking on the film's ideal viewpoint, it will seem to accompany it on its peregrinations through the filmic space.

The realism of 3D video game images clearly functions in the same fashion, which is not surprising given video games' aesthetic debt to cinema. The establishment of the first-person shooter is understood to be a watershed moment in the history of video games in no small part because of the way the genre created an unprecedented level of realism through the real-time plotting of perspective, by then long established as the ideal of representational realism.

The rendering of 'three-dimensional' environments in games is effected by simulating the trajectories of the rays of light that are captured by a film camera, mathematically plotting the lines of simulated light that will produce the effect of perspective. Of course, such 'three-dimensional' graphics are no more three-dimensional than movies: they are still produced as flat, two-dimensional renderings of space (even in a head-mounted display). What makes them seem 'more' three-dimensional than cinema is that the video game introduces a user interface that allows the player to manipulate the point of convergence within the image, whose movement causes an equivalent change in the ideal viewpoint attached to it. In effect, this means that the player can swivel the ideal viewpoint from side to side with a controller (and the greater realism of the head-mounted display comes from its replacement of a consciously manipulated controller with a motion sensor that automatically synchronises the movements of head and ideal viewpoint). Because the player cohabits the space of the ideal viewpoint, this in turn creates a sense that the player is moving around with it. This is entirely illusory, of course: not only does the player's body not move, but it also doesn't change its actual viewpoint relative to the image—it is only the relationship between the simulated space and the ideal viewpoint that changes as the image shifts its point of perspectival convergence in real time. If a player has a sense of travelling forward into the three-dimensional space of the game world, it is not because the player's actual viewpoint has changed—the player's body is in the same position it was in before, and her viewpoint relative to the screen is no different. Rather, the perspective constructed around the ideal viewpoint has shifted forward, and as long as the player identifies with that ideal viewpoint and feels that her perspective is meshed with that of the ideal viewpoint, then when the ideal viewpoint shifts perspective, the player will feel that her body is shifting along with it. Once again, as already seen with VR, this regime is as dependent upon kinaesthetic representation as visual representation; if what the player sees is not synchronous with and proportionate to the movements registered by an input device, the experience is no longer compelling.

What the video game adds to film's introduction of a mobile ideal viewpoint is an experience of not simply moving through the representational space, but of being able to physically act upon that space (see Calleja, 2007, pp. 254–255; Klevjer, 2013, p. 7). It does this by creating a sense that the ideal viewpoint is tied to a physical agent within the simulated space, usually a simulated body. The game's representational regime therefore adds a third viewpoint to the two already discussed in relation to painting and film, one that is *inside* the representational landscape.[6] With the perspectival painting, the ideal viewpoint is constructed at a fixed point, and the actual viewpoint can then occupy the same space as the ideal viewpoint. With film, the ideal viewpoint position is mobile, engendering in the actual viewpoint a sense of movement, but that ideal viewpoint is still physically disconnected from the space of the film itself: it is not tethered to anything inside the image, being able to switch between an infinite variety of positions relative to the features of the represented environment. In video games, this ideal viewpoint becomes physically manifested in the represented environment in some way.[7] And in games focused on a single protagonist, this ideal viewpoint enters into a fixed relationship with the posited viewpoint of a game character in order to create what I will refer to as the *avatar viewpoint*. Furthermore, in the FPS, the ideal and avatar viewpoints occupy the same spatial co-ordinates in order to create the sense of a simultaneity of not only ideal and actual viewpoints, but the viewpoints of player and game character.

The sense of agency created by this effect both heightens and obscures the relationship between the living body of the player and the phantasmal body of the ideal viewpoint that shares the same point in space. The ability to move the viewpoint through the representational space increases the illusion that there is only one viewing position—that of the player—that generates perspective, but at the same time other factors—for example the fact that the player cannot see her body in the space of the game, and that shifting her actual viewpoint independently of the game's controls (say, by moving her head from side to side in front of the screen) will cause the actual viewpoint and ideal viewpoints to fall out of alignment—highlights the differences between them. In contrast, the very immobility and lack of control of the film viewer makes such a loss of alignment less common.

Such complications notwithstanding, the creation of a convincing illusion that the perspectives of the ideal and actual viewpoints are perfectly meshed is a key tool used in video games to create a sense of visual realism. In the first-person shooter, the game creates a triple convergence between one real and two fictitious viewers: the actual viewpoint of the player, the ideal viewpoint outside the image, *and* the avatar viewpoint inside the game are all aligned in such a way as to create the illusion that they inhabit a single point in space, producing a sense that not only is the player's viewpoint moving around inside an illusory three-dimensional space, but also that this viewpoint is being shared with that of an illusory body inside that space.

And yet there are many examples of games that intentionally break up or complicate this stacking effect by situating the ideal viewpoint a short distance away from the avatar viewpoint. Some of the most successful video game franchises, such as *Grand Theft Auto* (1997), *Assassin's Creed* (2007) and *Tomb Raider* (1996), and most of the massively multiplayer online role-playing games, such as *World of Warcraft* (2004) seek to create (and succeed in creating if sales figures are anything to go by) a sense of acting upon a three-dimensional game space, and yet they primarily utilise a third-person viewpoint, in which the actual viewpoint is situated only *near* the game protagonist. In third-person games, the ideal and actual viewpoints remain anchored in the representational landscape, but the avatar viewpoint is not directly superimposed over the ideal and actual viewpoints; rather it is situated a short (but usually fixed and stable) distance away from the ideal and actual viewpoints, leaving them trailing around behind the game character's shoulder like a balloon on a string.

The third-person game should immediately raise a question about the role of viewpoint in games more broadly. If a video game is seeking to create a sense of 'immersion', of being a part of the simulated environment and acting upon it, isn't a third-person representation innately inferior to a first-person one? In a first-person game, the stacking of ideal, actual and avatar viewpoints creates the illusion that I am the hero moving through and acting on the game world, but wouldn't seeing the hero as a separate entity situated a short distance away from my simulated perspective break this illusion?

It may seem self-evident that the first-person point of view is the most engaging by virtue of being the most realistic, and the most realistic by virtue of being the closest to real-world sensory experience. After all, in our everyday embodied activity, we see the world from a viewpoint originating at our eyes, and our own bodies are largely invisible to us by virtue of being the point at which our sensory experience originates rather than being the object of that experience, and it is precisely this position that the first-person game seeks to reproduce. The development of virtual reality is motivated by a belief that a virtual environment seems most realistic and engaging if we view it through a convincing first-person perspective, and the very terms 'first-person' and 'third-person', with their implied relationships with 'me' as opposed to 'him'/'her' reflects this common-sense belief. Research into video gaming seems to confirm this: gamers interviewed by Kristine Jørgensen described themselves as 'merging' with the protagonists of first-person shooters (Jørgensen, 2009, pp. 2–3), and Chris Chesher claims that '[f]irst person games . . . give players a sense of visceral immersion' (Chesher, 2004). But if this is true, then when given a choice between first-person and third-person perspectives, why would game designers ever opt for the latter, and why wouldn't players experience the latter as fundamentally less involving than the former?

Two obvious motivations behind the use of third-person representations are the spectacularisation and commodification of game bodies. The spectacularisation of game bodies is well illustrated by comparing the classic 3D games *Doom* and *Tomb Raider*. In *Doom*, the first-person viewpoint is that of a masculine warrior, whose body—in line with traditional masculinist values—is simply a transparent, uncomplaining platform for acting on the world. In *Tomb Raider*, on the other hand, the female body of Lara Croft is part of the spectacle of the game: both her hypersexualised figure and acrobatic prowess are there to be admired, requiring that the player watch her from outside her body. Similarly, in the *Max Payne* (2001) games, the John Woo–style leaps and dodges of Max Payne as he engages in blazing gunfights are a key part of the game's visual appeal, but would not be available for aesthetic appreciation using a first-person viewpoint. The commodification of the game body overlaps to some degree with its spectacularisation: in both massively multiplayer and single-player role-playing games, for example, the game character's body is a project, customised and augmented by the player, and customisation of the game body's physical appearance, or the addition of new clothes, armour, weapons and so on, are best appreciated from an external viewpoint.

The spectacularisation and commodification of game bodies are both clearly influences on the decision to create a third-person rather than first-person game. At the same time, however, it seems unlikely that even both of these considerations combined would be enough to outweigh the disadvantage of a third-person position making the game less engaging for the player. Even if customising and improving the hero of an RPG made the player feel more invested in the hero and perhaps even generated additional revenue for the game's publisher, if a third-person representation simultaneously lessened the player's enjoyment of the game it seems highly unlikely that this would be considered a fair trade-off.

While the spectacularisation and commodification of game bodies are potential benefits of the third-person game, they don't explain how the third-person game can be as successful as the first-person. In fact, while gamers surveyed by Alena Denisova and Paul Cairns (2015) expressed the opinion that a first-person perspective was more 'immersive' than a third-person one, half of them still expressed a preference for third-person games, demonstrating that differing levels of engagement with the simulated space of a game cannot be explained simply by the degree to which it creates a sense of identicality between player and game character. This demonstrates that engagement with these games is more complex than naïve accounts derived from an 'immersive fallacy' (Salen and Zimmerman, 2004, pp. 450–451) would suggest.

The common and successful use of third-person representations should, in itself, establish that the player's relationship with the game character is not simply one of direct identification and immersion. If that were the case, then third-person games would always be less involving than first-person. Also, by contrast, in other audiovisual media such as film and television it is standard practice for the ideal viewpoint to be situated outside any particular body, and first-person point of view is rare, and fleeting when it does occur. Is their greater use of point of view the reason why video games supposedly produce a greater level of 'identification' than older audiovisual media? (Shaw, 2010, pp. 147–148). If so, why haven't these older audiovisual media simply adopted a more extensive use of point of view themselves? The technologies used to create and display these media forms are just as capable of doing so as video games.

Film Bodies and Game Bodies

When video games are heroised for putting the player inside a simulated world or decried for allowing players to act out violent fantasies, the implied relationship between player and game is quite straightforward: in effect, there is the player, and there is the game character, whom the player effectively becomes while playing the game. But, in reality, how the player is positioned relative to the game world, and which vantage point on it the player is invited to identify with, is much more complex. The actual, ideal and avatar viewpoints are separate and distinct in their attributes and, while the representational regime of the game seeks to create a sense that they have all been blended into a single coherent unity, they remain separate from one another, superimposed one upon another but quite unstable and vulnerable to dislocation. This should come as no surprise given existing investigations of identification as it occurs in film, a medium whose greater age has allowed for a more thorough theorisation than video games.

Vivian Sobchack's (1992) phenomenology of film spectatorship contains a refutation of the idea that the experience of film viewing is derived from a single, unified experience of vision. Where psychoanalytic accounts of spectatorship have cast the viewer as subordinated to the viewpoint of the camera—the viewer eagerly swapping her own imperfect subjectivity for 'the fantasy . . . of a "transcendental subject"' (Iversen, 2005, pp. 194–195)— Sobchack highlights the impossibility of the viewing body ever being suppressed or obliterated by the machinery of film. Technologies of vision have more widely and repeatedly been cast as replacing, or even transparently extending or transforming, human vision, but such descriptions ignore the fact that the images produced by such technologies are always, themselves, objects of human vision, rather than replacements for it (see Chapter 4). As Sobchack notes, when watching a film, 'we can see the seeing as well as the seen, hear the hearing as well as the heard, and feel the movement as well as see the moved' (1992, pp. 10–11). The camera–screen assemblage does not replace the eye and mind of the viewer; it presents another kind of vision, which then itself becomes the object of the viewer's vision.

> What is often regarded too quickly as a rivalry of vision is really a yielding to the mutual and intersubjective seeing and sharing of a visible world. This concession does not inherently entail a subjection to the vision of an other. It is also not a mistaking of the other's vision as my own in a false and alienating but necessary identification. Through acts of vision experienced as present to each other, communion or conflict may occur in the world, but one viewer does not, and finally cannot, 'usurp' the other viewer's situation, intentional and postural schema, and personal history.
>
> (Sobchack, 1992, p. 141)

Sobchack describes the viewer's relationship with the film as related to the subject's visual engagement with other viewing bodies; however, where this latter engagement is one in which we are presented with the physical presence of another body whose viewing subjectivity is hidden from us, film presents the viewing subjectivity of another whose body is hidden from us: 'Unlike other viewing persons I encounter, the film visibly duplicates the act of viewing from "within"—that is, the introceptive and intrasubjective side of vision' (1992, pp. 137–138). This leads Sobchack to give an account of a 'film body', that is, the viewing subjectivity that the technology of film creates between the film maker and film viewer.

While I do not endorse the degree to which Sobchack credits film as having its own body and subjectivity distinct from the viewer, her account of the film body is particularly useful for the current discussion given that games that utilise an avatar viewpoint explicitly seek to produce an equivalence between the player's point of view and that of the game character. This does not mean that the body of the game character is equivalent to Sobchack's film body—it is not—but the additional components and complexities introduced to Sobchack's account by the video game's avatar viewpoint allow a greater understanding of how the game player interacts visually with the simulated space of the game.

Of course, the film body's most direct correlate in the video game is the virtual camera, which, as noted previously, is necessary to the production of linear perspective. In other words, the film body possesses the ideal viewpoint that is shared by all perspectival representations. In a video game, this viewpoint can be shared by the game character (just as it can—more rarely—be shared by a film character (see the following discussion of *Lady in the Lake*), but it is not the point of view *of* the game character, even in an FPS where the two viewpoints are bonded together. At the same time, while the film body's viewpoint is that of the camera (and its video game equivalent has the viewpoint of the virtual camera), it is nonetheless not the *point of view* of the camera. Sobchack is at pains to make clear that, unlike other accounts of spectatorship that are mindful of the material technology of representation (of which apparatus theory is perhaps the most notorious), she is not claiming that the camera and projector *themselves* have a point of view, but only that they are the physical equipment necessary for the production of the film body's point of view. They no more have a point of view than the human eye has a point of view; both camera and eye are necessary components of seeing, but neither possesses in itself a subjectivity capable of having a point of view.

This highlights a key consequence of the previous discussion of perspective, viewpoint and point of view: in a visual representational regime like that of the video game, the player's primary object of visual identification is not the game character but the ideal viewpoint. The game character might be coincident with the ideal viewpoint in space, as in an FPS, but it might just as easily be entirely absent, as in the case of an RTS (real-time strategy) game. It is the ideal viewpoint that is indispensable, as this is what effects the player's relationship with the simulated space of the game. There is no need to fall back into the psychoanalysis of apparatus theory as a consequence of this, and conclude that the player is identifying with the computer producing the images or indulging in fantasies of being an omnipotent, invisible gaze—in fact, given that the video game's virtual camera is only a theoretical entity rather than a piece of physical machinery, and yet at the same time behaves much more like a physical part of the simulated world it inhabits—bound largely by the laws of Euclidean space and responding directly to the player's interactions with it—it provides less temptation to do so than the more free-wheeling, disconnected movements of the film camera.

Following Sobchack, we can maintain that the three different viewpoints—actual, ideal and avatar—while they can blend into one another in certain ways, are never a unified, homogenous whole. The player's visual relationship with the game world is therefore fluid and multiplex, and is further complicated by the nature of the player's capacity to act upon the game world. The player's visual relationship with the world of the game is determined by the ideal viewpoint of the virtual camera, but the player's capacity to act upon the virtual environment is tied directly to the game body[8]—regardless of whether the ideal viewpoint and game body occupy the same point in the representational space. As a result, and as illustrated by the third-person game, the player can be looking at the game body as a separate, externalised entity while still feeling that her capacity to act on and in the game is manifested in that separate, externalised entity.

Furthermore, a more explicit contrast between film and video game can be found elsewhere in Sobchack's characterisation of the film body. In seeking to establish the particularity of the film body and the visual experience that it makes available to the viewer, and its separateness from the points of view of the characters within a given film, she cites as evidence the fact that, not only does the viewpoint of the camera rarely take on the point of view of any of the characters in a film, but doing this seemingly renders the film's representational regime less viable. Sobchack's point, therefore, is that the film body has its own attributes that are quite different from living bodies, and which therefore seem jarring and strange if they are attributed to a living body; but it also raises the question of why, if Sobchack's claim about the irreconcilability of film body and first-person point of view is justified, the use of first-person point of view—in other words, the conflation of ideal viewpoint and avatar viewpoint—is a commonplace in video games.

In support of her claim for the awkwardness of first-person point of view in film, Sobchack cites what is considered to be the classic illustration of the non-viability of sustained first-person film narrative: the 1947 film noir *Lady in the Lake*, in which, for almost the entire film, the character of Philip Marlowe is positioned in the representational space in a way now familiar to players of first-person video games (Rehak, 2003, pp. 119–121).

> The protagonist and perceptual autobiographer, detective Philip Marlowe, is predominantly visible only *in* the perceptual correlations of 'his' (the film's) vision in the way that we appear materially visible to ourselves in our visual perception. That is, Marlowe sees himself *as* he sees only through his *visible reflection* in mirrors or other reflective surfaces. As well, he sees himself as directly and materially visible only in those *parts* of his body that are brought before his eyes— when, for example, the perceptual correlation makes visible a hand brought up to light a cigarette that hangs suspended from unseen lips. Otherwise, Marlowe is invisible to himself and to us but nonetheless constantly implicated as a *physically material* and *human presence* enabling the visible perception.
>
> (Sobchack, 1992, p. 230)

The 'strange discomfort, alienation, and disbelief experienced by the film's spectator' (Sobchack, 1992, p. 231) are taken as proof of the fundamental non-viability of this representational scheme, and the causes of this discomfort have since been discussed by numerous authors. But if watching a film with an almost uninterrupted first-person point of view is so off-putting,[9] why is it that many of the most successful video games of all time have utilised the same representational scheme without issue?

The simplest answer would be that the video game player feels like she 'is' the game character in a way that the film viewer does not feel herself to 'be' the film character. However, I hope that by now this response only seems to be begging the question. Does a first-person point of view seem natural because the player feels that she 'is' the character, or does the player feel that she 'is' the character because her viewpoint is aligned with the character's first-person point of view? Given the complexity of the relationship between actual viewpoint, ideal viewpoint and avatar viewpoint, how effectively can the player's viewpoint be aligned with a character's first-person point of view anyway? *Why* does the video game player feel like she is the game character, and what precisely does it mean to do so?

Alexander R. Galloway has sought to provide an explanation for the different status of point of view in film and video games, and furthermore has resisted the temptation to psychoanalyse viewers and players in order to do so (2006, Chapter 2). Galloway suggests that the subjective point-of-view shot, rather than working to make the viewer feel that her subjectivity and that of a character are the same, has been most successful in film when alienating us from the character whose subjectivity we are being presented with, and, furthermore, these alien subjectivities are often computerised in some way, suggesting an affinity with technologised vision that makes it more appropriate for a video game than a film:

> [T]he merging of camera and character in the subjective shot is more successful if the character in question is marked as computer- ized in some way. The first-person subjective perspective must be instigated by a character who is already mediated through some type of informatic artifice. Necessary for this effect are all the traces of computer image processing: scan lines, data printouts, target crosshairs, the low resolution of video, feedback, and so on. In other words, a deviation from the classical model of representa- tion is necessary via the use of technological manipulation *of* the image—a technological patina.
>
> (Galloway, 2006, p. 56)

This idea of an evolution from the cyborg vision of the Terminator or Robocop to that of the first-person shooter is an evocative one, but it fails to account for several aspects of the film–video game contrast in point- of-view representations. While Galloway gives an extensive listing of the successful use of point-of-view shots in films, not all of them represent computerised vision and none of them succeed where *Lady in the Lake* failed. That is, computerised vision is only a subset of a larger category of 'alienated, disoriented, or predatory vision' (2006, pp. 68–69) that also includes monsters and murderers, the drugged and insane, and their visual points of view are only presented fleetingly, rather than being the text's primary mode of representation as is the case with both *Lady in the Lake* and the first-person shooter (see Brooker, 2009, pp. 127–128).

Galloway does note the effectiveness of point of view in creating a sense of movement through space, however, and I think this suggests a slightly different explanation. Amongst other perspectives, Sobchack refers with (qualified) approval to an explanation for *Lady in the Lake*'s failure pre- sented in the 1960s by the French film theorist Jean Mitry:

> He sees the failure of *Lady in the Lake* to convince the spectator that s/he *is* Philip Marlowe as a failure based not so much on the invisibility of the character's body as on real *bodily difference*. Mitry emphasizes the difference between the spectator's body sitting rela- tively quiescent in a theater seat and the film's body invisibly living out, through the activity of the camera, a kinetic life and activity clearly not shared bodily by the spectator . . . [A]lthough we, as spectators, may be sympathetic to cinematic perception and, indeed, may intentionally parallel the film's and/or character's bodily position and perceptual bias as it intends toward and inhabits a world, we physically and materially occupy our *own* bodies and space. The per- ception whose intentional interest we share belongs always to *another*

perceiving and embodied subject, no matter how introceptively it is
visibly presented as visual for us.

(Sobchack, 1992, pp. 233–234)

Of course, the same could be said for the video game player, who is not
walking, jumping or shooting as the game character does these things.
At the same time, however, I think it draws attention to a more general
contrast between the levels of activity and agency in film and video game.
The video game produces an experience of being in and acting upon a
simulated space distinctively different from film.

Agency and Movement

Sobchack argues that the moving image of film produces a space of the
image in a way that still photography does not:

> Because a film behaves and acts, its present movement adds dimen-
> sion to the flat space of the photograph. Abstract space is dynamized
> as habitable, as 'lived in', as described in the depth that lived move-
> ment, not geometry, confers upon the world.

(1992, p. 61)

While this is true, it can be argued that the video game takes the generation of representational space further: while film turns the abstract space
of the representation into something 'lived in' by moving through that
space, the video game builds on this by presenting an experience of, not
just moving through the space, but of having an intentional relationship
to it. In fact, Lev Manovich has claimed that a shift in the status of space
sets computer graphics apart from other media technologies: 'For the first
time, space becomes a media type' (Manovich, 2001, pp. 251–252). With
computer-generated virtual environments, not only is a simulated space
presented to the viewer, but, by virtue of the fact that this space is generated in real time rather than being unspooled from a previously captured
viewpoint, it responds to the intentionality of the viewer's perception.

While the video game player to some degree and in some fashion shares
the experience of action in the video game world, the fact remains that
the video game player can never be claimed to have an experience of
simply *being* the video game body acting upon the virtual environment
in which that body is located. The player always is—and always must
be—an embodied physical presence who does not look out onto the virtual environment through the game character's eyes, but rather looks at
a screen with her own eyes; and does not engage in embodied activity in
the virtual environment, but rather manipulates one or more input devices
such as a game controller, keyboard or mouse. While skilled use of the
control device might cause its manipulation to withdraw from conscious

awareness, this manipulation nevertheless remains a part of the player's embodied experience of movement, an experience that is quite different from the bodily actions being represented in the game.

However, while the physical actions of the player and the represented actions of the game body might be quite different, the fact remains that the player is engaged in physical activity in a way that the film viewer, for example, is not, and furthermore—and crucially—that action is synchronised with the actions of the game body. That is, not only is the game player manipulating a control device while looking at the imagery of the game as opposed to the film viewer who is 'sitting relatively quiescent in a theatre seat', but the game body is responding to those manipulations. Human bodies are never completely passive or inactive, but if a film viewer shifts in her seat or stuffs a handful of popcorn into her mouth, this produces no effect on the images she sees.

I would argue that this disconnection between the embodied actions of the film viewer and the film's images facilitates the relationship between the film viewer and Sobchack's film body; there is no sense that the viewer's body and the film body are directly equivalent, as this would create a sense of dislocation or awkwardness where the visual experience of the film body follows a logic alien to embodied human perception. For example, if the viewer felt that she was directing or controlling the vision of the film body, common features of film such as the shot–reverse shot would presumably be jarring and disorientating, given that they are utterly alien to the attributes of embodied human vision. The other side of this, however, is that the use of a first-person point of view in film feels unpleasant and constricting; when the film body attempts to impersonate a living human body, its obvious lack of attributes fundamental to the viewer's embodied perception—such as a sense of agency and an intentional relationship with the environment—creates a sense of discomfort. Sobchack describes the experience of watching *Lady in the Lake* as one of claustrophobic constriction, and presumably this comes from the sense of being trapped inside a body over which one has no control; the viewer can only peer helplessly out of its eyes as it is propelled through the world by an alien subjectivity whose workings are hidden from its passenger. This explains the fact that point-of-view shots in film are largely restricted to depictions of 'alienated, disoriented, or predatory vision': these are subjectivities that, rather than inviting an expectation of familiarity and control in the viewer, have either had their capacity to see or act deranged, or are driven forward by a kind of monomaniacal automatism—these gun-toting cyborgs or psycho killers disregard all other possible actions or objects of attention as they single-mindedly hunt down their prey. Unlike Philip Marlowe in *Lady in the Lake*, these figures do not seem capable of distraction or shifts of interest; the viewer is not frustrated by her inability to control these bodies because they are bodies that are understood to be unable even to control themselves.

In the video game, on the other hand, the player has a sense of agency in the simulated space. In a first-person game, if an object in the virtual environment catches the player's eye, she can centre the ideal viewpoint on it, can move that viewpoint through the simulated space towards it, can possibly interact with it. The fact that the viewpoint being centred on the object is not the embodied viewpoint of the player but a viewpoint generated by the game, or that the player is not physically walking, or shooting or picking up the object, is not crucial here; what is crucial is the experience of agency and intentionality. The movements of the game body are not the same as those of the player body just as the viewpoint on the game world is not the same as the viewpoint of the player, but the movements of the player and game character are synchronous and seemingly generated by the player's intentionality. This is presumably why even games with quite rudimentary, low-resolution images can create a sense of involvement and immersion: the key factor is not a simultaneity of character point of view and player viewpoint—and in fact such a simultaneity can only ever be imperfect and unstable—but rather a simultaneity of the activity represented in the game and the actions of the player's body, which are generated in response to that activity in a circular fashion. This provides an answer to the question raised about third-person games: why does the separation of player and character viewpoints not lessen the player's sense of involvement? First, even in a first-person game the viewpoints of player and game character are never truly unified, meaning that the difference between first-person and third-person representation is only one of degree, and, second, a more important kind of simultaneity between player and game character—a simultaneity of action rather than viewpoint—is just as present in the third-person game as the first-person. In fact, given that the player has a greater awareness of the game body and its actions when the ideal viewpoint is situated outside the game body, it is possible that—at least in some instances—the third-person game creates a greater sense of simultaneity of action than the first-person.

Returning to the two examples of spectacularised third-person game bodies discussed earlier, it can be noted that both Lara Croft and Max Payne require carefully calibrated interactions with their environments— swinging off ledges or leaping backwards down flights of stairs, for example—which require the player to be able to see the spatial relationships between game body and environmental features in order to pull them off. Our lack of visual awareness of our own bodies in daily life is more than compensated for by proprioception; we don't need to look at our feet in order to walk or look at our hands in order to hammer a nail precisely because we have an unreflective awareness of where our limbs are, what they can do there, and how to go about making them do it. When given a proxy body by a game, proprioception might allow us to carry out complex and precise manipulations of the game controller while focusing on the action of the game world rather than the object in our hand, but it does not provide us with an innate sense of the movement and capacities of the game body. The result of this tends to be a game body whose capacities are extremely limited and predictable: it can move at a fixed speed, jump a fixed distance, fire a gun and so forth, but these actions are simple and small in number, and our understanding of them is based purely on the predictability of their results, rather than being equivalent to the intricate and adaptable array of actions possible when using our own bodies.

Seeing the game body from a third-person viewpoint, therefore, might facilitate a more natural relationship with it than a first-person one by allowing the player to evaluate and contextualise the body's capacities and interactions in a way that more closely approaches her ability to do so with her own physical body. Not having access to a pre-conscious awareness of it as she does with her own body, she can at least engage other senses in order to understand the game body's attributes. Because the game's representational schema cannot directly engage our sense of proprioception, the third-person game substitutes visual for proprioceptive information, an externalised representation of the game body providing a sense of the character's bodily disposition in space where proprioception cannot. In this sense, the third-person game is perhaps a more effective attempt to simulate physical presence than the first-person game, which lacks such a detailed, surrogate proprioceptive experience. Proprioception is itself produced through the integration of multiple sensory experiences, and so visual information always constitutes a part of proprioception; in this case, it perhaps simply constitutes its entirety.

Shared Embodiment

Just as the film viewer's visual experience becomes a synthesis of viewing body and film body in Sobchack's account, rather than either a replacement of viewing body by film body or a clinical, disengaged inspection of the screen, so the game player experiences a coming together of playing body and game body. As noted earlier, if this did not happen, video games would presumably not be as successful as they are.

Research into how we experience our own living bodies and understand those of others demonstrates how natural and basic such a relationship can be. For example, the discovery of mirror neurons in the brain suggests that, at a basic level, we share an experience of the actions of other bodies (see Chapter 2). In other words, when we see another person perform an action, our own brains rehearse that action, on some level sharing the experience of the other person based on an innate understanding of their movements. This helps us to understand and empathise with other living bodies, but is it not possible that it can produce a sympathetic sharing of the bodily movements represented to us by a video game?

More directly relevant might be experiments that have manipulated subjects' sense of body ownership. Neuroscientist H. Henrik Ehrsson has become well-known for experiments that cause subjects to believe that part or all of another body—living or artificial—belongs to them. In the most famous of these experiments, a team lead by Ehrsson fitted each subject with a head-mounted display that fed her images from cameras attached to the head of another person standing behind her. In other words, the experiment set up a visual relationship much the same as that between FPS player and game body, but with a real living body substituting for the virtual body of the game character. When this was combined with tactile stimulation widely used in body-ownership experiments, subjects could be made to feel that they were having an 'out-of-body experience', looking at their own bodies from outside themselves, or, in a variation on the format, even feel that their bodies had been replaced by a mannequin or doll (Petkova and Ehrsson, 2008; van der Hoort, Guterstam and Ehrsson, 2011; Guterstam and Ehrsson, 2012).

Because the subjects' movements were manifested by the body being looked at, the overall effect was not really like that of playing a first-person game, but rather of playing a third-person game. The loci of viewpoint and action were disarticulated, seemingly occupying different points in space so that the subject's capacity for action was exercised by the body being seen in front of her rather than by the one she seemed to be watching it with. Our capacity to have such an experience makes a close identification between game player and game body in third-person games seem more natural and attainable than it might otherwise appear.

Significantly for the discussion of action and perception when successfully employing a third-person viewpoint in video games, a key component of all such body-ownership illusions, from the originary 'rubber hand illusion' onwards (see de Vignemont, 2011), has been the subject's observation of tactile stimulation of the surrogate body that is synchronous with the feeling of tactile stimulation of her real body. Again, it is the perceived simultaneity of what the subject sees happening to the simulated body and what the subject does or feels with her own body that creates a sense of commonality, and this effect has even been produced using a computer-generated 'virtual arm' rather than a physical prop (Slater et al., 2008). More generally, temporal synchronisation can be seen to function as the glue that holds these experiences together. Where sensory experiences contradict one another or arise from differing sources, it is the fact that they share an experiential rhythm that allows them a degree of unity. This is clear also from the history of virtual reality, in which latency has been the traditional enemy: the complex processing required to generate VR's computer graphics inevitably produces a delay of some kind between the movement of the user's body and the response of the image, which can cause the simulation to falter, producing nausea and disorientation.

In fact, it has been suggested that human experience arises from the synchronising of different kinds of perceptual information at a more fundamental level. The research of David Eagleman and his colleagues on time perception has addressed the question of how, given that it takes the brain differing amounts of time to process sensory stimuli in differing modalities (and tactile stimuli can take different amounts of time to arrive at the brain depending on how far from the head it originates), how can our brains accurately discern the temporal relationship between them? (Stetson, Fiesta and Eagleman, 2007). For example, if you click your fingers in front of your face, your brain registers the sound made slightly before it processes the visual information produced by seeing your fingers move; so how do we attribute what we see and what we hear to the same event? In the case of the clicking fingers, this attribution can be based on our awareness of a single, unified action originating at our own bodies— in other words, we know that the different sensory stimuli are connected because we created them—and Eagleman and his colleagues suggest that this fact is used to calibrate our synthesis of different kinds of sensory information from external sources too. So even when making sense of real rather than simulated sensory experiences, our bodies are always serving as nexuses in flows of perceptual stimuli whose relationships to one another are never direct or self-evident, and it is only by actively fixing the temporal relationships between these stimuli and the actions of the body that they can be effectively synthesised to create an integrated and coherent experiential unity.

These examples draw attention to the fact that my sense of what is and isn't my body, and the relationships between the different kinds of sensory information it receives, is not fixed and predictable, but rather is generated dynamically through interaction with the environment and is always quite fluid. A blind person senses her environment through the end of a cane; someone else will flinch while watching a third person fall over as if afraid that any resulting injury will be manifested on her own body. We routinely shift the boundaries of our bodily experience in multiple ways and to multiple degrees, and the simulated spaces and bodies of video games generate sensory, kinaesthetic and affective engagement by inviting us to extend this capacity into their virtual worlds.

Conclusion

Far from being particular to digital simulations of space, questions about how human–machine interfaces can allow technological devices to fundamentally alter our sense of who and where we are have been lurking in the background throughout human history. When Galileo put an eye to a telescope, did he have an experience of being a human being with radically different perceptual powers standing on the earth, or of being a human being with unremarkable perceptual powers floating in space above the moon, seeing its features close at hand? (see Ihde, 2011a, p. 81).[10] Or of simply being a man looking at a representation of the moon in a glass lens? By integrating external artefacts into our sense of our bodily boundaries in such a way that we feel ourselves to be sensing and/or acting at a location beyond the skin, interfacing necessarily alters our perception of space. But it is perhaps easier to consider these questions using video games because the representational regime of the video game requires that some of this complexity be managed by identifying the player's capacity for action at a distance with a separate and fictitious game body, making this spatial distribution clearer. The third-person game is analogous to Galileo putting an eye to his telescope and having the uncanny experience of seeing a double of himself floating far away in space, sharing his close vantage point on the moon.

The third-person video game makes visible the multiplication and distribution of perception and action that takes place when experiencing a digital simulation of space by introducing another body—that of the game character—whose confusing relationship with the game player literalises the way in which a close engagement with an artefact can change our relationship with space. Does the game player feel that she 'is' the game character, 'inside' the simulated space of the game? And, if so, how does the technology of representation on which the game depends enable such an experience?

Video games have demonstrated an ability to create a sense of immediacy and involvement in players, which suggests that a sense of involvement in their represented events and agency in their simulated environments is a key part of their appeal. At the same time, however, to suggest that players experience games in the same way that they experience embodied everyday activity, or that the simulated characters and events of games can swamp their existing subjectivity or embodied experiences, is implausible. Like any media form, the video game creates new experiences by producing another layer of embodied experience that articulates with the foundation of embodied experience that is with us all the time, creating novel combinations. But how can video games do this? A naïve (but common) answer would be through their simulational realism. Certainly, the creation of greater representational realism (e.g. more convincing facial expressions or more true-to-life water movement) has been a key concern of the video game industry. But this goal is founded on the idea that human action and perception is a stable, 'natural' thing, a fixed point with which the representational and control regime of the video game must be aligned; if the body of the user can be inundated with simulated experiences, her experience of the physical world—of sitting in a chair looking at a screen and manipulating a game controller, for example—will be blotted out and replaced with the experience of being someone else, somewhere else. This idea of course underpins much of the discourse of virtual reality, but the fundamental problem with it is simply that the physical body of the user is the surface upon which these simulated experiences play out; if the physical, embodied experience of the user were removed from the equation, there would no longer be any perceptual experience of the simulated space. Virtual reality is not an illusion produced by digital technologies that can trick the human mind and perceptual apparatus— on the contrary, it is a subjective experience created *by* the human mind and perceptual apparatus as they synthesise a varied and often contradictory array of perceptual stimuli to create a coherent unity.

Rather than the replacement of one kind of experience with another, the sense that my body has a spatial relationship with a simulated environment is dependent upon me having multiple kinds of experience simultaneously, of feeling that I am simultaneously here and there, me and him. Again, the often simplistic accounts given of realism in video games or the experience of video game playing themselves result from how naturally, how effortlessly, we can generate such experiences. The video game player does not feel disorientated, is not troubled by the irreconcilability of different kinds of perceptual experience; like the blind person who senses the world from the end of a cane but can still use this sensory information to manoeuvre her fleshy body around the obstacles that are sensed there, the game player is simultaneously sensing and acting on the chair and in the game world, without even being conscious of the distinction between the two. Interfacing with the representational and control schemata of the video game allows both of these things to exist simultaneously, being superimposed one upon the other to create a unified experience without them ever resolving into a single, unambiguous thing.

VR does not work by simply replacing existing sensory experiences with new, alternative, computer-generated ones in order to dupe the brain. Rather, it adds a variety of additional stimuli, and the brain is capable of weaving the resulting multiplicity of often contradictory stimuli into a new, coherent experience—just as it does with the multiplicity of sensory experience it receives at all other times. Rather than replacing embodied human experience, it is dependent upon embodied human experience in order to function.

The digital simulation of space more generally demonstrates the expansion and multiplication, rather than replacement, of perceptual experience via engagement with technological artefacts, and our capacity to spread our sense of action and perception beyond the boundaries of our bodies without our bodily experience ever being lost. Simulated environments such as video games or virtual reality therefore demonstrate that the capacity to seamlessly incorporate technological artefacts into our embodied experience of action and perception—already seen in examples such as hammering or typing—can bear a much greater load of sensory stimuli and complexity of interaction than seen with these less complex devices. While interacting with a virtual environment might seem like a form of engagement with technology that is fundamentally different from hammering a nail, for example—one being about sensory stimulation while the other is about practical action in the physical world—in the last chapter we saw that even wielding a hammer is an experience foundationally dependent upon the hammer's capacity to itself generate new kinds of sensory experience. A technology like virtual reality is distinguished by its capacity to generate sensory stimuli independent of a physical source, as well as the greater volume of stimuli produced; however, while virtual environments deliver a constant stream of compelling sensory stimuli, our brains remain able to absorb this stimulation and fuse it with stimuli coming from other sources to create a unified experience.

No matter how elaborate the simulationary technology used to create virtual spaces might become, it will never be able to replace or overwhelm physically embodied experience; but, at the same time, not only does it not need to, but its simulations would not be possible if it did. The interfacing of body and technology means that the user's embodied perception and agency stretches out to meet the simulation and incorporate it, rather than simply being a static, passive dupe of its cleverly wrought illusions. As we have seen, key to this incorporation is the temporally synchronous, multi-sensory synthesis of stimuli, and the final two chapters will investigate the ways in which this relationship between the senses and time operate.

Notes

1. Some of the material in this chapter has previously been published in Black, D. (2017). Why Can I See My Avatar? Embodied Visual Engagement in the Third-Person Video Game. *Games and Culture*, 12(2), pp. 179–199.
2. Krueger (1991, Chapter 4) remains a good brief overview of VR's origins.
3. Jaron Lanier's book *Dawn of the New Everything* (2017) gives a good sense of the early days of VR. Perhaps the film that best illustrates the virtual reality mania of the time was *Lawnmower Man* (1992). The fact that this VR-themed film was marketed as an adaptation of a Stephen King story from which VR was conspicuously absent demonstrates that the addition of VR was considered a sure-fire way to guarantee popular appeal.
4. A prominent recent illustration of this fact was the 'What colour is this dress?' Internet meme (Trendacosta and Gonzalez, 2015), and related illusions like the chequerboard illusion, which demonstrate the degree to which our perception of colour also results from our brains negotiating different kinds of visual information in order to produce a single, synthetic perceptual outcome. The attribution of colour arises from an assessment of contextual information such as spatial and lighting qualities; in a photograph where some of these contextual cues are missing, different viewers can attribute it with different colours (see Gegenfurtner, Bloj and Toscani, 2015; Lafer-Sousa, Hermann and Conway, 2015; Winkler et al., 2015). For further discussion of this problem with Hansen's perspective, see Chapter 4.
5. One of the many definitions of VR offered by Jaron Lanier is 'A media technology for which measurement is more important than display' (Lanier, 2017, p. 170).

6. Of course, painting and film can create an awareness of, or even a sense of identification with, the viewpoint of a figure 'inside' the representation, but cannot produce a sustained merging with this viewpoint because they cannot respond to shifts in the viewer's focus of attention. It is this experience of merging two viewpoints in a manner similar to the merging of ideal and actual viewpoints that I am concerned with here.

7. This is the case for 3D spaces across game genres—even in, for example, the real-time strategy game, which presents the player with a godlike viewpoint able to pan and zoom across battlefields or continents to impersonally scrutinise armies and cities. While the RTS's ideal viewpoint is disembodied, it is still depicted as manifested in the space of the game and subject to its laws as it travels about within it. Even if it can move instantaneously within the game space, for example in response to clicks on a particular location in a 'minimap', there is still a clearer sense of travelling between spatial locations with a clear and consistent relationship to one another (a relationship itself manifested in the minimap) than the filmic viewpoint's staccato shifts through space and even time.

8. My use of the term 'game body' throughout this chapter should not be considered in any way based upon or equivalent to Vivian Sobchack's film body. I am simply using this term to refer to the simulations of physical bodies produced within video games.

9. The recent film *Hardcore Henry* (2016) was an attempt to revive the idea of the first-person film in the GoPro era. However, the generally negative response of audiences, not to mention the recurrent critical complaint that it simply mimics the experience of playing first-person video games, doesn't suggest that it has established the viability of this approach in film.

10. See Ihde, 1990, pp. 42–58 for a deeper phenomenological account of Galileo's experience of telescope use.

4   Aesthesiogenesis

When they are concentrating hard on writing, some people poke out their tongues. Other people can be seen to jiggle a leg or fidget in some other way while engaged in work that requires more concentration than physical exertion.

Such behaviour is likely to be dismissed as incidental, a non-generalisable quirk in one individual's relationship with her or his body, or as evidence that the proper mode of reading or writing—in which all effort is confined to the brain—has not been mastered; but it seems to me that there is a larger significance in this. If I poke out my tongue while writing, as some people do, then poking out my tongue is part of the act of writing for me. The physical act of writing does not only consist of manipulating a pen, but additionally includes poking out my tongue. The fact that poking out my tongue does not, itself, produce written words does not disqualify it from inclusion in the act of writing; if someone pokes out their tongue when writing, this is clearly, in some way, a necessary or at least facilitatory part of the act of writing for them, whether they are aware of it or not. Writing never consists entirely of the physical movements that make the marks or symbols; there are always numerous other physical and cognitive processes necessary to get the writing done, and for some people they include the poking out of their tongues.

I think the larger point to be taken from this example is that, while the productiveness of the human body and mind are central to an understanding of interfacing, it would be a mistake to see this productiveness in purely linear terms—for example, the linear movement of words from the mind of the writer to a page, or the movement of information from a machine into the mind of a user. This linear back and forth is, of course, precisely the model that traditionally informs both the design and analysis of user interfaces, whether it be the rational user's transmission of instructions to a computer or even the technology company's projection of a certain logic of use into the work habits of the user. But the user interface is never simply a conduit for forces and influences that originate elsewhere; while all sorts of constraints can be designed into an artefact, and the user's mode of engagement will always be shaped by existing habit, interfacing cannot help but produce some excess.

The productiveness of the human body is never linear and unified. Because the body is not simply a tool utilised by a disembodied, rational consciousness to carry out singular, well-defined aims in the most efficient way possible, it is constantly throwing out tangential energies and actions. Poking out one's tongue might not be integral to the business of writing in the same way that making marks on a page or screen is, but the writer who pokes out her tongue is producing branching or cascading flows of bodily movement and energy that spill out from the central business of manipulating a keyboard or pen to become part of writing's larger context. Could poking out one's tongue be integrated more fully into the business of writing? Perhaps—maybe someone will design a keyboard that sprays a bad-tasting mist when a word is misspelled in a word processor—but my point is about something more general than the possibility of our having underestimated the potential usefulness of tongue-poking. Picking up on a theme introduced through my discussion of natural user interface design in Chapter 2, this broader point is that the productiveness of interfacing, and its potential to create new kinds of experience, needs to be appreciated more and understood better so that we can move away from conservative and normative frameworks for understanding our relationships with technology.

Chapter 2 asked where bodies end and objects begin, and this chapter will swing back around to that question and try to make further progress towards an answer using sensory experience as a measure of human engagement with the world. In it I will work to clarify the distinction between interfacing as the replacement or supplementation of existing capacities or practices, and interfacing as harnessing a multiplication of energy flows to produce new kinds of action and perception.

The Problem With Prosthesis

Our increasingly intimate relationships with an ever-growing panoply of technological artefacts is often presented as following a logic of prosthesis. From Freud's suggestion that the machines at the disposal of the Victorian gentleman had transformed him into a 'prosthetic god' (2015, p. 69),[1] to Marshall McLuhan's claim that electronic media had created an external nervous system (1964, pp. 3–4), to a more recent fascination with certain kinds of technologised amputee bodies such as sprinters with high-tech 'cheetah' legs (Össur America, 2016) that allow them to outperform non-amputee athletes, it has been suggested that our contemporary dependence upon various technological artefacts and their near-seamless integration into our habitus has made prosthesis an almost universal experience. The term 'prosthesis' might seem, therefore, to be a useful complement to the investigation of interfacing. On the contrary, however, I believe that prosthesis as trope brings with it a real danger of fundamentally compromising and misdirecting any investigation of technologised embodiment.

In 1999, Sarah S. Jain described prosthesis as 'a tempting theoretical gadget with which to examine the porous places of bodies and tools' (1999, p. 49), and, in 2006, Joanne Morra and Marquard Smith commented that '"the prosthetic" has . . . begun to assume an epic status that is out of proportion with its abilities to fulfil our ambitions for it' (2006, p. 2). The fashionability of prosthesis as a trope around the turn of the century provoked an effective critique from writers such as Steven L. Kurzman (2001) and Vivian Sobchack (2004, pp. 205–225), scholars who saw little connection between their experiences of prosthetic embodiment as amputees and the more abstract, metaphorical deployment of the term in reference to contemporary experiences of technological dependency:

> Sometime, fairly recently, after the 'cyborg' became somewhat tired and tiresome from academic overuse, we started to hear and read about 'the prosthetic'—less, in its ordinary usage, as a specific material replacement of a missing limb or body part than as a sexy, new metaphor that, whether noun or (more frequently) adjective, has become tropological currency for describing a vague and shifting constellation of relationships among bodies, technologies, and subjectivities.
>
> (Sobchack, 2004, p. 207)

In her essay, Sobchack is careful to make it clear that she is not seeking to disqualify those who lack her more 'genuine' experience of prosthesis from talking about it, but rather to argue that the deployment of this 'sexy new metaphor' shows little interest in the embodied experience of those thousands of people who are best described using the term. That is, by employing prosthesis as a trope, many writers miss the important insight into the nature of prosthesis to be found in its actual lived experience, which is that the prosthetic experience is multiple and contradictory, shifting according to circumstances and evading any simple, singular significance. At one moment the prosthesis might feel like a part of the body and at another like something alien; at one moment it seems to render invisible the boundary between body and artefact, while at another it works to accentuate it (Sobchack, 2004, pp. 205–225, 2010).

There has been a tendency to deploy the prosthesis as part of an attack on a humanist conception of the human body/subject as isolated and self-contained, an unproblematically and self-evidently independent and discrete unit (see Chapter 2). The fact that technological artefacts can come to feel like a part of our bodies, this argument goes, demonstrates that this conception of the self is fallacious. And of course it does, but leaving the argument there doesn't really get us very far, and certainly does nothing much to problematise the simplistic understanding of the self on which this humanist ideal rests. At its most unsophisticated, this line of argument ends with a pop-posthumanism or pop-transhumanism that takes it as proof that the body is simply a kind of fiction constructed by the mind, one that can be partially or completely replaced with machinery; but even less naïve accounts tend to declare victory after problematising atomistic conceptions of the self and so never grapple with the details of what, exactly, prosthetic experience does and does not say about embodiment. While it might demonstrate that our sense of self is not fixed and does not simply arise from the physical and biological fact of our bodies, the fact remains that our sense of who we are is still *largely* confined to the boundaries of our biological bodies, and I certainly don't find my sense of embodiment constantly threatening to dissipate across the many different technological artefacts with which I engage in the course of any given day. Only after dispensing with an either/or approach that pits the body as fixed, contained and self-evident against the body as polymorphous, illusory or a social or technological construction can we begin to appreciate the complexity of our relationships with the things around us.

There are multiple criticisms that can be raised concerning the broad application of the term prosthesis, but here I will focus on one that I think makes it fundamentally inappropriate for the discussion of interfacing outside specific and limited cases. I will call this *the problem of redundancy.*

A prosthesis is generally understood to be a replacement for part of the body.[2] A prosthetic arm, for example, is a replacement for an arm that is missing from a body when it is compared to a standard body considered to be 'normal'. But when the term prosthesis is used to refer more broadly to instances of well-integrated technology use, it becomes unclear what, exactly, is being replaced. In fact, such usage often explicitly takes these technological 'prostheses' to be replacing specific bodily capacities despite the fact that these capacities are clearly neither missing nor inactive.

For example, in Marshall McLuhan's argument that the media function as 'extensions of man', his model of auto-amputation (1964, p. 42ff.) suggests that sensory capacities are removed from the body and replaced with technological prostheses, but the logical problem with this account is that the appearance of television, for example, is not accompanied by a loss of the power of sight, and if it were then television would have no value precisely because it is dependent *upon* the human power of sight rather than interchangeable with it. The same problem obviously exists regarding McLuhan's central and repeated assertion that electronic media constitute a new, external nervous system. On the face of it, such a claim might seem to blur the distinction between human body and electronic artefact, suggesting as it does that we and our electronic media devices have come to function as unified, seamlessly integrated entities. However, in important ways, McLuhan's approach maintains an untenable belief in a radical difference between 'direct' sensory experience and that produced by electronic media, and where it does suggest a seamless joining of the two it does so in ways that obscure its significance.

According to McLuhan's account, 'In the physical stress of superstimulation of various kinds, the central nervous system acts to protect itself by a strategy of amputation or isolation of the offending organ, sense, or function' (1964, p. 42). Television, therefore, can be understood as a prosthetic sensory organ deployed as part of a defensive disconnection from direct sensory engagement with the hyper-stimulation of modernity. It might be countered that the introduction of television only increases our sensory load, rather than limiting it; however, I would argue that the opposite is true, and there is perhaps more value in McLuhan's argument if we highlight its suggestion of media technology as reducing, rather than extending, our sensory experience.

The fact that sensory experience is always produced through interaction with our environment makes the sensory stimulation produced by electronic media different more in quantity than quality from other technological artefacts. For example, a Palaeolithic hunter would have evaluated the damage done to his prey by feeling the distance travelled through its body by his spear, and the resistance of different parts of the animal's body to its penetration. In other words, the spear mediated between the sensory organs of the hunter's biological body and the wounded animal, transforming the hunter's sensorium in a way that produced new and different ways of experiencing the world. The sensorium of all living things extends out beyond the boundaries of their bodies at all times—this extension is definitional to the word sensorium—but, furthermore, the use of technological artefacts to produce new kinds of sensory experience, rather than appearing with mass media, has been a feature of human life for as long as human beings have existed.

And if we compare the hunter's spear with the television, we find that the spear seems more amenable to claims about replacing sensory experience than the television (although, in reality, neither actually does). An artefact like a spear, or a blind person's cane or carpenter's hammer, functions much more clearly to extend its user's sensorium, producing sensory information that is tightly and often unconsciously integrated into that person's experience of the world than is a television set. A television viewer looks at a television, which exists as a clearly separable locus of sensory investigation for the viewer, but the carpenter does not look at her hammer and see it as an isolated generator of sensation; rather, the hammer operates as an extension of the carpenter's body *through* which she experiences part of her environment as well as acting upon it. Contra McLuhan's claims, the mass media do not extend our nervous systems out into the world, enlarging their reach; they are, rather, largely self-contained artefacts that we look *at*, rather than look *with*. The much older and less complex artefact of the blind person's cane, on the other hand, is very much something that its skilled user can sense *with*. As a result, McLuhan's claims are not open to criticism because artefacts cannot change our sensory relationship with the world around us, but rather because our capacity to do this is actually the norm, rather than an exception produced by mass media—which are, ironically, quite poor at doing this when compared to all sorts of other technological artefacts. Rather than prosthetically adding to or replacing the human organs and tissues that produce sensory experience, the mass media only produce new kinds of sensory stimuli for them to register.

Prosthetic Memories

A broader illustration of the problem of redundancy can be found in the idea of 'prosthetic memory'. Freud's 'prosthetic god' of the Victorian age was claimed to have a prosthetic memory due to the technologies of gramophone and photography (2015, p. 68); André Leroi-Gourhan's account of the development of human technics progresses from the replacement of bodily capacities by tools and machines to the replacement of cognitive capacities through the externalisation of memory (1993); and Clark and Chalmers claim that, for their Alzheimer's disease–suffering character Otto, 'his notebook plays the role usually played by a biological memory' (1998, p. 12). But what, precisely, *is* a prosthetic memory, and how can it replace regular, old-fashioned memory if that original memory is still present and functioning?[3] The idea of prosthetic memory rapidly begins to fall apart when these kinds of questions are asked about what it is and how it works.

Bernard Stiegler's *Technics and Time* (1998, 2009, 2011) takes up Leroi-Gourhan's claims about the industrialisation of memory to provide the central conception of technology from which it works, especially in its second and third volumes. According to Stiegler, technologies of information storage and retrieval are a kind of artificial memory that, by virtue of being prosthetic in nature, are integrated directly into the process by which memory informs our experience of the present. New technologies of information, therefore, produce new ways of understanding the world, replacing older ways of engaging with the information available to us. Stiegler's negative account of the effects of contemporary mass media hinges on the idea of 'industrial tertiary retention'. His claims for tertiary retention are in turn founded on Edmund Husserl's phenomenology of time perception, which breaks the experience of time down into primary and secondary retention, or memory (Husserl, 1991). Husserl uses the term 'secondary retention', or 'secondary memory', to refer to what we generally mean when we use the term 'memory'. The contemporary technical term for this is *episodic memory*, the kind of memory where you recreate the experience of living through a particular experience.[4] Primary retention, on the other hand, is a short-term retention of sensory experience, a provisional chunking of perception before it is filed away in secondary memory. The classic example of primary retention's explanatory usefulness is the experiencing of melody: my perception of each note in the melody is generated, not by that note alone, but its relationship with the notes that came before it (and those that will come after). There would seem to be a kind of memory in play there because the significance of the current note arises only through an awareness of past notes, but clearly it's something quite different from what we usually think of as memory because that kind of memory is something completed and separate from our current moment in time. According to Husserl's account, secondary memory can't have a constitutive effect on current perception because it is a discrete representation of a past experience separate from what is happening now.

Central to Stiegler's analysis is the claim that '[t]echnics does not aid memory: it *is* memory, originarily *assisted* "retentional finitude"' (2009, p. 65). Stiegler's aim is to establish that human memory is always 'prosthetic' in the sense that it has always been reliant on external records—just as humanity has always been 'prosthetic' in the sense of having always been reliant on tools. But to do this, Stiegler must reject Husserl's depiction of time perception as beginning with a neutral perception of the world, a 'primal impression' that consists of a pure sensory experience untouched by memory, context or interpretation, from which trails primary memory. According to Husserl,

> The primal impression is something absolutely unmodified, the primal source of all further consciousness and being. Primal impression has as its content that which the word 'now' signifies, insofar as it is taken in the strictest sense. Each new now is the content of a new primal impression. Ever new primal impressions continuously flash forth with ever new matter, now the same, now changing.
>
> (Husserl, 1991, p. 70)

But if primary memory is generated by such primal impressions, then clearly our relationship with technology cannot be constitutive of memory, as the primary impression is produced by our human sensory apparatus alone. To refute this, Stiegler presents examples of media reception that make a belief in such a pure relationship with sensory stimuli untenable. For example, if I listen to a music recording on one day, and then listen to it again on the following day, it is likely that my experience of the music will be to some extent different each time (Stiegler, 2011, pp. 18–19). However, given that the recording technology produces an exact reproduction in each case, my primal impressions should also be identical. Stiegler presents this and other examples of the capacity of media representations to inflect perception[5] as evidence that technologies of recording and representation, while constituting a tertiary retention, or third phase of memory that falls after the primary and secondary retentions that take place in the human body, can actually inform primary retention. Thus Stiegler concludes that,

> consciousness is always in some fashion a montage of overlapping primary, secondary, and tertiary memories. Thus, we must mark as tertiary retentions all forms of 'objective' memory: cinematogram, photogram, phonogram, writing, paintings, sculptures—but also monuments and objects in general, since they bear witness, for me, say, of a past that I enforcedly did not myself live.
>
> (Stiegler, 2011, pp. 27–28)

Stiegler presumably puts inverted commas around 'objective' when describing mechanical recordings as memories because an objective memory—like an objective emotion—is an impossibility. But if it is impossible for memories to be objective, then how can these non-subjective mechanical recordings actually be memories in the first place?

The problem with Stiegler's engagement with Husserl is not that there isn't really a flaw in Husserl's account, but rather that Stiegler has identified a flaw, not in Husserl's understanding of technology, but rather in his understanding of secondary retention. According to Husserl, secondary retention must be something separate from primary retention because it is a representation, a recording of perceptual experience that must therefore be separate from it and come afterwards, thereby having no capacity to be involved in the creation of what it records. For Husserl, primary retention is inhabited wholly by perception, and secondary retention wholly by what he calls imagination.[6] Stiegler complains that Husserl refuses to acknowledge that imagination is always also present in primary retention, but he doesn't acknowledge the complementary problem that perception is also always present in secondary retention.

Stiegler seeks to improve Husserl's account of memory by adding to it the role of media technologies, but what it really needs is for media technology to be taken away. Husserl's understanding of secondary memory—like most people's understanding of memory—is clearly already based on a metaphor of recording technology. The separation of secondary memory from perception is justified on the grounds that secondary memory is a representation, a record, of a completed event, which can be replayed repeatedly after that event has finished; rather than needing Stiegler's account of listening to a gramophone record, Husserl's account already contains one, in that secondary memory is described as a kind of biological gramophone. Consequently, rather than correcting Husserl's account of memory, Stiegler's shares its reliance on an inaccurate mechanical model.

The Memory Machine

Memory researcher Daniel L. Schacter has noted the past influence but present untenability of the myth 'that memories are passive or literal recordings of reality', like 'a series of family pictures stored in the photo album of our minds' (1996, p. 5):

> Twenty years ago, when I first entered the field of memory research, it was fashionable for cognitive psychologists to compare memories to computer files that are placed in storage and pulled out when needed. Back then, nobody thought that the study of memory should include the subjective experience of remembering. We now believe with some degree of certainty that our memories are not just bits of data that we coldly store and retrieve, computerlike.
>
> (Schacter, 1996, p. 4)

The flaw in Husserl's account is ultimately the same flaw that underlies any account of prosthetic memory: it's the isolation and limitation of the role of perception. Rather than making a crude division between primary retention, which is attached to perception, and secondary retention, which is a mental representation of something previously perceived, it makes much more sense to see the formation of memory as a continuous, recursive chunking of perception that produces ever-larger aggregates that are always interacting with an ongoing continuity of perception. Perception always has a temporal existence—as we saw in David Eagleman's account of sensory experience in Chapter 3, even the neurological process of gathering sensory stimuli takes place over a short but significant duration rather than occurring in an instant of the now—but, in addition, perception is always a part of memory. Rather than secondary memory as like a gramophone recording or home movie that represents a static object of perception after the fact, remembering is a much more dynamic experience, and a form of perception itself.

Alison Winter's book *Memory: Fragments of a Modern History* (2012) provides an account of the historical evolution of understandings of memory in which the enduring influence of metaphors of media technology is clear. Even though nineteenth- and early twentieth-century pioneers of psychology such as Hugo Münsterberg and Frederic Bartlett foregrounded the instability of memories, their insights struggled to make headway against a popular, common-sense belief that the brain operated like a recording or information storage device (Winter, 2012, p. 198). Probably more than anything else, the work of Wilder Penfield in the mid-twentieth century gave this common-sense understanding of memory an air of scientific validity. While performing surgery on the brains of conscious epilepsy patients, Penfield reported, electrical stimulation of the brain could initiate a 'replaying' of memories. Penfield explicitly characterised memory as operating like a recording technology; his account of electrical stimulation causing a woman to repeatedly hear a popular song evokes an image of the brain as biological gramophone: Penfield needed only to drop his electrode into the grooves of the brain to play back a perfect reproduction of the music over and over again (Winter, 2012, p. 78; The Brain as Tape Recorder, 1957). This understanding of memory was contradicted by other research being done in his time, and today this belief in a stable, mechanical recording of experience in the brain has no scientific validity, but Penfield's claims were popular in the media, presumably because they fitted with everyday experiences of using media technologies (Winter, 2012, p. 96).

While Husserl might not have referenced the gramophone, he does illustrate his understanding of the relationship between secondary retention and perception using the example of remembering a visit to a theatre. Husserl argues that we don't remember the act of perceiving an object, but only that the object was perceived; as a result, memory records the object, not the perception, which is therefore outside secondary retention.

> I remember the illuminated theater means: 'in my interior' I see the illuminated theater as having been . . . The theater then hovers before me in the representation as something present . . . This re-presentation of the perception of the theater must not be understood to imply that, living in the re-presentation, I mean the act of perceiving; on the contrary, I mean the being-present of the perceived object.
>
> (Husserl, 1991, pp. 60–61)

The 'illuminated theatre' that 'hovers' before Husserl's mind's eye is strongly evocative of a cinema image—still a curious novelty at the time Husserl was writing—or at least some other method of still photography and projection. And, while this recording might have been produced by the machinery of human perception, it is like a photographic image in that it has an enduring existence divorced from human perception. Husserl imagines himself watching an image of the remembered theatre inside another theatre, the Cartesian theatre of his own mind.

However, while it is true that memory is not a memory of the act of perception, it is also more than a 'reproduction' of perception as Husserl claims. Memory is more a re-enactment of perception, which rehearses a specific act of perception in order to generate it anew. This is why human memory is so unreliable: rather than its unreliability being the result of some flaw in its operation as suggested by analogies with recording technology, it actually results from the fact that human memory does not retrieve static reproductions of events, but rather arises from a dynamic re-experiencing of them, which can cause memories to change or be recontextualised each time they are revisited. To quote a contemporary scientific understanding of remembering:

> Information retrieval is a reconstructive process. The memory for an event is not stored in its entirety, as an exact replica of the event. Rather, the event is broken and organized into personally meaning-ful pieces. These mental representations capture the gist or essen-tial meaning of the event. The retrieval process involves a mental re-enactment of the original experience, reproducing as many details as possible.
>
> (Pickrell, Bernstein and Loftus, 2004, p. 346)

After all, while memories can be lost, they can also be gained, as in the case of false memories; rather than being wholly the result of a stream of 'primal impressions' that originate a linear procession from 'now' to 'then'—and thus being nothing more than more or less faithful records whose status only changes if they are degraded or lost—they are actually shot through with perception from beginning to end.

Not only does this quality of memory have no parallel in media tech-nology, but it demonstrates why media technologies can never be inter-changeable with human memory. Recording technologies can serve as a prosthetic memory for Stiegler because, like Husserl, his understanding of human memory is already based on the analogy of recording technologies, which therefore seem interchangeable with it. But if human memory is characterised as having an endlessly dynamic relationship with percep-tion—both by informing perception of the now and existing through the re-invocation of perceptual experiences from the past—then the qualities that justify the analogy (separateness from perception, separateness from immediate experience and static reproducibility) become points of differ-ence rather than similarity. Memory is not simply the recording of a linear series of instants caught by the human perceptual apparatus, like film spooling through a movie camera. Stiegler's addition of external objects as tertiary retention does not fundamentally change the logic of Hus-serl's account because Husserl's account already contains objects: external things like the theatre are stored in memory as recoverable, static entities that are themselves analogous to mechanical recordings. Stiegler's only point of difference is that he argues for the interchangeability of these mental recordings and externally produced mechanical recordings.

It might be objected that both common sense and Husserl say that memory can't exist without some direct relationship with a temporally located now. The example of false memories immediately problematises this claim, but in any event my argument does not require that it be rejected. Memories—at least in the majority of cases—are initiated by a particular perceptual experience that takes place at a particular moment, but they are not then instantly disconnected from perception. Rather, each evocation of the memory is itself an echo of that initial perceptual experience that re-enacts and inevitably inflects it.

Stiegler's claims concerning 'industrial tertiary retention' treat mechanical recordings as a kind of memory; but in reality they are recordings of sensory stimuli that can be the *objects* of (human) memory, but cannot overwhelm the dynamism and instability of individual instances of embodied perceptual experience such that memory becomes standardised and de-individuated in the manner he suggests. Perhaps the best illustration of this aspect of media recording as 'memory' is the clichéd question, 'Do you remember where you were when you heard that John F. Kennedy was assassinated/Kurt Cobain was dead?': the question is never, 'Do you remember *that* Kennedy *was* assassinated/Cobain *is* dead?'—such a question is rendered meaningless by the very fact of media's recording of events. The question is about your memory of a particular, individual experience of perceiving a mediated event, rather than the content of the media representation itself: the importance of that first experience of a mediated event is dependent upon the fact that its status as memory is distinct from that of any other audience member, or even the same person's memories of subsequent exposure. In other words, while the media produce the event, the media production of the event is not itself the memory.

Stiegler's claim that memory is always technicised—like his Gourhanian account of tools—depends on an untenable division between the technical/prosthetic and the environment as a whole. Memory can be exteriorised in all sorts of ways, such as a prisoner making marks on a wall to memorialise the passage of time, but this externalisation produces an object of sensory experience that can trigger memories, rather than determining perceptual experiences so completely as to cause the spontaneous appearance of mental phenomena divorced from the context of specific perceptual events. Perhaps a better example of this is that I can extend my memory by, for example, speaking a phone number out loud over and over so that I don't forget it while looking for a pen and paper with which to write it down. In doing this, I am externalising the information, throwing it out into the environment and catching it again in a loop between mouth and ear, and thus turning the information into a sonic artefact. I remember the telephone number because it is being continuously re-presented to my sensory experience: as the movements of mouth, diaphragm and jaw that shape the words and the sound of the numbers in my ears. This is an external 'technology' of memory, but one that uses the air and the human body itself rather than arising from some special quality of recording technologies. And rather than the information having a significance independent of specific instances of its perception, it is the repeated experience of perceiving the information that allows it to exist.

Interfacing with external artefacts creates new kinds of embodied perception. This coming together of body, artefact and world generates new kinds of sensation and thus new kinds of human experience. However, while those experiences are never simply the sum of the entities that compose them, they also never represent a homogenisation of them, or a replacement of one component with another. But Stiegler is certainly not alone in lumping these different possibilities together. In the study of cinema, apparatus theory was guided by the same misconceptualisation of the role of technology in human sensing, understanding the machinery of the cinema as *a replacement for* human vision, rather than simply *the object of* human vision (see Chapter 3). In both cases, a mechanistic analogy between technology and body (gramophone record as memory storage, camera as eye) allows body and machine to be conflated. The resulting account of prosthesis is simplistic because, since the bodily capacity in question and the technology that engages with it are being treated as fundamentally the same, it isn't possible to give any meaningful account of how they come together or what new system results. If each term is ultimately the same (camera = eye, CD = memory, electronic media = nervous system), then one can only replace the other and render it redundant—adding them together can produce nothing new because it doesn't introduce anything new into the system. As a result, these accounts ultimately can't say anything meaningful about how human–machine couplings arise or function, as they can't acknowledge any kind of productive engagement between two entities they treat as indistinguishable.

In other words, these explanations of body–technology relationships ignore interfacing. Lacking any framework for understanding how the materiality of body and machine engage one another or how they productively function together, they come to describe technological artefacts as simply replacing (parts of) the human body or its capacities in a way that supposedly demonstrates the interchangeability of body and technology.

Possible Prostheses

The logic of technological replacement can be seen as implicitly limiting and regressive, as it depends upon a belief in some stable, fixed, originary system that is being replaced or repaired. Even where a prosthesis is understood to improve the function of the body beyond what is considered 'normal' this remains the case; while Cassandra Crawford has argued that, in medical prosthetics, 'design is no longer inspired by the desire to return bodies to "normal" states but rather by the desire to transcend the inadequacies of the human body' (2014, p. 245), this desire for transcendence is still dependent upon a normative understanding of the body that seeks to increase its performance and efficiency without making any fundamental change to existing understandings of what it is.

There is an important difference between reproducing or improving an existing way of engaging with one's environment and creating a new way of engaging with one's environment. The traditional understanding of a prosthesis is of something that, rather than producing a new way of engaging with an environment, maintains the viability of an existing set of expectations and assumptions about the proper way of doing so by mediating between the environment and a body that does not conform to those expectations and assumptions. In other words, it is a technological artefact that is produced by working backwards from an existing or extrapolated state, rather than working forwards towards a new conceptualisation of how a human body might engage with the world around it. For example, a prosthetic leg—even one that allows you to run faster or jump higher than a biological leg—does not seek to create a new relationship between human body and ground (as a skateboard, for example, does), but rather seeks to re-establish a relationship with the ground that has previously been established as 'normal'.

If we return to the example of the hammer, the act of hammering didn't begin with an animal deciding to hammer something and so looking around for an object suitable for the job. That scenario is impossible because the act of hammering simply didn't exist before an animal first hefted an object and swung it at the end of its arm. To quote Bruno Latour's appeal to a famous image,

> One can easily understand the anthropoid monkey in Stanley Kubrick's film *2001*, stupefied and surprised when faced with the world opened up by a jawbone held like a hammer—and as a club handy for killing. If, in a famous swirling movement, he flings it so high and far that it becomes the space station of the future, it is because all technologies incite around them that whirlwind of new worlds. Far from primarily fulfilling a purpose, they start by exploring heterogeneous universes that nothing, up to that point, could have foreseen and behind which trail new functions.
>
> (Latour and Venn, 2002, p. 250)

Hammering didn't exist as a possibility until a certain object was transformed into a hammer by a body interfacing with it; the tool reconfigured the potentiality of the human body. That having happened, the act of hammering exists as a possibility; I can look at a hammer, a mallet, a rock or even a book or smartphone, and perceive hammering as a possible outcome of my bodily engagement with it. But who knows how many other forms of engagement with these things I don't see because they remain confined to the virtual rather than the possible? The prosthetic leg begins with an understanding of the possibilities for human locomotion derived from the biological leg, but what would it look like if this wasn't the case? The running blade (Figure 4.1), while still ultimately derived from the model of the biological leg and its form of locomotion, nevertheless results from an attempt to expand this set of possibilities by seeking to follow its model less slavishly (by replacing jointed rigid sections with a

Figure 4.1 The 'Cheetah' running blade
Source: Image courtesy of Össur

single flexile strip). The result is a body whose potential for action has been reconfigured—for example, in contrast to locomotion using biological legs, moving rapidly through space using running blades is very easy, while moving through space slowly, or stopping, is difficult.

In the words of Pierre Lévy, 'A tool is more than just an extension of the body; it is the virtualization of an action' (1998, p. 95). Lévy is here calling on Gilles Deleuze's differentiation of the virtual and the actual from the possible and the real:

> [T]he possible is open to 'realisation', it is understood as an image of the real, while the real is supposed to resemble the possible. That is why it is difficult to understand what existence adds to the concept when all it does is double like with like. Such is the defect of the possible: a defect which serves to condemn it as produced after the fact, as retroactively fabricated in the image of what resembles it. The actualisation of the virtual, on the contrary, always takes place by difference, divergence or differentiation. Actualisation breaks with resemblance as a process no less than it does with identity as a principle. Actual terms never resemble the singularities they incarnate. In this sense, actualisation or differentiation is always a genuine creation . . . For a potential or virtual object, to be actualised is to create divergent lines which correspond to—without resembling—a

virtual multiplicity. The virtual possesses the reality of a task to be performed or a problem to be solved: it is the problem which orientates, conditions and engenders solutions, but these do not resemble the conditions of the problem.

(Deleuze, 1994, pp. 211–212)

The virtual is therefore a configuration of energies and phenomena that can be actualised in a multiplicity of ways. The possible, on the other hand, is restrictive and limiting where the virtual is creative—the possible is a projection of things as they are into the past or future, while things as they are never look like the virtual, despite the virtual being in them. The term prosthesis as it is usually employed understands interfacing in terms of the possible. While every new configuration of body and object transforms the virtual, the logic of the prosthesis forces it into a restricted set of possibilities. The prosthesis is like an arm, or a leg, or an eye, or a nervous system, or a memory; even when the prosthesis is not the result of a conscious attempt to emulate some existing solution to a problem (such as the problem of human locomotion), it must be subordinated to some existing phenomenon or physical model that can serve as an analogy for it.

Of course, any prosthetic leg will inescapably have properties that are different from a biological leg, and so, like any artefact, will unavoidably smuggle in the possibility of a different relationship with the environment, but this is generally considered a by-product, rather than the aim, of the prosthesis's creation. The logic of redundancy or replacement tends to ignore, or attempt to minimise, such 'by-products', but they are an inevitable and integral attribute of the experience of interfacing. Rather than seeking to side-line or ignore them, then, my account of interfacing seeks to place them at the centre of the analysis. Our relationships with technology never simply replace something; even when an attempt is made to do so, interfacing always produces new kinds of action and perception. These new kinds of action and perception should be the focus of the analysis, rather than the always limited and partial ways in which experiences of interfacing replace or replicate what has come before.

Mind Control

In 2012, quadriplegic American woman Jan Scheuermann volunteered to have implanted in her brain two electrodes that could send signals to a robotic arm. This research project, which came after an earlier demonstration that monkeys could be habituated to perform tasks using brain signals and a robotic arm (Lebedev and Nicolelis, 2006, p. 542), was funded by DARPA (the US Defense Advanced Research Projects Agency), for whom brain–machine interfaces, or BMIs, are of ongoing interest. The most obvious appeal of BMI research for the US Department of Defense relates to the large number of US veterans who have lost limbs or body function, but BMIs are also hoped to offer a solution to information overload amongst the human operators of ever-more complex military systems. For some time, the cockpits of military aircraft have been at the cutting edge of new user interface development, as these highly complex, highly technologised environments have seemingly reached the limits of a human operator's capacity to comprehend and respond to flows of information at the split-second speeds required for air combat.

The hopes for this longer-term application of BMIs beyond the treatment of disability were illustrated when, in 2015, Scheuermann's electrodes were connected to a simulation of the F-35 Joint Strike Fighter, and it was demonstrated that she could send commands to the simulated aircraft. Given that publicity surrounding Scheuermann's brain implants had previously revolved around her ability to eat a chocolate bar held in a robotic hand (Foley, 2016), a capacity to pilot the most expensive and high-tech weapon of war ever created seemed like a dramatic escalation of the research's ambitions.

Shortly after Scheuermann's experience with the flight simulator, Arati Prabhakar, the director of DARPA, publicly expressed her belief in the revolutionary potential of such a military BMI:

> In doing this work, we've also opened this door. We can now see a future where we can free the brain from the limitations of the human body and I think we can all imagine amazing good things and amazing potential bad things that are on the other side of that door.
>
> (quoted in McGarry, 2015)

For Prabhakar, at least, the development of BMIs falls within a long history—and is perhaps the apotheosis of—attempts to transcend the human body using technology. This belief is encouraged by descriptions of BMIs in popular reporting—as well as in public statements by some researchers—as 'mind control', 'thought control', or even 'telepathy' or 'telekinesis'. These terms suggest that BMIs allow technological devices to be plugged directly into Descartes' *res cogitans*—an immaterial 'stuff of thought' that exists independently of the body and matter more generally.

If the bottleneck in user interfaces for military aircraft is a pilot's capacity to deal with the cognitive load of their high-volume, high-speed flows of information, then creating more work for the mind to do would seem to be counterproductive; but, according to Prabhakar, BMIs can make more brainpower available by liberating pilots from a need to think about controlling their own bodies:

> Instead of thinking about controlling a joystick, which is what our ace pilots do when they're driving this thing, Jan's thinking about controlling the airplane directly.
>
> (quoted in McGarry, 2015)

But is 'thinking about controlling a joystick' really an accurate description of what an ace pilot is doing when flying a jet fighter? By the same token, is 'thinking about turning a steering wheel' an accurate description of driving a car, or 'thinking about moving a pen' an accurate description of handwriting? Surely a prerequisite for becoming an ace pilot is an ability to fly an aircraft without thinking about controlling the joystick at all.

Or to put it another way, the value of the direct brain–machine interface is thought to be that when the pilot formulates an intention to bank right, the aircraft banks right, as opposed to current aircraft controls, where the pilot formulates an intention to bank right, then thinks about how to manipulate the joystick to bring this about, and then physically executes the manoeuvre. The problem with this reasoning is obvious: the trained pilot never *does* carry out the additional step in the latter sequence because using the joystick to control the aircraft has become second nature, meaning that the BMI does not shorten the process or render it more efficient or effective.

To bring the example down to a more everyday level, let's shift to BMIs that can allow a person to type on a computer using neural impulses (Metz, 2017). Again, while this is obviously a huge breakthrough for those without the use of their hands, claims that such an approach is more effective than current input devices for people *with* the use of their hands are less convincing. As I touch-type this chapter, I formulate in my mind a string of words and my fingers move in such a way that they appear on the screen—I already seem to have a brain–machine interface, given that my intentions are immediately expressed in the operation of the device without any consciously controlled intermediate steps. In short, the underlying problem with this whole approach is that the human body already has a direct, brain–controlled interface with the things around it: the hand. In fact, it has two!

Even more than BMI research, this issue is illustrated by related research into direct–brain interfaces which can connect two people (through the medium of a machine), rather than a person and a machine. In 2012, following on from previous research demonstrating the principle with rats (Pais-Vieira et al., 2013), two researchers at the University of Washington created a system by which they could be connected to one another using one cap that registered brain activity through external electrodes, and another that delivered transcranial magnetic stimulation to produce movement (Rao et al., 2014):

> Rao looked at a computer screen and played a simple video game with his mind. When he was supposed to fire a cannon at a target, he imagined moving his right hand (being careful not to actually move his hand), causing a cursor to hit the 'fire' button. Almost instantaneously, Stocco, who wore noise-cancelling earbuds and wasn't looking at a computer screen, involuntarily moved his right index

finger to push the space bar on the keyboard in front of him, as if firing the cannon. Stocco compared the feeling of his hand moving involuntarily to that of a nervous tic.

(Armstrong and Ma, 2013)

After a few more years of research, we could imagine a brave new world in which technology gives us the ability to press computer keys with all ten of our fingers, rather than just one!

Of course, I'm being unjust to this research project, which is about the ability to register and reproduce brain signals at a distance, rather than more efficient user interfaces as the military BMI research is. At the same time, the description of this system includes an aside that is relevant to the discussion: 'he imagined moving his right hand (being careful not to actually move his hand)'. This is significant because it suggests that the use of this system requires *more* mental exertion than simply using one's hand: where playing the game directly would involve formulating an intention to press the button and so pressing the button, the direct–brain version involves formulating an intention to press the button and then mentally suppressing the action of *actually* pressing the button. There is real importance in this point, because, where older models of the relation-ship between thought and action from artificial intelligence and robotics research relied on an assumption that action followed a series of discrete steps that moved from the mental formulation of a plan to its execution in the physical world, later research into cognition has shown that this is not the case, and 'thinking about' a particular action (which does not simply mean the action of moving a hand, but also, for example, the action of speaking a word) engages the parts of the brain responsible for taking that action, and so thinking about the action and the action itself are inextricably linked at their origin. When we are 'only thinking' about performing an action, we are actually formulating intention and action as an integrated whole, and then suppressing the execution of the action. (This is why some people mouth words while reading silently, and even those who don't still subvocalise to some extent: thinking about words is inextricably tied to the action of speaking those words, and so we must actively suppress their enactment.) The upshot of this is that acting through a brain–machine interface can be expected to be less efficient and produce more cognitive load than simply pressing a button.

Hand and brain have been evolving in a reciprocal relationship for millions of years to produce a system that is vastly more effective and complex than any interface device that can currently be made in a research lab. This point might be dismissed on the grounds that BMI research is only in its early days, and far more sophisticated systems are likely to be developed in the future, but the real issue is not the relative complexity of the hand and any particular artificial control system; rather, it's the nature of embodied action itself.

The most direct result of BMI research is the possibility of better prosthetic limbs and the rerouting of neural signals past obstructions caused by spinal cord injuries. But even in the proposed scenarios for able-bodied usage, it subscribes to the logic of prosthesis. While BMI research follows a logic of subtracting from the body rather than adding to it as in standard medical prostheses (removing the actions of limbs rather than replacing them), its underlying assumptions are nevertheless fundamentally the same. Any attempt to add to, subtract from, replace or augment embodied human capacities using external artefacts shares a common understanding of how body and artefact function together. Both body and artefact are understood as fixed collections of independent capacities; the capacities of a new artefact might be added to the existing capacities of the body in order to augment it, or might replace them with a more efficient equivalent— as with the BMI, where the supposedly less efficient form of control given by the hands is replaced by a computer—but there is no belief that the coupling of body and artefact can produce new capacities. BMI researchers might claim that their work is actually *all about* providing people with new capacities, but for Arati Prabhakar's ace fighter pilot the payoff is understood to be an increase in the efficiency of what pilots are already doing, rather than the creation of any capacity that is genuinely novel. In this case, the fighter pilot's body is seen to be dead weight, an inefficient biological mechanism controlled by a disembodied intellect; the pilot's performance can be improved by bypassing this limiting intermediary and plugging the pilot's brain directly into the aircraft's systems. The possibility that some of the pilot–aircraft assemblage's capacities might actually be generated, not in the pilot's disembodied intellect or in the machinery of the aeroplane, but rather at their point of physical contact, does not appear in this understanding. The wider prevalence of this negative attitude is reflected in the following description of brain–machine interface research from some of the leading researchers in the field:

> Brain–machine interfaces (BMIs) have emerged as a new paradigm that allows brain-derived information to control artificial actuators and communicate the subject's motor intention to the outside world without the *interference* of the subject's body.
>
> (Pais-Vieira et al., 2013, p. 1, my emphasis)

The body is understood to be nothing but a source of interference or inefficiency; any novel phenomenon generated by the meeting of body and machine is understood to be necessarily negative and undesirable. The appeal of the BMI is thought to lie in a capacity to purge the human–technology relationship of any new or unexpected phenomenon generated by physical interaction. But escaping the body's productivity is not so easy.

In fact, rather than simply being a conduit directing an innate or previously learnt language of mental commands to a piece of technology, BMIs

are dependent on a user developing an ability to exert control by responding to the sensory feedback generated by interactions with the system,
and this process of reciprocal adaptation between technological system
and body produces physical changes in the user's brain (see Upson, 2014;
Lebedev and Nicolelis, 2006; Balasubramanian et al., 2017). In other
words, BMI technology doesn't simply eavesdrop on a user's mind and
then act on the wishes or commands found there; rather, it is dependent
on user and machine changing one another through an ongoing process
of feedback generated by loops of interaction. Rather than conforming
to a hierarchised model of 'mind control' or telepathy, in which the BMI
empowers an isolated and omnipotent user to exert control over machines
using the disembodied power of thought, it actually operates in a much
more lateral and collaborative way that remains dependent upon the
materiality of the body. Claims that BMIs can remove the 'interference'
of the body somehow forget that the brain is, itself, a part of the body,
and BMIs are dependent upon, not thought, but the brain as a physical,
bodily system. Acknowledging this underlying mechanism deflates the
rhetoric of bodily transcendence often used to refer to BMIs, and once
again highlights the degree to which user interface research is wedded
to a model of user and device as isolated from one another, in which the
optimal model of interaction is one in which the machine serves the user
without interfering with a set of fixed, 'natural' bodily constraints that
the user is supposedly subject to.

   An ability to remove the hand from the business of control is, in reality, far less significant than has been suggested; it merely replaces one
physical control system with another. In addition, there is no reason to
believe that the hand was a significant liability in the first place. The
high cognitive load of the fighter pilot does not come from the effort of
working a joystick, which, as I hope I've already established, is largely
non-conscious and habitualised and thus requires little attention. The
high cognitive load comes from the need to absorb and respond to the
flood of information produced by the cockpit, and this draws attention
to the fundamental failing of the brain–machine interfaces that have
been produced so far: they're not actually fully fledged user interfaces
at all.

   They're not full user interfaces because they only allow information
to move in a single direction. A fighter pilot might be able to use a BMI
to send a command to an aircraft to bank right, but the pilot receives no
information *from* the BMI that could lead to a decision to bank right,
nor does s/he receive information from it about the results of this action.
As a result, the understanding of user interfaces reflected in these BMIs is
even more limiting than those discussed in Chapter 1. While it completely
depends on an idea of the user and machine as self-contained and isolated
from one another, it's not even a conversational model as deployed in
early user interface design, because the machine has no way to reply to

the user. It positions the user as a completely isolated figure, shouting imperatives into a void.

The cognitive load of the fighter pilot using a brain–machine interface as described by Arati Prabhakar would be more or less the same as a fighter pilot without one. With practice, the mental effort of sending commands to the aircraft through the BMI presumably could be reduced to the level of a non-BMI control system, but all the information coming *from* the aircraft would presumably still be relying on the eyes and ears of the pilot, just as it is today, meaning that the cognitive load of interpreting it would be unchanged. Any potential that BMIs have to reduce information overload resides, not in an ability to issue commands, but rather in an ability to receive incoming information (see Kercel, Reber and Manges, 2005; Danilov and Tyler, 2005).

An assumption that a user interface is just something a user employs to tell a machine what to do is prevalent more generally. In the University of Washington direct–brain interface experiment described previously, the command to press the key might have been communicated using a high-tech brain interface, but information from the computer concerning when to press the key and the results of doing so was presented on a bog-standard computer screen using video game graphics that would have looked underwhelming twenty-five years ago. The depiction of an imagined future gestural interface in the Steven Spielberg film *Minority Report* (2002) is still highly influential, with the term 'Minority Report interface' or similar being shorthand for a futuristic gestural interface design, and yet, while Tom Cruise's character is shown controlling a computer by moving his tracking-gloved hands around like an orchestra conductor, the output from the computer—the feedback from his movements and the information he summons up—is presented as simply a two-dimensional, windowed screen of a kind that would have been instantly recognisable to Doug Engelbart in the 1960s. John Underkoffle, who designed the *Minority Report* user interface (Shedroff and Noessel, 2012, p. 95), seemingly imagined that, while the input component of user interfaces would progress in the fifty years between the film's production and its future setting, the output component would remain largely unchanged over the course of a century.

Once again, the immaturity of BMI research might be invoked as a defence. This technology is only the subject of early lab experiments; mostly these experiments are merely crude demonstrations of the viability of the technology, and much more—including the addition of direct–brain feedback—would have to be added before they could provide a true, viable user interface.[7] This is no doubt true, but, at the same time, it remains the case that the research does not at all establish the viability or usefulness of BMIs for general, everyday use. It only suggests that it would be possible to replace *part* of a user interface with a BMI, and, despite the lofty promises made for it, there doesn't seem to be any clear advantage for an able-bodied user in adopting even that part. Furthermore, the very fact of breaking the proposed system down into separable binaries of input and output, user and machine, reflects a lack of appreciation for interfacing as a phenomenon that arises *between* these things rather than being simply the sum of their parts.

The examples of BMI research given previously leave unaddressed the most important aspect of any proposed brain–machine interface. Generating input for a technological system *from* brain activity fits neatly within a framework that takes the body as fixed and separate from that system—it is easy to conceptualise this process because we're aware that our brain activity is tied to our desires and actions, and so can imagine the markers of that activity being registered and responded to by a machine. But can we imagine how a machine would send information directly *to* the brain of a user, and how that user would make sense of it? This would require a retreat from a belief in the autonomous, fixed user, because it would require a model of reciprocal influence between machine and body, in which the body adapts to the technological system with which it interfaces in such a way that human experience is transformed. While replacing a joystick with a BMI would be of questionable value to a fighter pilot, replacing a screen with a BMI would be of tremendous value; but how would an aircraft's systems indicate its current heading, or the range of an enemy aircraft, in a way that bypassed the pilot's eyes and ears? Would it be possible to develop a new sense that directly incorporated the output of machines?

A New Sensation

Could it be possible for a technological device to produce a new sense? It's actually quite difficult to answer this question, not because of a lack of clarity concerning the potential of technological devices, but rather because it's not entirely clear what a sense is, or how we come to have the sensory experiences that are already familiar to us.

At first blush, this claim might seem absurd. A sense is something that arises from having a sense organ, it might be argued, and sensory experience results from this sense organ functioning as an interface between the brain and stimuli arising from the environment. So vision is a sense that results from having eyes, and the sensory experience of vision is produced by photosensitive cells inside the eye producing nerve impulses that are fed into the brain. Going by this understanding, we would conclude that a machine could only produce a new sense if it were some kind of artificial, cyborg sense organ plugged directly into the brain, and even then it would only work if its output perfectly reproduced that of the biological sense organ it replaced. (This is the prosthetic logic of the cochlear implant and bionic eye, and, where BMI research *is* working on direct sensory input, it follows the same model in attempting to create a sense of touch in prosthetic arms.) But this line of reasoning is built on a misapprehension.

Take, for example, the blind spots in your eyes. Each of your eyeballs has a region on its inner rear surface where the optic nerve and blood vessels enter, and which, because of this, is not equipped to register light. Therefore, if vision was simply caused by light being registered by your eye, the view from each of your eyes would have a circular blank spot in it that corresponded to this location;[8] but nobody is able to 'see' this absence of sight. Or, more exotically, consider the condition known as 'blindsight' (Weiskrantz, 1990): a person with blindsight has eyes that function perfectly well, but is nonetheless at least partially blind. And this is not because of some disruption in the connection between eyes and brain—in fact, if pressed to do so, a person with blindsight can reach out and pick up an object, or even catch a ball, despite not being able to see it (Gallagher and Zahavi, 2013, pp. 57–61). The reason why such a condition can exist, of course, is that the stimuli registered by our eyes only serve as a kind of raw material from which various processes within the brain assemble our sense of the visual qualities of the world, and those with blindsight have sustained damage to a part of the brain where visual information is made available to the conscious mind.

But this doesn't simply mean that seeing is something that takes place inside the brain rather than the eye; I am not advocating the so-called grand illusion theory, which presents our sensory experience as a kind of internally generated simulation of our environment produced by our brains (see Noë, Pessoa and Thompson, 2000; Noë and O'Regan, 2000). It is only common sense that an eye alone cannot see, but it is equally common sense that a brain alone cannot see (Noë, 2004, Chapter 2)— rather, a whole body sees. And, furthermore, even a whole body cannot see anything without an environment that produces stimuli amenable to perception. But the very necessity of this larger assemblage of body and environment demonstrates that senses are not simply produced by sense organs.

Another reason to doubt the sense organ–based explanation of perception can be seen in some of the sensory experiences prominently discussed in this book: proprioception (discussed in Chapters 2 and 3) and chronoception (which will be discussed in Chapter 5) aren't attached to any particular sensory organs. In fact, while human beings have traditionally been understood to possess five senses—seeing, hearing, touching, tasting and smelling—it is now widely accepted that this schema is inadequate (Kiverstein, Farina and Clark, 2015, p. 659; Keeley, 2015, pp. 853–854). The Aristotelean schema of five senses itself results from a belief that our senses are produced by our five organs of perception—the eyes, ears, skin, tongue and nose—but this is highly questionable.[9] Smell and taste arise from a single set of sensory equipment, the different orifices used to communicate with it notwithstanding (Bayne and Spence, 2015, p. 604);

does this mean that we really only have four senses? Obversely, on closer consideration, it can be seen that 'touch' actually bundles together a number of quite distinct sensory experiences registered through the skin; if we compare a sensation of pressure, the pain of a cut, or the registering of temperature, it's quite clear that each is very different. Tactile, thermal, pruritic (itching), painful and (arguably) pleasurable touch stimuli all have their own receptors and are processed separately in the brain (McGlone and Reilly, 2010, p. 157), as well as producing further cutaneous perceptions through their interaction (for example, tactile and thermal sensations together allow the perception of wetness). So does the sense organ of the skin actually account for five senses on its own?

We actually experience the world far more richly than in five senses; exactly how many sensory modalities we understand ourselves to have depends both on how we want to divide this complex and overlapping combination of sensory experiences, and also what kinds of perception we have developed through our various modes of interaction with the world around us. It is now widely acknowledged that different sensory modalities do not work in isolation, but rather produce a more integrated perceptual whole, and this goes beyond sensing multiple things about a feature of my environment (for example, vision telling me what something looks like and olfaction telling me what it smells like); it means that how something sounds to me can be altered by a visual experience, and how it looks can be altered by a tactile experience (see Bayne and Spence, 2015). Paul Schilder claimed that all sensory experience is primarily synaesthetic, the isolation of different sensory modalities being introduced later (1950), and studies of new-born infants (especially those of Meltzoff and Moore [1983]) have shown their innate cross-modal comprehension of sensory data (for example, they can visually recognise a shape that they have only previously felt in their mouths, and know how to make the muscular movements necessary to create facial expressions they have only seen). In other words, our physical, sensory experience of the world should not be understood as a small number of watertight pipes directing flows of discrete stimuli from the world 'out there' through individual sense organs and on into the brains in our heads; rather, various flows are always mixing and branching off into other areas, creating cascading experiences and mixtures of stimulation that form a complex whole.

But it's one thing to claim a mixing of our sensory modalities and another to claim that non-living artefacts can be swept up in this promiscuous intermingling. It might be hard to differentiate between taste and smell, but the mouth and nose are nonetheless parts of a single, living body and are connected to a brain able to blend different kinds of stimuli together. However, sensory experiences are always and necessarily generated by a combination of a body and things external to it—for example, we cannot see in the absence of a light source. Sensing is by its very nature about extending our embodied experience out into the world. Our modes of sensing are potentially very flexible and adaptable: not only can the absorption of objects into our sensory experience extend and alter it, but more complex technological devices have the capacity to present new kinds of sensory stimuli that can generate new kinds of sensory experience.

Research on neural plasticity has highlighted the degree to which parts of the brain associated with sensing can be repurposed to best serve the needs of an individual. Brain plasticity refers to the capacity of the brain to physically adapt to changes in the circumstances of its use:

> It is . . . possible to modify, fine-tune and adapt . . . 'blueprints' of harmonious development with changes in nurture background. This adaptation phenomenon is called brain plasticity and refers to the life-long changes in the structure of the brain that accompany experience (experience-dependent plasticity) . . . Hence, plastic changes across brain systems and related behaviors seem to vary as a function of the timing and the nature of the changes in experience.
>
> (Ptito and Kupers, 2005, pp. 479–480)

The potential significance of this for perception has been demonstrated in a number of cases. It is possible to destroy the visual cortex of a ferret and then reroute signals from its eyes into the part of the brain associated with hearing and have the ferret continue to make sense of visual information, demonstrating that a part of the brain previously associated with audition has been repurposed (Roe et al., 1992; von Melchner, Pallas and Sur, 2000). A blind person can employ the brain's capacity to understand spatial information, but bring it to bear on auditory stimuli, rather than visual as would be the case with a sighted person, and various well-known experiments with vision (for example, making subjects wear goggles that distort or upend what they see) have shown that the brain has a capacity to reconfigure its response to sensory stimuli in order to adapt (Hurley and Noë, 2003, pp. 148–150). The precise nature and mechanisms of this plasticity—and even the degree to which some of these changes in perception actually require physical changes to the brain—are still not completely understood, but they do importantly establish that our sensory experiences are not simply determined by either the sense organ that receives a stimulus, or the brain region that processes it, but arise in a manner far more flexible and responsive to circumstance.[10]

Probably the most striking—and contentious—demonstration that sensory experience is not simply produced by fixed anatomical or neurological features can be found in sensory substitution devices. Efforts to develop technologies able to effect sensory substitution have been around for some time; the work of the late Paul Bach-y-Rita and his colleagues, beginning at the end of the 1960s, is probably the best-known early attempt to create electronic sensory substitution devices, although Bach-y-Rita himself pointed out that the idea was not new then, either.

> The most successful sensory substitution system to the present is Braille. Information usually acquired visually (reading) is, instead, acquired through the fingertips. We suggest that reading can itself be considered the first sensory substitution system, because it does not occur naturally but rather is an invention that visually presents auditory information (the spoken word).
>
> (Bach-y-Rita and Kercel, 2003, p. 541)

Bach-y-Rita's work focused on 'tactile–vision sensory substitution' (TVSS), through devices that could substitute tactile stimuli for visual stimuli for the blind. Beginning with a dentist's chair that pressed a grid of 'pixels' of varying 'intensity' into the user's back (Bach-y-Rita, 1972), Bach-y-Rita and his colleagues ultimately created the 'tongue display unit' or 'brainport', a device that converts visual information into signals that are then delivered as electrical impulses to a 'lollipop' on a user's tongue (Bach-y-Rita and Kercel, 2003).[11] Peter Meijer's 'vOICe' system, which substitutes sound for visual information and can run on a smartphone, has also been very successful (Meijer, 1992; Trivedi, 2010).

Sensory substitution seems to be telling us something important about perception, but precisely what is a matter of debate. This debate has primarily revolved around the degree to which sensory substitution devices (SSDs) can be said to transform sensory experience from one modality to another. For example, can a brainport device turn touch into vision, or does it only allow a user to employ touch in an atypical way to map space or identify distant objects?

The experiences of SSD users have certainly been taken to suggest the former, rather than the latter, conclusion; that is, that the brains of users can actually remap their processing of sensory information to produce, for example, an experience that is as direct and spontaneous as seeing despite not addressing the eyes—something that has even been described as 'acquired synaesthesia' (Ward and Meijer, 2010, p. 494). In the 1970s, Paul Bach-y-Rita recorded how, while a test subject was using the sensory substitution chair, the camera's zoom was activated, causing the image being translated into tactile stimuli to seemingly rush forward. Bach-y-Rita describes how the subject responded as if seeing this sudden visual change:

> The change in visual angle produced by the zoom lens change produced a looming effect, and the startled subject raised his arms and threw his head backwards to avoid the 'approaching' object. It is noteworthy that, although the stimulus array was, at the time, on the subject's back, he moved *backward* and raised his arms in front to

avoid the object, which was subjectively located in the three-dimensional space before him.

(Bach-y-Rita, 1972, p. 99)

In other words, the subject reacted as if unexpectedly perceiving something looming up in front of him, rather than unexpectedly feeling pressure on the skin of his back. Similarly, the merging of auditory and visual experience can be fundamental enough that some users of sensory substitution technology, such as vOICe user Claire Cheskin, started seeing shapes when hearing loud, unexpected noises unrelated to the vOICe system.

'There was kind of a spiky shape this morning when my pet cockatiel was shrieking, and [the warning beeps of] a reversing lorry produce little rectangles.' Only loud noises trigger the sensations and, intriguingly, she perceives the shape before the sound that sparked it.

(Trivedi, 2010, square brackets in original)

However, no one has reached into these SSD users' heads and rewired their brains, as was the case for Mriganka Sur's unfortunate ferrets mentioned previously (Roe et al., 1992; von Melchner, Pallas and Sur, 2000), and these experiences can arise too rapidly to be dependent upon the gradual shifts associated with brain plasticity[12]—or they might not happen at all (not every SSD user will have them). Given that analyses of these changes are reliant on subjective reporting by SSD users, there has been some scepticism regarding the claim that perceptual experience has really changed in any meaningful or fundamental way (see Kauffmann, 2011, p. 61; Wheeler, 2015; Kiverstein, Farina and Clark, 2015, p. 670), but a growing body of scholars argues that such an either/or account of sensory substitution is unhelpful. Rather than substituting one kind of sensory experience for another (or not), they argue, SSDs should be understood to create novel sensory experiences by addressing human perception in novel ways (Farina, 2013; Deroy and Auvray, 2015), and 'we should speak of sensory extension, supplementation, or transformation, rather than substitution' (Auvray and Myin, 2009, pp. 1037–1038). While there is an important difference between extension or supplementation on one hand and transformation on the other, the broad suggestion is nevertheless that these technologies can add something new to the human sensorium, rather than simply swapping one existing feature for another.

These devices cannot themselves create new sensory experiences—only living bodies can do that. As with tools, they simply lend themselves readily to the human capacity to integrate objects into a field of action and sensation in order to produce new kinds of embodied experience, and the blind man's cane is itself a pre-digital sensory substitution device. While the previous examples have resulted from attempts to replace lost sensory modalities, there is no reason why the same approach could not be applied to the creation of entirely new ones. Stephen Kercel, Arthur Reber and Wayne Manges have explicitly called for the incorporation of Bach-y-Rita's research into the creation of new user interfaces, pointing to SSD users' ability to perceive a variety of different inputs as intelligible sensory stimuli even when they record input with no correlation to existing human senses (Kercel, Reber and Manges, 2005).

There have been cases of informal attempts to create new sensory experiences by implanting a rare earth magnet in the tip of one finger, thus creating a sensitivity to the electromagnetic fields that invisibly permeate the contemporary urban environment:

> [T]he magnet works by moving very slightly, or with a noticeable oscillation, in response to EM fields. This stimulates the somatosensory receptors in the fingertip, the same nerves that are responsible for perceiving pressure, temperature and pain . . . [R]ecipients found they could locate electric stovetops and motors, and pick out live electrical cables.
>
> (Norton, 2006)

More formally, lab rats have had their eyes sutured shut and geomagnetic compasses implanted in their brains, leading them to develop an ability to navigate a maze using a new directional sense (Norimoto and Ikegaya, 2015), and a similar principle has been demonstrated in humans by the feelSpace project, led by Peter König at the University of Osnabrück Institute of Cognitive Science (Nagel et al., 2005, p. R14). Rather than sewing subjects' eyelids together and implanting devices in their brains, the feelSpace project sought to create a completely novel form of sensory experience through the more humane intervention of a belt of thirteen vibrators that girdles the midriff. At any given time, one of these vibrators will be active, indicating the subject's orientation relative to north. Obviously, human beings have no natural awareness of magnetic north, and thus the project was able to investigate our potential to make use of a new kind of sensory information. Of the four subjects initially fitted with the belt, two gave strong indications that this new sense had been incorporated into their pre-conscious sense of bodily orientation, changing their powers of navigation and their spatial awareness. To quote one of the subjects:

> During the first two weeks, I had to concentrate on it; afterwards, it was intuitive. I could even imagine the arrangement of places and rooms where I sometimes stay. Interestingly, when I take off the belt at night I still feel the vibration: When I turn to the other side, the vibration is moving too—this is a fascinating feeling!
>
> (quoted in Nagel et al., 2005, p. R22)

Our awareness of our orientation in space arises from a combination of information from different senses, and this device addresses the sense of touch rather than being introduced directly into the brain as with the rats, making it unclear to what extent the feelSpace belt truly can be said to constitute a new sense in itself, rather than being an additional form of stimuli feeding into an existing composite awareness (see Nagel et al., 2005, p. R24), but, even so, it demonstrates our ability to seamlessly incorporate new kinds of sensory stimuli produced by technological artefacts.

David Travieso and colleagues argue that this kind of direct, pre-conscious awareness is definitional to true sensory substitution, which they contrast with the use of a 'cognitive aid':

> In true sensory substitution users report perceiving objects out there, in the environment, rather than attending to the stimulation on the sensory surface. The term distal attribution is devoted to this conscious experience of external objects. On the contrary, a cognitive aid is a device that translates information about the external world into arbitrary signs. In this case, users perceive the signs and infer the objects through association. Whereas cognitive aids require explicit learning of signs, codes, and the corresponding meanings, true substitution is intended to make distal attribution emerge through a lawful coupling of perception, action, and sensorimotor information, without the explicit learning of codes . . . A related criterion to classify a device as belonging to the true substitution category or the cognitive aid category is the analysis of how the sensory information is transformed in stimulation. In true substitution, one may argue, the contingency of the perceiver's movements and the stimulation should be derived from certain physical laws, such as the laws of optics or acoustics, whereas this is not the case for the relation between external objects and the (arbitrary) codes of cognitive aids.
>
> (Travieso et al., 2015, pp. 130–131)

The distinction they are putting forward here is precisely that already made by Don Ihde between embodied and hermeneutic relationships with technological artefacts (see Chapter 2), and thus it hinges on differences in the experiential relationship between user and device. Putting aside debates about which sensory modality these experiences 'really' take place in, it is clear that this aspect of these experiences is significant to our understanding of our broader relationship with technological devices. Even if we feel compelled to confine sensory substitution within the boundaries of one or other existing sensory modality, the fact remains that these are sensory experiences of a kind not possible without the creation of an intimate, experientially seamless relationship between human user and device. I find the argument for these as novel kinds of sensory experience more persuasive, but even if they are 'only' examples of people sensing the speed of a distant object through the skin on their backs, or hearing the shape of a statue, they are singular and novel enough to demonstrate that we can incorporate objects into our sensory experiences in a direct and meaningful way.

Senses and Sensors

In his book *Feed-Forward* (2015), Mark Hansen argues that what he calls 'twenty-first-century media' have created a novel human–technology relationship precisely because they do not follow a prosthetic model in their engagement of the human sensorium:

> With twenty-first-century media, in short, we witness the advent of a media system that no longer directly mediates the human senses or any other *faculty* specific to human experience (e.g., memory). In a fundamental break with the lineage of media prosthetics that runs from Plato via McLuhan to Derrida and Stiegler, twenty-first-century media directly mediate the causal infrastructure of worldly sensibility. Whatever impact they have on human experience specifically is a part of this larger mediation: by mediating worldly sensibility, twenty-first-century media simultaneously modulate human sensibility, as it were, beneath the senses.
>
> (Hansen, 2015, pp. 51–52)

I have already noted (in Chapter 3) a claim from Hansen regarding the stereoscopic display as 'body–brain achievement' that follows a similar logic: while older media such as still or moving analogue photography simply present pre-formed sensory experiences to us (e.g. the photograph is simply a mechanically produced equivalent to what we see), the stereoscopic image requires that the brain combine two images to 'add' a perception of depth that is not captured by a camera or encoded in the photographs themselves. Twenty-first-century media more generally, according to Hansen, are differentiated by an ability to engage with human sensation upstream from the fully formed perceptions that are its products. Thus, Hansen argues, where older media can only create representations addressed to existing modes of perception, twenty-first-century media can create new modes of perception, most importantly through their ability to register phenomena at speeds exceeding the threshold of human perception and then present it in a humanly comprehensible form so that it 'bypasses the slow time resolution of consciousness' (Hansen, 2015, p. 52).

Using the term 'twenty-first-century media' rather than 'digital media' or some other technologically specific name—and also acknowledging that these attributes can be found in media prior to the twenty-first century—allows Hansen to leave the matter of how new this really is somewhat vague. Nevertheless, Hansen begins with a prosthetic model of media, explicitly drawn from the work of Stiegler, and then notes that this model does not apply to the media he is investigating. But, as I have already argued—and illustrated with the example of stereoscopic display—media never functioned as sensory prostheses in the first place.[13]

In the discussion of stereoscopic display, I have already highlighted the degree to which all the ingredients of visual perception are not present in the photograph, the photograph only providing certain sensory cues that feed into the assembly of visual perceptions within the human body. If we move onto the example of film, this becomes even more apparent. Rather than the film camera reproducing human vision, it registers light on silver halide crystals (once) or photosensors (now) of a size too small and at a speed too fast for the human eye to see. It is a mechanism for registering optical phenomena that occurs, through and through, 'beneath the senses'. And it is this non-equivalence between the camera mechanism and human sensing that allows film to work: when the captured information is played back, our inability to visually discriminate at the spatial and temporal scale of the film camera causes the individual crystals/pixels and frames to smear together in a way that produces in us a perception of unified moving images. The human experience of seeing a living, dynamic world isn't inscribed in the film at all; rather, seeing the film causes the human body to *generate* a human experience of seeing unified, coherent, moving images that is absent from the film.

Media technologies have never prosthetically done the work of human perception themselves, and have never operated as 'the technical inscription of human experience' (Hansen, 2015, p. 43); at the same time, perception always exists as an interpenetration of our bodies and the things around us that cannot be separated into its constituent parts so as to plot a set of discrete steps in its construction. No technology of representation functions as a sensory prosthesis because no technology of representation replaces or reproduces human sensation; rather, it can only become a part of the material assemblage that includes the perception that takes place in a human body. Therefore, what Mark Hansen has argued for 'twenty-first-century media' is potentially true for objects of all kinds: in fact, the simple, non-digital technology of the blind man's cane reconfigures the human sensory relationship with the world far more radically than most complex digital media technologies. But does this mean that digital media are simply 'more of the same' in how they address the human sensorium? My answer is no, not on the grounds that they address the human sensorium in a new way or at a different scale, but rather because of what happens in the space between the technology's registering of environmental phenomena and the (re)presentation of these registered phenomena to the human body. The film camera does not simply capture an object of human vision and then pass that to a human viewer; rather, it captures something fundamentally different from human vision, which, when presented to a human viewer in a certain way, can initiate a particular visual experience in the viewer's body. However, this process is nonetheless largely linear and predictable: the kinds of phenomena captured and how they are presented to the viewer remain more or less the same on each occasion, and the design of the film camera as a technology of realistic representation results in it being both predictable and fixed in what it does, and producing a sensory experience readily understandable in terms of non-mediated visual perception. Digital media technologies can operate in the same way and according to the same logic—and most of them do—but they possess a capacity to autonomously and adaptively reconfigure their own registering of external phenomena—and thus the human sensory experiences that can collaboratively arise through them—that greatly exceeds that of pre-digital technological artefacts.

The power and ubiquity of digital data relies most importantly on its 'technical capacity to encode, digitize, and transcode various "things" from the real world' (Thacker, 2004, p. 9): disparate phenomena can be translated into digital data, which can then be worked upon and/or retranslated into still other phenomena. When this capacity is combined with devices that are becoming ever better at sensing us and sensing our sensing in ever more sophisticated ways, the possibilities for new kinds of sensory experience are dramatically expanded.

In Don Ihde's existential technics, it is claimed that the technological transformation of sensory experience is a zero-sum game, in which any sensory gain made through the use of a technological artefact brings a loss somewhere else:

> [T]he transformation itself displays an invariant feature which I shall now call the *amplification–reduction* structure. This structure is constantly two-sided. With every amplification, there is a simultaneous and necessary reduction.
>
> (1979, pp. 21–22)[14]

This may or may not be true of perception through pre-digital artefacts, but I do not believe it to be an 'invariant feature' of the digital. This belief is not based on a naïve conviction that digital technologies allow for more accurate or 'realistic' representation—and, in any event, how realistic a depiction is would not be directly relevant to the point that Ihde is making. Rather, it is informed by the fact that digital technologies can supplement or transform sensory stimuli in ways not possible for older technologies.

Older technologies can of course transform sensory stimuli in significant ways—they would have no purpose if they did not—and yet there is a fundamental level at which the stimuli remain the same. If we take a telescope or microscope as examples, we can see that they function by working on the flow of light to the eye, thereby altering what we see, and Ihde's point is that they bring the ability to see something far away or very small but at a cost in other areas—for example, in both cases depth perception is lost. However, as a first response, we could imagine the use of digital technology to replace what is lost: we could create a device that utilised several microscopes or telescopes to reach certain conclusions about the volumetric properties of an object that is very small or far away, and then present the user with a 3D model of the object through a stereoscopic display. While it might be objected that this case is different because a single device has been replaced with a number of different systems working together, and the user isn't really seeing the object any more but only a computer-generated simulation, I hope it's clear on reflection that these objections can't be maintained because, first, almost any technological artefact can be decomposed into a number of constituent systems, and, beyond a very basic level, what is important is the unity of the user's experience, not that of the artefact itself. Second, claims about how real or direct the sensory information about the object of scrutiny are are similarly unproductive; whether an image of an object is seen in a manufactured glass lens or in a computer representation, we can never have a direct, objective perception of it, but neither is what we see unrelated to its objective properties. We can only speak of the reality of the sensory experience itself.

But going beyond these issues, I am thinking primarily of a more fundamental difference, which arises from digital technology's capacity to encode, transcode and decode sensory stimuli. In the examples of the telescope and microscope given previously, the transformation is from one kind of visual experience to another, but digital technologies can effect more fundamental transformations, such as from visual stimulus to aural. A key difference between analogue and digital representation is that the analogue arises through a direct physical relationship with what is being represented that establishes a stable analogical relationship; the digital, on the other hand, creates a more open and fragmented relationship, whose lack of direct physical connection opens up space for more radical transformations.

Analogue technologies can also translate stimuli from one modality to another—for example, the kymograph, an instrument key to the development of physiology in the mid-eighteenth century, could create visual information from non-visual temporal phenomena such as a heartbeat by inscribing changes in pressure (Borell, 1987). However, the wavy lines on a kymograph drum, while they are visual stimuli, need to be read and interpreted; that is, the relationship between this visual information and the phenomena that produced it is not apprehended simply through the experience of seeing it, but requires expert knowledge. Again, in Ihde's terms the user has a hermeneutic relationship with this information, rather than an embodied one. There is also an important difference between the transformation of sensory stimuli using digital technologies and non-digital sensory substitution devices such as the blind person's cane, in that the cane itself does not transform a sensory stimulus: the cane is a conduit for touch only. Even if using the cane is described as transforming touch into vision, if such a transformation takes place it does so in the human body holding the cane, not the cane itself.

Of course, digital technologies can work in exactly the same ways as these analogue examples, but their employment in sensory substitution devices illustrates their capacity to fundamentally transform the flow of sensory stimuli to the body. Such cases could be described in zero-sum terms—when visual information is translated into sound, the ability to hear something is gained while the ability to see it is lost—but this tells us very little. At a finer grain equivalent to the extension of visual range at the loss of depth perception seen with the telescope, the question of gain and loss would seem to be meaningless because of the incommensurability of the two sensory experiences being compared.

Digital devices' ability to generate sensory stimuli underlies the tendency to misrecognise user interfaces as systems of representation, as it means that they present sensory experiences just as representational media do; the difference is the relationship between this sensory information and the other systems (the human body, the environment, other devices) with which they are in interaction, as well as the way in which the user experiences that sensory information. What enables these capacities in digital devices is the matching of human senses to machine counterparts: sensors. The sense–sensor circuit creates the loops that enable the kind of real-time interactivity that underlies all digital interfacing, but it has become massively expanded and elaborated since the popularisation of mobile devices. Input devices such as keyboard and mouse can be understood as limited sensors: they sense the movement of fingers and hands/arms, which are brought into a loop that feeds back into the human sensorium primarily through the visual medium of the computer screen. However, the role of sensors is greatly expanded with the smartphone, with its accelerometer, gyroscope, light sensor, infrared proximity sensor, and perhaps a magnetometer, barometer or eye tracker. Once digital devices become mobile, they leave the predictable and constrained environment of the computer desk (see the introduction), and so their context of use becomes unpredictable, meaning that it becomes necessary to register where they are and what their users are doing; for example, the infrared proximity sensor can be used to determine if the user is manipulating the phone in her hand or holding it to her head to make a telephone call. And the capacity to transcode sensory stimuli, or to augment stimuli or create new stimuli ex nihilo, allows sensory experiences to be radically transformed during the execution of these loops between body and machine. Unlike older sensory devices such as the telescope, which have a fixed effect on sensory stimuli, it is possible to create digital devices that adapt to their context of use, registering the actions and habits of their users and modifying the sensory stimuli they generate in response.

There is no hard boundary between what digital and analogue technologies allow in sensory transformation, and in the majority of cases digital devices are designed to mimic the attributes of analogue technologies or unmediated sensing in any event, suppressing their potential. But it does seem clear that the sense–sensor circuit, and the temporal loops of interaction that enable it, bring interfacing possibilities that could not exist without them, and which have yet to be fully harnessed or explored.

Acting on or with the object causes an answering action; the object is designed to non-consciously sense the user's sensing of it or with it. A useful artefact is designed to 'turn towards' the body, to use Henri Bergson's expression (2004, p. 29), presenting a facet of itself conducive to interaction and seeking to define the potential for action of the body. With digital user interfaces this is carried further by the artefact's efforts to reactively shape itself to the actions of bodies and to respond directly to the rhythm of their actions. The artefact is designed to produce an ongoing rhythm by echoing the actions of the body, generating this through a sensing of the body of the user even as the body of the user is sensing it—sensing the sensing of the user. The rhythms of our interactions with digital and other artefacts will be the subject of the following chapter.

Conclusion

The most obvious question to ask when trying to understand our mode of engagement with technological artefacts is, how does the user control the artefact? The second most obvious question to ask is, how does the artefact communicate feedback to the user? These questions produce a focus on 'the interface' as a discrete, usually highly engineered, entity that sits between user and artefact, passing commands and reports back and forth. But because interfacing always produces something new, something that is a product of both user and artefact while at the same time having qualities present in neither, a deeper understanding requires that these three terms not be analysed in isolation from one another.

When attempting to either understand how we engage with an existing technological device or imagine how we might engage with a future one, the initial focus should not be on how the user might act upon or perceive the technological device, but rather on how the user–device assemblage might act upon or perceive its environment. Doing so need not entail a naïve belief in the irrelevance of any distinction between human body and machine; in fact, it must be fundamentally informed by an understanding of how these two components remain distinct while simultaneously transforming one another.

The dynamism of our engagement with artefacts and environment means that our sense of where our bodies are and where they end is always to some degree negotiable. The boundaries of embodiment are not biologically fixed, but nor are they endlessly adaptable and elastic. The reality lies somewhere in between, but in making this point I am not trying to pinpoint where bodies *really* end and objects *really* begin. Rather, my point is that the real value in discussing experiences of prosthesis or other instances of interfacing between bodies and artefacts is that they seem to transcend the spatial logic of boundaries and linkages altogether. Interfacing does not work according to an additive logic of *this* + *this* = *that*, just as the logic of prosthesis is not that of (one-legged person) + (prosthetic leg) = 'normal' body. Interfacing works according to a different logic, one in which the body as a physical reality remains crucial and central even as its boundaries and capacity for experience become dynamic and multiplex.

Whether using the most high-tech digital device to perform a complex task, or an unworked object found on the ground as a makeshift hammer, to speak of any mode of interacting with the world as natural or unnatural has little value—each is simply an example of the interplay between human bodies and features of the environment that produces sensory experiences and capacities for action. All sensory experience and action arises this way, regardless of the features of the environment involved, and there is no natural dimension to these things that exists within any human body in isolation from its surroundings. To speak of artefacts as extending or replacing the capacities of the human body reflects an assumption that bodies *have* a clearly defined collection of innate capacities that can be artificially supplemented, but in reality bodies can't do anything without interacting with their environment; the question is never *whether* a body's capacities are inflected by features of its environment, but rather *how* the inevitable inflection of a body's capacities will take shape according to the specificities of a particular set of environmental circumstances (cf. Gibson, 1986, p. 8).

Understanding our relationships with technology in terms of how user and machine, as distinct entities, communicate with one another creates an unnatural division in an integrated system, one that always leaves some excess that cannot be attributed to one or other term and so must be disavowed or ignored. While understanding it in terms of prosthesis, extension, augmentation or substitution might seem to provide a means of acknowledging this integration, in fact this logic of replacement or redundancy, and the modification of the body in ways that might magnify but nonetheless never expand its possibilities for action and perception, misses both the factors that give that integrated relationship its character, and the reason why we have relationships with technology in the first place—namely in order to transform our mode of engagement with the world around us.

Notes

1. Even as his own experience with a prosthetic palate following throat cancer surgery was far from divine (Jain, 1999, pp. 31–32).
2. The pre-medical etymology of the word actually suggests an addition rather than replacement (Jain, 1999, p. 32; Davis, 2006, p. 91), and it is part of the nature of prosthetics to problematise distinctions between the two. Nonetheless, the history of medical prostheses does depend on the idea of a replacement for something that has been lost.
3. Admittedly, in Clark and Chalmers's story, Otto *doesn't* have a functioning memory; however, if he truly, completely lacked a biological memory their claims would be untenable (how would Otto find the information in his notebook and act on it if he had no persistent information about himself and the world?).
4. The science of memory accepts that this is only one of a number of different kinds of memory. For example, there is also the *procedural memory* that allows us to learn skills: when I drive a car, for example, I don't need to revisit the experience of learning to drive in order to figure out what I need to do—my body just seems to know.
5. Most notably his discussion of the 'Kuleshov effect' (Stiegler, 2011, p. 13ff.).
6. Imagination in the sense of mental phenomena that, unlike perceptions, are created independently of external stimuli.
7. And attempts to do just this are already underway (Foley, 2016, pp. 4–5; O'Doherty et al., 2012; Weber, n.d.; Oddo et al., 2016).
8. Not to mention the fact that the image would be upside-down.
9. In fact, Aristotle believed the heart to be the seat of the sense of touch (Jütte, 2005, p. 42), but the principle remains the same.
10. See, for example, Hurley and Noë (2003) and Kauffmann (2011) for an indication of some of the mysteries and complexities inherent in such phenomena.
11. The tongue having been chosen because of its density of nerve endings and conductivity.
12. Although it is possible that sensory experience might have more short-term plasticity than has previously been appreciated (Lo Verde, Morrone and Lunghi, 2017).
13. In fact, later in the same book, Hansen expresses a loss of confidence in the prosthetic account of media he endorses here (2015, p. 162).
14. See also McLuhan's 'closure' principle regarding media: 'because there is equilibrium in sensibility, when one area of experience is heightened or intensified, another is diminished or numbed' (McLuhan and McLuhan, 1988, p. viii).

5 Real Time

In the previous two chapters, a passing suggestion has been made that time plays a central role in our sensory experiences, and through this to the capacity of artefacts to inflect those sensory experiences. In Chapter 3, we saw that the synchronisation of different perceptual experiences is what allows them to be synthesised into a coherent whole. In Chapter 4, I argued that the rhythms of the temporal loops that join senses and sensors is key to digital devices' potential to create new perceptual experiences. Time can perform these functions because it is both anchored in and constitutive of perception; time is flexible and interacts dynamically with our bodies and the world around us.

Changes in our experience of time are possible because time is something we each perceive using a bodily sensory capacity: chronoception. Chronoception can shift in response to changes in the environmental circumstances of our bodies, and no set of environmental circumstances has been more strongly associated with changes in our experience of time than modernity (Rosa, 2013, pp. 35–45).

A key experience of modernity is acceleration, a sense that the pace of life is increasing, and the ongoing nature of this acceleration is tied to the continuous appearance of new technologies: from clocks, to trains, to production lines, to Twitter feeds. As a result, digital technologies have widely been associated with an acceleration in the speed of modern life, one that further ratchets up a sense that the human body and mind are struggling to match the relentless pace of machines—perhaps even suggesting that the speed of digital technologies has created a final annihilation of the human temporal scale.

In her book *Pressed for Time*, Judy Wajcman argues that 'there is no temporal logic inherent to digital technologies' (2015, p. 176). But, while the larger argument that this claim serves is valid—that particular human experiences of time are not simply produced by digital technologies in a technologically determinist way—it's nonetheless the case that this claim is not. In fact, key to digital technologies' successful integration into everyday life and habits is the fact that they have been explicitly designed to conform to a very specific temporal logic called 'real-time interaction'.

And while such a temporal logic cannot simply be imposed on a human user by a technological device, and the human experiences of time it produces can be different, and even antithetical, to its motivating aims, the fact remains that this is a crucial part of digital devices' ability to inflect our perception of time.

Interactive computing, whose appearance in the mid-twentieth century brought into being the model of temporalised interaction upon which all personal digital devices now rest, has a more complex relationship with time than, for example, the steam train, which, for all its associated new experiences (Schivelbusch, 1980), still followed the horse-drawn carriage's logic of travelling from A to B; or the production line, which forced the factory worker to align the pace of her actions with the inhuman regularity of an engine's revolutions. For writers like Paul Virilio (2005), the technology of speed is exemplified by machines like the car that project a still body through space, but interactive computing works on a time that is anchored in the speed of the animated human body itself. In fact, interactive computing represents an attempt to introduce a human temporal scale into the time of the machine rather than a machinic temporal scale into the time of the human, producing not an economy of speed but an economy of waiting. This can introduce resistance to human interfacing through, not a human inability to keep up with the pace of machines, but rather the breaks in engagement caused by waiting, and this waiting long ago shifted from one in which the human waits on the machine to one in which the machine waits on the human.

And yet this stuttering articulation of the time of the machine and the time of the human user is not inevitable. There are choices other than that between a machinic time of maximum efficiency that outstrips human perception and thought on one hand, and an economy of waiting where the times of machine and user must constantly be realigned on the other. There exist examples of body and machine interfacing in a way that seems to transcend, rather than annihilate, human time, producing an uninterrupted flow rather than a succession of breaks and wait states. This chapter will look at how interfacing can alter our perception of time, and what this tells us about our current relationships with digital technology, as well as the potential for these relationships to evolve in the future.

Time Bomb

The time of digital technology has commonly come to be referred to as 'real time', a term that originated in the study of human–computer interaction but has since been adopted by cultural criticism. 'Real time' has repeatedly been used by multiple authors to mean a kind of non-time, an inhuman instantaneity of operation that is characteristic of the operation of the computer, and which squeezes out any space for human comprehension or deliberation in its constant drive towards greater mechanised efficiency (see Virilio, 1995b, 1995a, 1997; Stiegler, 2009; Hassan, 2003, pp. 231–233, 2007, pp. 48–51, 2009, pp. 88–91; Hope, 2006, p. 276), rendering the human body obsolete (Virilio, 2005, pp. 123–126). The work of Paul Virilio is only the most hyperbolic in describing real time in apocalyptic terms:

> Albert Einstein, in fact, had already prophesized as much in the 1950s, when talking about 'the second bomb'. The electronic bomb, after the atomic one. A bomb whereby real-time interaction would be to information what radioactivity is to energy. The disintegration then will not merely affect the particles of matter, but also the very people of which our societies consist.
>
> (Virilio, 1995b)

According to Bernard Stiegler, real time is 'the industrial production of time by the programming industries whose products suspend all traditional programs. Thus so-called real time is not time; it is perhaps even the de-temporalization of time, or at least its occultation' (2009, p. 63). Real time has come to be used to refer to the arrival of an apotheosis of modernity's technologised acceleration, in which time has sped up to the point where it reaches the point of instantaneity.

The name 'real time' seems counterintuitive as a way of describing a kind of non-time, a time of machinic operation that seemingly occurs in no time at all. But this usage of the term can be seen to arise from a lack of consideration for the ways in which technologised systems—and technologised time—arise, not from technology in isolation, but rather from interactions between machines and human bodies.

Robert Hassan, through his writing on 'network time', has already considered this usage of the term real time enough to notice that it is logically flawed:

> If one thinks about the nature of time, however, it can be recognized that the concepts of 'timeless time' or of the 'killing' of time make no sense at all. Ontologically it is an impossibility. We are temporal beings living in a temporal environment—whether inside or outside the network.
>
> (Hassan, 2007, p. 49; 2009, p. 90)

It is true that human beings can't exist in a world without time, but machines can't either. In fact, it makes less sense to talk about computers working instantaneously or simultaneously than it does human beings. Computers can work very quickly, of course, but it is this very fact—that their operations are measured in ever-smaller increments, that further improvements in processing speed are constantly being sought and attained—which means that instantaneity can never be achieved. Any computational operation must take some amount of time, and no matter how fast a computer might operate, the speed of that operation will still be measurable. At the much coarser temporal grain of human thought and action we might say that an action is instantaneous: we might say that someone instantly thought of the solution to a puzzle, or caught a dropped object 'as quick as a flash', but, of course, by the standards of computer operation, these supposedly instant actions took place very slowly. And this is the source of the fundamental error in interpretations of real time as meaning an instantaneous machinic time: its instantaneity is measured, not by the time of the computational machinery itself, but by the time of the human observer, leaving it fundamentally human in nature.

In answer to the question 'What is real time?', Robert Hassan replies,

> Computer programmers and systems designers coined the term to describe operating systems that could respond at high speed to the input of data. The computer technicians' online dictionary of Internet terms defines real time as something 'occurring immediately', and on a surface level, at least, this is how most people would conceive of real time.
>
> (Hassan, 2007, p. 49, 2009, p. 91)

However, what Hassan and other writers on this subject have not considered is the larger significance of this high-speed response to the input of data. Why the time of real time is supposedly real is that it is fast enough to represent or respond to external events seemingly as they happen. As Wendy Hui Kyong Chun notes, 'The notion of real time always points elsewhere—to "real-world" events' (2008, p. 316); that is, the time is real precisely because it is not the time at which the computer functions, but is the time at which events transpire in the world outside the computer. The online dictionary previously cited by Hassan continues from 'occurring immediately' to further elucidate: 'For example, real-time operating systems are systems that respond to input immediately . . . *Real time* can also refer to events simulated by a computer at the same speed that they would occur in real life' (Beal, n.d.). In other words, 'occurring immediately' is intended to mean matching the speed of events outside the operation of the computer without any lag; rather than the time of the computer replacing the time of things external to it, the time of the computer is actually *subjugated to* external time. If a computer is providing real-time stock market analysis, this means that it is providing information about the stock market that is (nearly) synchronous with the rate at which the stock market operates; real-time weather information is (nearly) synchronous with changes in the weather. That is—and as reflected in the name itself—the term 'real time' does not refer to the speed of operation of computers at all; it is actually defined in contrast to it. Furthermore, as noted previously, the idea of instantaneity or non-time in the operation of the computer makes no sense in relation to the internal logic of the computer itself; it only makes sense according to the time perception of a human operator or observer, and her sense that the outputs from the computer and events in the wider world occur simultaneously.

As a result, when Robert Hassan seeks to problematise the concept of real time in the following terms, he fundamentally misconstrues the place of the human in its operation:

> To be able to achieve true real-time response would mean the ultimate surrender of human agency to digital technology, where latencies have been driven out and where lags no longer occur. This would . . . be unrealizable because imperfect humans constantly get in the way of perfect systems.
>
> (Hassan, 2007, pp. 49–51, 2009, p. 91)

Following the understanding of writers such as Virilio and Stiegler even as he seeks to problematise their claims, Hassan understands the human user as the fly in the ointment, the impediment to real time that can never be completely assimilated to its perfect efficiency. But in fact the logic of real time seeks to assimilate the computer to the time of the user, not vice versa; the speed of human perception and action is the benchmark for the measurement of the computer's speed of operation. While this might result in attempts to make the computer respond instantly, this is only because the physical, everyday world doesn't have any perceptible latency: I don't perceive a lag between the movement of a speaker's mouth and the sound of her words, and I don't perceive a lag between pressing my hand to a wall and feeling pressure on my skin.

Wait State

Bernard Stiegler's *Technics and Time*, and particularly its second volume, *Disorientation* (2009), directly concerns itself with the idea of real time, arguing that real time exemplifies 'the industrial synthesis of memory' (2009, p. 146). Stiegler's arguments regarding the pernicious effects of real time require further interrogation here because, rather than seeing real-time operations as synchronised to human time, he associates them with an inhuman, effectively instantaneous, 'speed of light':

> On the networks, information circulates at the speed of light across network interfaces, processing systems also working at light-time, and this data-processing is anticipation: under these conditions, the usual receiver of information, the thinking who, seems to be dismissed, since it cannot think fast enough and must automate the process of anticipation. In order to do that, it employs the cybernetic tool called 'real time'.
>
> (2009, p. 141)

Stiegler's analysis of modern information technologies is founded on a belief that these technologies have rendered the human body and human action more or less redundant—something clearly antithetical to the larger argument of this book—and his analysis of 'real time' is a key part of this belief. To make his argument he presents real time as a technologised time that is effectively instantaneous and thus makes human reflection or intervention impossible.

We saw in Chapter 2 how Stiegler, in volume 1 of *Technics and Time*, was working very much as a continuation of André Leroi-Gourhan's account of technics, and the second volume of this work perpetuates the key problems of that approach. Leroi-Gourhan argues for a movement from a technics of physical work to a technics of memory (see Chapter 4), and just as Stiegler considered Leroi-Gourhan's work the last word on human evolution, remaining largely indifferent to further developments in fields such as animal behaviour and paleoanthropology since Leroi-Gourhan referenced them in the 1950s, he also does not acknowledge any substantial change in the development of our relationship with machines since the account based largely around factory machinery given by Leroi-Gourhan in the mid-twentieth century, when he could only gesture vaguely towards the possible future significance of 'electronic brains' and their punchcard memories (Leroi-Gourhan, 1993, pp. 264–266). He therefore carries forward the trajectory Leroi-Gourhan identified decades earlier, in which the human body has an ever-more diminished role to play; in which automation makes human beings increasingly redundant and leaves them struggling to keep up with the relentless speed and efficiency of the independent machine. For Stiegler, therefore, 'real time' is a further point in this development, where the operation of the machine becomes effectively instantaneous in human terms and therefore renders critical engagement with its operations impossible. But why would Stiegler understand the words 'real time' to refer to the antithesis of 'real' human time?

The answer is that Stiegler's understanding of the term is based, not on human—computer interaction, but rather media representation. 'As an expression, real time is always a matter of transmission' (2009, p. 136) he says, but, writing in 1996, he is thinking of television transmission more than networked data transmission. For Stiegler, real-time transmission is emblematically the transmission of real-time television coverage (see Crary, 2014, pp. 52–53). Real-time news coverage claims to bring global events to your television screen 'as they happen', with no delay; for Stiegler it is this (near) instantaneous transmission that illustrates the concept of real time:

> Conjoining the effect of the real (of presence) in image capture, in which event and input of the event coincide in time, with the real-time or the live aspect of transmission, in which the captured event and reception of this input coincide equally and simultaneously, analogic

and numeric technologies inaugurate a new collective as well as individual experience of time as a departure from historicity.

(2009, p. 115)

But seeing events 'as they happen' cannot be instantaneous. A television news report is not itself instantaneous: while it might produce a representation of an event in a format that greatly condenses the entirety of its temporal duration, it nonetheless presents it as a series of short snippets of representation that, themselves, unfold on the human temporal scale of both the viewer's perception and the actions of the human bodies likely to be depicted on the screen.[1] As with the application of the term real time in other areas, it is not defined by its instantaneity or lack of duration; rather it is defined by a duration that is matched to the time of human perception and action. The term 'real-time coverage' is intended to (always falsely) suggest that you can experience events 'as they happen', as if you were physically present, and at the temporal scale of their participants—in other words, in human time, not that of the technologies of media representation being employed.

Here's an easy experiment. Put a video file on the hard drive of your computer—it doesn't matter what the video depicts or what format it is in. Now play the video, and take note of how long the video clip runs for (this should be easy, as most video player applications display a time counter). Now transfer that video file to some other drive (for example a USB drive plugged into the computer) and time how long this operation takes. Moving the file takes much less time than watching it. What does this tell us?

It tells us that the time of the video clip has nothing to do with the time of the computer's operation. The time of video playback, the real time of representing things as they happened, is human time, the time of human perception. When the computer does not have to cater to human perception, it will read the file at a rate set by its physical hardware specifications, a rate that will therefore vary from one computer to the next; but the video file always takes the same amount of time to play because the computer must play it back at the speed of human perception regardless of its physical capacities. If the machine's hardware is not capable of playing back a file at human speed, it will still try to do so, skipping, stumbling and failing in its attempts to exceed its own specifications. Again, 'real time' doesn't mean machine time; it doesn't even mean the industrialised time of the worker struggling to keep up with an assembly line. Real time is as close to being a human time as the computer can manage.

So the real time of media coverage is not a machinic time, but rather a(n almost) human time, and, in fact, it is this very matching of real-time processing to external events on a human timescale that underlies Stiegler's argument for its danger. According to Stiegler, real-time transmission allows media representations to match the speed of human perception and consciousness so neatly that they effectively becomes interchangeable *with* human perception and consciousness. For Stiegler, the instantaneous production and dissemination of media representations effectively makes them interchangeable with what they represent; rather than being a representation of something that happened, they actually cohabit the temporal co-ordinates of the events to which they refer, allowing media technologies to present them to us as a pre-digested stream of experience that replaces a direct, critical engagement with the events themselves.

But there are reasons to be sceptical about the possibility of such a neat relationship. The first problem, as already discussed in the previous chapter, is its logic of prosthesis. Media technologies do not allow memories or perceptions to appear in my brain fully formed—my perception of the world is never the unmediated view of a prosthetic video camera eye, but rather I have my own, individuated perceptual experience of looking at a screen that displays sensory stimuli produced by a technical assemblage of which the video camera is a part. In other words, Stiegler depicts technology as an immaterial force that can engage directly with the human mind, rather than as comprising assemblages of artefacts with which we have embodied relationships.

The second problem is that real-time operation never simply equates to human time; rather it is a hybrid, a series of fits and starts in which the human–machine assemblage switches back and forth between machine time and human time through the implementation of rhythmic interruptions. News coverage never equates to a smooth 'stream of consciousness' but is constantly interrupted, and the hybridity of real time is much clearer in the context of human–machine interaction, in which the rhythmic switching back and forth between human and machine operations is an explicit feature. When Stiegler refers to real time in computing rather than television, the incompleteness of his account is readily apparent. Take, for example, this passage:

> A computer keyboard is a data-upload terminal in which a datum's input virtually coincides with its processing since the machine operates in real time, in what I have called 'interactivity'.
>
> (2009, p. 125)

For Stiegler, real-time, interactive computing is characterised by instantaneity because the computer can 'instantly' perform operations on the words I type on the keyboard. The weakness of this account is partly illustrated by the fact that this instant result is not a troubling novelty produced by the computer, but rather the computer's attempt to simulate the kind of direct articulation of human action and result seen when writing with a pen or manual typewriter. But it is identifiable on a larger scale in that the process of writing on a computer of course and necessarily progresses at a speed set by the action of the human body; in writing this book, I am (lamentably) not working at the near-instantaneous speed of the computer, and there is no possibility that I will ever fall behind the speed of the computer's operation and so find the book continuing to be written without me.

As with the application of the term real time in other areas, it is not defined by its instantaneity or a lack of time; rather it is defined by a duration that is matched to the time of human perception, action and understanding. In focusing on instantaneity of transmission, Stiegler is only acknowledging the sliver of nearly atemporal machinic time that is sandwiched between the human time of the news report's production and reception, and moving from this partial account of real time to make claims about its significance for things like human action and understanding is highly problematic, given that it completely ignores the ways in which human beings engage with real-time technology and its dependence on them. Information technologies are of course capable of outstripping human perception and action, but this represents a fail point in the system, one that real-time computing was developed to avoid.

Interactive Computing

Real time is a key principle in interactive computing, the philosophy of human–computer interaction that underpins the role of digital technology in contemporary everyday life. According to Lucy Suchman,

> The technical definition of interactive computing . . . is simply that real-time control over the computing process is placed in the hands of the user, through immediate processing and through the availability of interrupt facilities whereby the user can override and modify the operations in progress.
>
> (Suchman, 2007, p. 38)

This logic of human–computer interaction is today so well established as to seem inevitable, but it results from a change in direction in the field that took place in the late 1960s/early 1970s (Utterson, 2013, pp. 67–68). According to a periodisation of the development of human–computer interaction by Autodesk founder John Walker (1990, pp. 439–443), the first generation of 'knobs and dials' computing relied upon a direct, embodied relationship between user and machine:

> In the first generation, the user went one-on-one with the computer, in the computer room, operating the computer at the switch and knob level. Because the user was the operator of the machine and controlled it with little or no abstraction, there was essentially no mediation between the computer and its expert user.
>
> (Walker, 1990, p. 440)

However, beginning in the 1950s, this relationship was severed by the rise of computers that were 'programmable without hardware reconfiguration' (Walker, 1990, p. 440). Second generation, batch, computing meant that 'the machine could be turned from task to task as rapidly as new programs could be loaded into memory', greatly increasing its efficiency, but also separating computer and user from one another. No longer dependent on the direct and ongoing guidance of a human being, the computer could perform actions without interruption at the greatest possible speed, and the user's role shifted from directly manipulating the computer to handing a pile of punchcards over a counter to a specialised operator, then returning later to collect a printout that she 'hoped would contain the desired result (but more often consisted of a cryptic error message or the Dreaded Core Dump)' (Walker, 1990, p. 440).

If there has been a general trajectory towards ever-greater autonomy amongst technological artefacts (see Chapter 2), then batch computing was a breakthrough that maximised the autonomy and thus the efficiency of the machine, in turn maximising its usefulness. After all, the original value of the computer came from its ability to perform reliable calculations at a speed impossible for a human being; batch computing gave the computer the autonomy necessary to make the best use of the inhuman timescale of its calculations. However, this same inhuman timescale also maximised the computer's greatest weakness: its inflexible response to instructions and indifference to outcomes. One small error in a user's program, and the computer would diligently occupy itself with the business of producing useless or nonsensical outputs, and the radical incommensurability between the time of its operation and the time of human perception and action meant that there was no way to discern or respond to such problems.

> Second-generation operation introduced many important levels of mediation and abstractions between the user and the computer hardware. First and probably most important was the time shifting performed by a batch system and the autonomy this gave to the computer (or its operator) at the expense of the user's direct control.
> (Walker, 1990, p. 440)

Walker's third, fourth and fifth generations of computing ('timesharing', 'menus' and 'graphics') all responded to this problem by reducing, rather than extending, the autonomy of the computer. In an absolute sense, this slowed the computer down and decreased its efficiency, as well as tending to shift more work back to the human user; but the payoff came from allowing the user to monitor the computer's operation (although with varying degrees of granularity) and intervene to modify its course along the way. This is the 'real-time control' Suchman presents as definitional to interactive computing, and 'real time' in this sense is synonymous with 'human time', as opposed to the inhuman time of the computer that ruled batch computing. Although the computer can (and does) operate on a timeframe that is utterly alien and incomprehensible to the human user (and would lose most of its usefulness if it didn't), interactive computing introduces a series of delays in this operation, during which the computer presents the user with some kind of report on its current state and awaits further human input before continuing. A naïve analogy for this process might be the computer as like Aesop's hare, stopping partway through the race to allow the tortoise user to catch up, although, unlike the fable, the computer always resumes the race upon the user's arrival. However, this would be inaccurate as it portrays the time of the computer as ultimately reconcilable to human time, only passing at a different rate.

What is most significant about this development is that it was a movement *against* automation—and perhaps also autonomisation—in technology. While, as discussed in Chapter 2, writers on technology such as André Leroi-Gourhan saw a progression from man as the autonomous wielder of tools, to man the subservient helper of semi-autonomous tool-wielding machines, to man as spectator in a world of fully autonomous machines, interactive computing moved in a direction contrary to this posited trajectory. This reaction against automation provides one explanation for the fact that futurists' regularly repeated predictions that greater automation and more sophisticated information processing technology will lead to shorter working hours have been discredited time and again by the reality of increased labour (at least of the white-collar variety) produced by the information society, and the way in which this labour has further bled into social and recreational time. The expectation that more automation and more computing would create a future where those who once worked would either be left to put their feet up while autonomous technology did everything for them, or become a disenfranchised, unemployed underclass surviving by crime (see Granter, 2008), was contradicted by changes in work habits—both professional and domestic—that for decades have run in the opposite direction (see Wajcman, 2015, p. 1). While this paradox can to some degree be explained with reference to social and psychological factors (Rosa, 2013; Wajcman, 2015), the appearance of interactive computing can also be seen to have played a part: while there are far more computers in the world now than there were when those predictions were first made, most of those computers have been intentionally set up to *not* realise their full potential for automation, but rather to remain dependent on human input.

And this movement against the spread of automation was an intentional one. The aims of the originators of personal computing were 'augmenting human intellect' (Engelbart, 2003) and producing 'man–computer symbiosis' (Licklider, 2003). Rather than computers being automated and autonomous workers performing tasks in isolation, figures like Doug Engelbart and Joseph Licklider sought to make them powerful tools that extended the human capacity to work rather than replacing it. Of course, doing so itself required certain kinds of automation: those operations and input requirements of the computer that were disruptive to the articulation of user and machine had to be, as much as possible, taken care of in the background, and the computer needed to consistently match its behaviour to a conceptual model (see Chapter 1) that facilitated human interaction. But, nevertheless, this kind of automation was intended to fit the computer into human rhythms and habits of work, to put the computer at the service of the human user through the introduction of the 'interrupt facilities' referred to by Suchman previously.

It would be a mistake to understand the interruptions introduced by real-time computing as just being about the computer 'slowing down' to allow the human user to catch up with its operation; if just slowing the computer down produced real-time computing, then the time of computer processing would already be human time (just human time playing out at an accelerated rate) rather than the inhuman time of a machine. That would imply that the computer's processes follow the model of human perception, thought or action, only occurring more rapidly, but a computer does not function in a way that is the same as or reducible to human action or perception, only faster. Interactive computing might seek to produce an impression that it does (i.e. that the computer responds to human commands by carrying out a set of tasks in a human-like way, checking in with the user at regular intervals so that the user can evaluate its progress), but this anthropomorphism is always an illusion.

Returning to the tortoise and hare analogy, rather than computer and user as following the same track at different speeds, it would be better to conceptualise the computer and user as following tracks of completely different shapes with completely different topographies; however, the computer's track is designed in such a way that it crosses the user's track at multiple points, and the computer must stop and wait at each of these intersections until the human passes by before it can continue. Real-time computing never actually means that the computer operates in real (i.e. human) time, but it seeks to, to some degree, simulate real time by introducing a succession of breaks in the operation of the computer that allow the time of the computer's processes to be periodically synchronised with the time of the human user. It is in these delays that the 'tit-for-tat' (Laurel, 1993, p. 2), 'ping-pong' (Pias, 2011) or (more problematically) 'conversational' (Laurel, 1993, pp. 2–4; Walker, 1990; Winograd and Flores, 2003, pp. 552–553; Munster, 2006, p. 123) qualities of human–computer interaction arise.

Being Waited On

But, it might be objected, if real-time computing does not entail a supplanting of the human temporal scale with an ever-accelerating machine time, then why are so many of us frantically responding to social media notifications, taking our work home with us at night, and feeling a generalised anxiety about the constant demands of our digital devices? (see Wajcman, 2015, pp. 1–2). If interactive computing was intended to create a man–machine symbiosis that would produce effortless mastery over work and information flows—would perhaps create something approaching a smooth and effortless interfacing of user and computer—then why do so many of us seem harried by our digital devices and unable to keep up with their demands?

In his expansive and carefully reasoned book *Social Acceleration: A New Theory of Modernity* (2013), Hartmut Rosa places at the centre of his investigation the claim that our collective blaming of new, ever-faster technologies for our feelings of time-poverty makes no sense. That is, while 'the subjective phenomena of stress, hecticness, and lack of time are traced back over and over again in pop science literature to the immense *technical acceleration* of numerous processes, which at first glance appear to be the most powerful drivers of a ubiquitous social and cultural acceleration' (2013, p. 67), logically, such technical acceleration should have the opposite effect. Rosa points out that

> the heightening of the pace of life is a paradoxical phenomenon in view of the continual technical acceleration of transportation, communication, and production. Technical acceleration shortens the time bound up in such processes and partially frees considerable time resources such that for a constant quantity of actions and experiences *more time* is available: thus one would expect a *slower pace of action, longer breaks*, and *less overlapping of actions*.
>
> (Rosa, 2013, p. 131)

If transportation technology gets me to and from work twice as rapidly, this acceleration of technology should *add* to my free time, not reduce it. Similarly, if technological advances make a factory twice as productive, then logically the workers in the factory should only have to work either half as long or half as hard, meaning that their lives should feel less hectic. Of course, things don't really pan out that way under a neoliberal economic regime (the management of a factory that doubles its output is likely to either sack half of its workforce or simply double its production targets), and it is precisely the ways in which such social values rather than the direct effects of technology produce an experience of time poverty that Rosa is interested in. But even aside from this there are limitations to Rosa's underlying understanding of the logic of technological acceleration.

Of course, transportation and manufacturing operate according to logics of human–technology interaction that are importantly different from that of interactive digital technologies, but even if we take the model of the factory floor things are more complicated than faster machines producing products more rapidly. Modernity's exemplary factory technology associated with increased production and human time pressure is the production line—just look at Charlie Chaplin in *Modern Times* (1936). But the production line isn't intrinsically a technology of acceleration; it doesn't *cause* any of the machinery utilised in production to operate any faster, and the production line can be set to any speed, fast or slow, that factory administrators desire. Rather than a technology of acceleration, the production line (like real-time interactive computing) is a technology of *synchronisation*—that is, however fast or slow the machinery and factory workers work, their pace of work and even individual actions are locked to one another. Of course, once the actions of the worker have been synchronised to the operation of the machinery, the speed of the worker's actions can be accelerated by increasing the speed of the machinery to which they have been synchronised, but even without doing this productivity can be increased simply because the synchronisation of worker with machine, and the synchronisation of workers with one another through their synchronisation with the single external rhythm of the machinery's operation, decreases delays and mismatches in pace. So a first point to make about Rosa's reasoning regarding technological acceleration is that technologically produced increases in factory productivity could never allow workers to work half as hard or half as long because they work within a system where they must work at the pace of the production line regardless of how many products have been manufactured. Consequently, it could never produce an experience of deceleration.

With digital communication technologies this relationship is reversed, with the machine being synchronised to the user rather than vice versa. So why doesn't this solve the problem by forcing the technology to work at whatever pace is most comfortable for us? Again, there are obviously larger human factors at play (such as pressure from our bosses for greater productivity), but even at the level of the technology's operation we can see that this reversal creates new problems through the introduction of delays and interruptions.

Email is widely seen as an exemplar of the anxieties produced by the fast pace of digitally mediated communication (see Wajcman, 2015, p. 95). Various personal habits and technological fixes are offered for achieving the state of 'inbox zero', or the ability to deal with emails at the pace at which they arrive (e.g. Ars Staff, 2018). However, while email is differentiated from physical mail by the near-instantaneity of its delivery, on reflection it is clear that the anxiety produced by email does not directly result from this speed.

The term 'inbox zero' is an indication that the anxiety created by email is not a product of the speed at which emails arrive, but rather the number of emails awaiting response. The large number of emails in an inbox might indirectly result from the speed and convenience of digital technology (in that people are more likely to send more emails more often as a result of this speed and convenience), but it's also possible to imagine a scenario in which we start sending an increased number of physical letters to one another, leading to mounting piles of paper letters that similarly engender guilt and anxiety amongst recipients struggling to reply to them all. Assuming a steady flow and roughly consistent speed, the amount of time the physical or electronic missive takes to arrive at its destination does not have any influence on the amount of anxiety caused because this anxiety is generated by volume rather than velocity.

In fact, the email inbox is not a Chaplinesque production line where the hapless human fails to match the speed at which the technology operates. If it were, we would all achieve 'inbox zero' because we would have no choice but to operate at the speed of the technology and so respond to emails as they arrived. Rather, the anxiety-inducing count of emails in the inbox is produced by the fact that the speed of the system is set by the human user, not the machine, which puts aside messages until the human user has the time and inclination to deal with them. Rather than forcing us to match the speed of its operation, the digital device in fact largely leaves us alone, letting us know that the emails are there but imposing no timetable on our response. Ironically, it is the machine's deferral to the time of the human user that can generate a panicked sense that we can't keep up, rather than its enforcement of a relentless time of its own. The reason for this is the logic of the interrupt facility that Suchman refers to in her definition of interactive computing. Rather than driving the user to conform to its inhuman speed, or simply continuing to function automatically without human intervention, in email, as in many other cases, the computer patiently waits until the user is ready to proceed. But this allows emails to accumulate over time until the user becomes depressed at the thought of the amount of effort required to respond to them all.

The logic of real time is not one of instantaneity, but rather one of waiting. We are waited on by our machines, both in the sense that they serve us, and in the sense that they do so by interrupting their operation until we provide input. However, the greater the number of activities and interactions that take place using digital devices, the greater the number of inputs being waited for and the rate at which they accumulate. In addition, the larger the role of digital devices in social and communicative activities—in which we're aware that, not only is the device itself waiting on us, but there are other human beings awaiting the results of our input—the more anxiety is likely to be generated.[2]

The speed at which the technology operates outside moments of human interaction (for example, the near-instantaneous speed at which a character appears on screen in response to a keystroke or an email arrives in the inbox of its recipient) does not generate anxiety or alienation—in fact, rather than feeling harried by this machine time, we don't even register it. Anxiety is not caused by the time of the machine in itself, but rather the imperfect articulation of machine and human time, which produces the never-ending succession of interruptions that characterises interactive real-time computing. Waiting arises from the ultimate irreconcilability of human time and machine time, and the resulting need to endlessly stop to resynchronise them. While interactive computing seeks to fit the computer into the flow of human time, that flow is unavoidably cut through by periods of interruption and waiting, and the more we use interactive devices the more cuts are made, reducing human experiences to smaller and smaller slices of continuous time.

Flow

However, it would be a mistake to exaggerate the degree to which machines can produce any particular relationship with time in a deterministic way. The clock is the archetypal tyrannical mechanical regulator of temporalised experience (Mumford, 1963, pp. 12–18; Thompson, 1967; see also Rosa, 2013, p. 98), and yet on a personal level it's common to be surprised by how slowly or how quickly it has registered the passage of time. Looked at in one way this is just evidence of the clock's tyranny: no matter how much time we feel it has taken up already, the clock maintains that the meeting has not gone for very long at all and we cannot leave; no matter how much more time we think it would take to experience enough enjoyment of the party, the clock insists that it has gone on too long already and must end. But looked at another way, this very mismatch between chronoception and clock time demonstrates the degree to which our experience of time has *not* been subjugated to the clock. In the words of Tim Ingold, 'We may seek to attune our activity so that it resonates with the repetitions of the clock . . . but that does not turn our bodies into pieces of clockwork' (1995, p. 20).

Then there is the question of our relationship with artefacts that are not intended to have any particular relationship with time or timekeeping at all, but which nonetheless do seem to have a more profound and direct effect on chronoception than any clock ever could. Take the video gamer who recovers from a reverie induced by a focused engagement with the equipment of game console, screen and controller to discover that hours of clock time have passed in what her chronoception registered as almost no time at all; or the woodcarver who puts down a spokeshave and notices that it's dark outside, despite the fact that he last registered his temporal location when it was lunchtime. It is a common experience for those who drive to and from work regularly to pull out of their workplace's car park and have their awareness of the passage of time seemingly suspend itself until they are dropped back into normal chronoceptive experience as they pull into their driveway at home, with only a vague awareness of what happened in the interim. The very fact that these experiences defy the laws of clock time illustrates the degree to which these kinds of embodied, enactive relationships between individual human beings and technological artefacts are far more important to our experience of time than the impersonal technologies of timekeeping themselves.

Such experiences have most famously been described by psychologist Mihaly Csikszentmihalyi's work on happiness as produced by a state of 'flow':

> One of the most common descriptions of optimal experience is that time no longer seems to pass the way it ordinarily does. The objective, external duration we measure with reference to outside events like night and day, or the orderly progression of clocks, is rendered irrelevant by the rhythms dictated by the activity.
>
> (1992, p. 66)

Csikszentmihalyi's work does not claim any special significance for objects in the production of flow states, and his focus on flow as producing happiness also skews his account in certain ways (the state of flow produced by driving home from work, for example, doesn't really seem to generate any feelings of happiness, or even enjoyment). However, his account does associate this loss of time awareness with a loss of self, in which the distinction between body, environment and action seems to dissolve.

> [O]ne of the most universal and distinctive features of optimal experience . . . [is that] people become so involved in what they are doing that the activity becomes, spontaneous, almost automatic, they stop being aware of themselves as separate from the actions they are performing.
>
> (1992, p. 53)

This provides an indication of why this state is often associated with a deep engagement with features of the physical environment: when the body is closely engaged with something outside itself in order to act as part of a tightly integrated assemblage, awareness of the distinctions between body, external object, and even action, fades from consciousness, whether that external object be the mountain into whose fissures the climber wedges her fingers, the bat being swung by a baseball player, or the motorcycle straddled by a member of a Japanese *bōsozōku*, or 'speed tribe' (Greenfeld, 1994):

> The loss of the sense of a self separate from the world around it is sometimes accompanied by a feeling of union with the environment, whether it is the mountain, a team, or, in the case of [a] member of a Japanese motorcycle gang, the 'run' of hundreds of cycles roaring down the streets of Kyoto.
>
> (1992, p. 63)

There are, of course, experiences that can be described as flow states that do not feature discrete external objects. At the same time, however, flow states are commonly produced by close bodily engagement with an artefact, and, as discussed in Chapter 2, these are in turn part of a continuum with a wider engagement with physical features of the environment. We can more broadly associate the change in chronoception associated with flow with the experiences of acting and perceiving with and through objects discussed throughout this book, as this mode of close engagement with external objects can be understood to alter our sense of time by to some extent inflecting our habitual experience of time's passage with the rhythms of the object and its mode of use.

Natasha Dow Schüll's analysis of 'the painstaking efforts of the gambling industry to organize the kinesthetic and temporal elements of machine play into a streamlined economy of production' (2012, pp. 56–57) provides a good example of a technology specifically designed to produce a flow experience through a rhythmic kinaesthetic engagement between body and machine: the slot machine. Schüll quotes players' explanation of gambling's appeal in terms of a rhythm of rapid user–machine interaction that keeps them 'in the zone' to such an extent that they sometimes discard winning combinations rather than break the flow to collect money (2012, p. 54).

Machine Time

Despite the suggestion of objective reality in the term 'real time', it is generated by human perception. This is explicit in Henri Bergson's pre-digital investigations of what he, too, called 'real time': for Bergson, real time is real precisely because it is generated by human consciousness, without which time can only exist as a spatialised abstraction made up of disarticulated instants. As explained by David Scott, '"Real time", as such, is only ever lived, and perceived in this continuousness of its being lived' (2006, p. 186).

The nature of temporalised engagements between bodies and artefacts can be explored more broadly through a discussion of Bergson's work, particularly the account of time presented in *Matter and Memory* (2004 [1896]). Bergson's account of matter is helpful because it depicts objects as always fundamentally bodily significant: while every object has a ('virtual', in Bergson's terminology) existence independent of us, the object only becomes actualised for us in its human significance, embedded in human memory. The very title *Matter and Memory* suggests a model of time as arising from the interaction of a material object (matter) and human experience (memory); in Bergson's words, 'Memory . . . is just the intersection of mind and matter' (2004, p. xii).

But could we take this further and credit some artefacts with a more active role in the way in which they become actualised for human beings?

After all, while a hammer might be used in all sorts of ways, it has been consciously designed to encourage us to integrate it into a particular model of perception and use. Bergson refers to objects that 'appear to turn towards our body the side . . . which interests our body' (2004, p. 29), and when we move on to contemporary digital devices that are intended to adapt dynamically to our modes of use, and perhaps even to pre-empt our needs, we can take this theme further. Does this mean that these artefacts are themselves now 'zones of indeterminacy', capable of 'movements spontaneous and unforeseen'? (Bergson, 2004, p. 331). Absolutely not, but they are intended to play off the indeterminacy generated by the human user, both shaping, and shaping themselves to, its contours.

So what exactly happens when a human body interacts with a useful object? In Gilles Deleuze's redeployment of Bergson's work, a key concern is the way in which human recollection combines with material objects to produce the capacity for physical action. Most important is the process of actualisation, which pulls a certain actuality out of the realm of the virtual (see Chapter 4). Deleuze tells us that there are

> four aspects of actualization: translation and rotation, which form the properly psychical moments; dynamic movement, the attitude of the body that is necessary to the stable equilibrium of the two preceding determinations; and finally, mechanical movement, the motor scheme that represents the final stage of actualization . . . The first moment ensures a point of contact between the past and the present: The past literally moves toward the present in order to find a point of contact (or of contraction) with it. The second moment ensures a transposition, a translation, an expansion of the past in the present: Recollection-images restore the distinctions of the past in the present—at least those that are useful. The third moment, the dynamic attitude of the body, ensures the harmony of the two preceding moments, correcting the one by the other and pushing them to their limit. The fourth moment, the mechanical movement of the body, ensures the proper utility of the whole and its performance in the present. But this utility, this performance, would be nothing if the four moments were not connected with a condition that is valid for them all.
>
> (1988, pp. 70–71)

What this means can be made clearer if we take driving a car as an illustration of how a human actor and a physical object come together to produce directed and meaningful movement. When I am presented with a car, translation consists of rendering the car intelligible to me as something that brings the possibility of meaningful action: all of my previous interactions with cars mean that I know what the car is useful for and understand how the car can be used to effect certain kinds of action. Rotation refers to a kind of 'turning towards' the car and its various systems by my body; there is a way in which my body and the car 'fit together' physically, but there is also a set of prior knowledges regarding cars that are applicable. For example, when I sit in the driver's seat of a car, I am not consciously aware of the texture of the upholstery, but I am intimately attuned to the feedback produced by the steering wheel. How I make sense of the car and interact with it results from my 'pulling out' certain aspects of the car's material attributes and imbuing them with a particular significance—understanding them to invite or operationalise certain kinds of sensing and action—and not others. Deleuze's third aspect, dynamic movement, is the translation of this potential from the generality of previous actions and current options to the specificity of a particular body and a particular object interacting in the idiosyncratic context of this particular, unique set of circumstances; and the fourth, motor movement, is the means of producing this action in a unified way. Of central concern in this account is its claim that the human user brings duration—that is, the component of time and memory, which in turn produce conscious understanding and experience—and the object brings matter—that is, the space in which action and perception can take place.

Memory is constantly interacting with the world by providing the context that makes it intelligible to us and available for action; it is a store of previous experience, like a great ring of keys we can fit into the present in order to open it up, and we are constantly adding new keys to the ring. Not only that, but each time we use a key, the key changes. Without the key ring of memory, a car would mean nothing to me, and driving it would be unimaginable. We pull out the key that fits most closely and usefully with our presently unfolding experiences, and we are constantly and fluidly plugging memory into the present, producing new interactions between the two. The insertion of memory into the keyhole of the present is not in any way organised by the chronological order of memory or experience, but is ordered more by the relative applicability of past experiences, and the most appropriate grain of detail. And every time we fit memory to the present, we cause a change in the nature of memory.

A similar process is taking place in the realm of matter, too. This 'lock' is not a fixed or given attribute of the material world, even though it might appear to be so as we fit the key of memory to it. In fact, both the lock and the key are created by us at the moment of their use. We perceive the world like the kind of optical puzzle where a jumble of dots becomes an image when we look at it through glasses with coloured lenses; in this case, our perception of the world is tinted, not by coloured cellophane, but simply our requirements for action and the patterns of perception established by previous experience. This is what is meant by the *virtual*: it is all the things the material world *could* mean and *could* do given its endless jumble of potential. The *actual* is the pattern we *do* see in that potential, and the pattern of actions that arises from it. We only actualise the pattern that fits memory and circumstance; everything else remains non-actualised.

However, this model should not be taken as a simple dualism, where the human and duration sit on one side and the objective and matter sit on the other, as Deleuze reminds us that it is not possible for either to exist in pure isolation. At the same time, even though Deleuze is careful to make this clear, it is also the case that, if we consider the process in closer detail than either Bergson or Deleuze do in their description of it, the practical details become even less clear-cut.

Let's take matter first. Returning to the example of the car, the car is an object, a structure of objective matter, that brings with it a set of possibilities. Is it a mode of transport, an object of trade, an occasion for aesthetic contemplation, a faulty system in need of repair, a fashionable personal accoutrement requiring further decoration? When I perceive the car, these possibilities resolve themselves into something clearer: for the sake of argument, let's say a simple mode of transport, although of course none of these options are really mutually exclusive. However, when I drive the car, I am not simply an immaterial enduring consciousness applying itself to the material system of the car; on the contrary, I am myself material. I am an acting body, and that body is itself a set of material potentials. Rather than the car as transportation being actualised directly through the application of duration, duration is working on a subset of the car's potentiality, that fraction that intersects with the potentiality carried by my body. Imagine a Venn diagram showing the set of potentiality that is my body and that of the car, and then the region where the two sets overlap. This region of overlap is partly generated by duration already, as memory holds a set of previously established possibilities for interaction with the car, but it is also partly generated by the physical properties of both my body and the car—the car, for its part, has been intentionally imbued with certain material properties that facilitate certain kinds of interaction with my body and impede others.

Now let's take duration. When I apply myself to the driving of the car, I do so with the benefit of memory. If I had never seen a car before, let alone driven one or seen someone else drive, the car would not even exist for me as a mode of transportation. At the same time, however, as a habitual driver I am not aware of any engagement of memory here. The car just 'makes sense' to me as available for a certain kind of use: the windscreen is in front of my eyes, the steering wheel falls into my hands. More baffifingly, my engagement with the car might sometimes seem to exist outside duration: I might have the previously noted experience of driving home from work with my mind on something else, finally dropping back into the normal flow of time in my driveway with no recollection of the series of complex actions, perceptions and decisions that lay between my work carpark and my home. This experience of flow associated with skilled physical activity is precisely a falling away of temporal awareness, a non-linear rhythm of movements that seems to exist outside time and memory. Deleuze is aware of this complexity, and takes the time to explicitly assert that duration remains a factor here, even when it seems not to.

> Sometimes perception is extended naturally in movement; a motor tendency, a *motor scheme*, carries out a decomposition of the perceived in terms of utility. This movement—perception relationship would, on its own, be sufficient to define a recognition that is purely automatic, without the intervention of recollections (or, if you prefer, an instantaneous memory consisting entirely in motor mechanisms). However, recollections *do* intervene. For, insofar as recollection-images resemble actual perception, they are necessarily extended into the movements that correspond to perception and they become 'adopted' by it.
>
> (1988, pp. 67–68)

At the same time, however, both Bergson's and Deleuze's accounts don't tell us a great deal about what's happening in such cases. It is certainly true that duration and memory are in play here; we might not be conscious of them, but Bergson's account is specifically about opening up the role of memory in such cases where its role has otherwise been missed. And yet cases like these, where duration has become sedimented into the materiality of the body to such an extent that its relationship to our traditional notions of memory is unclear—where it has become what is sometimes referred to as muscle memory—make the relationship between matter and memory seem much messier than it appears in a general account. The same can be said for matter if we return to my description of the Venn diagram of body and car: the possibilities of the body are shaping those of the car, and the matter of the body that is doing this shaping seems to already be infused with memory. This infusing with memory of course arises from the fact that we are not simply incorporeal entities composed of memory and consciousness, but are ourselves matter, so that matter and memory are already brought into interaction by the very fact of our being alive. None of this is meant to imply that either Bergson or Deleuze were oblivious to this fact, but only to point out that describing this relationship in terms of general principles makes it appear much neater than it does when we look at actual instances of body—machine interaction.

So why do different kinds of objects seem capable of producing different kinds of time? Bergson describes human perception as cinematographic in nature (1975, pp. 331–333), cutting into frames what are more properly indivisible continuities; but why does the craftsman intent on his work seem to make fewer incisions into the flow of time and movement? Why does the very process of chronoception as Bergson describes it seem to break down when we are intimately engaged with some objects, causing time itself to seemingly stop?

Habit

As already described by Deleuze, for Bergson, chronoception is driven by the process through which the past of memory is brought into interaction with the present of movement. Bergson famously illustrates this with a conical diagram (2004, p. 211), whose sharp tip marks the point where different levels of past experience, contracted by a tight focus on their relevance to the current moment, drill into the present. The engine that drives this boring into the now is the constant oscillation between different layers of the past and the present, a piston-like movement that draws past experience into the present with reference only to relevance, rather than chronology. This oscillation is fast; in fact, the value of memories and habits is that they are ready to hand and the process of activating them is much quicker than the business of analysing the unfamiliar perceptions arising in the present; as a result, the specificity of the present has a tendency to be lost beneath our projections of the past into it:

> With the immediate and present data of our senses we mingle a thousand details out of our past experience. In most cases these memories supplant our actual perceptions, of which we then retain only a few hints, thus using them merely as 'signs' that recall to us former images. The convenience and the rapidity of perception are bought at this price; but hence also springs every kind of illusion.
>
> (Bergson, 2004, p. 24)

However, while this oscillation is rapid, it cannot be instantaneous—it is a process that must have its own rhythm, rather than being an indivisible, instantaneous event. But can this process occur more or less rapidly, depending on the circumstances? I would argue that it can, given that it is a process of negotiation between the specificity of past and present; logically, some pairings of past and present will be more similar and amenable to one another than others, and so require less negotiation.

Deleuze broke the process down into four parts: translation, rotation, dynamic movement and mechanical movement. In the first two stages, past experience is adapted and made relevant to the particularity of the now; in the second two, the body is adapted and made relevant to the instantiation of the resulting action in the present and then carries it out. If a past experience of action is almost identical to the action called for in the present, and the body is trained in the ready execution of the necessary movements, then the progress of this process will surely be smoother, more natural and rapid than if it is very different. I am thinking here of the role of habit.

What lies at the heart of our pleasure in watching a skilled sportsperson, dancer or acrobat is their ability to make something entirely unnatural seem entirely natural. That is, they can perform contrived and complex movements seemingly without any conscious reflection. Their ability to do this has arisen, not simply through a reshaping of the physical capacities of their bodies, but also through the repetitious application of conscious reflection to those movements until they become submerged beneath consciousness as 'motor tendencies', 'motor schemata' or 'motor programmes' (Deleuze, 1988, p. 67; Gallagher, 2005, pp. 47–48). Or, rather, the shaping of the body and the habituation of movement have progressed in tandem: an ability to instantaneously actualise the principles of the movement has been coupled with a shaping of the body's attributes such that it is suited to their enactment. Bergson acknowledges this kind of process with his own example of habituated movement:

> In learning a physical exercise, we begin by imitating the movement as a whole, as our eyes see it from without, as we think we have seen it done. Our perception of it is confused; confused therefore will be the movement whereby we try to repeat it. But whereas our visual perception was of a *continuous* whole, the movement by which we endeavour to reconstruct the image is *compound* and made up of a multitude of muscular contractions and tensions; and our conscious-ness of these itself includes a number of sensations resulting from the varied play of the articulations. The confused movement which copies the image is, then, already its virtual decomposition; it bears within itself, so to speak, its own analysis. The progress which is brought about by repetition and practice consists merely in unfolding what was previously wrapped up, in bestowing on each of the elementary movements that *autonomy* which ensures precision, without, how-ever, breaking up that *solidarity* with the others without which it would become useless. We are right when we say that habit is formed by the repetition of an effort; but what would be the use of repeating it, if the result were always to reproduce the same thing? The true effect of repetition is to decompose, and then to recompose, and thus appeal to the intelligence of the body. At each new attempt it sepa-rates movements which were interpenetrating; each time it calls the attention of the body to a new detail which had passed unperceived; it bids the body discriminate and classify; it teaches what is the essen-tial; it points out, one after another, within the total movement, the lines that mark off its internal structure. In this sense, a movement is learnt when the body has been made to understand it.
>
> (2004, pp. 137–138)

According to Bergson, then, the physical action of another body is con-verted by visual perception into a unified image, which we then decom-pose by converting it back into physical action with our own bodies. This decomposition then allows our bodies to reconstitute the action as unified, integrated movement (cf. Merleau-Ponty, 2002, pp. 164–165).

This is an account of the development of muscle memory, with its 'appeal to the intelligence of the body'. This decomposition of the movement, the embodied understanding of its component parts at a fine grain, enables its ready re-enactment at a future moment, as a command over its small details allows it to be easily and precisely modified to account for circumstances that differ from those of its past enactment. The movement is digested to produce a collection of small parts, each of which can be readily and flexibly arranged to map new parameters of enactment by a body that has developed a habituated, unreflective capacity to reproduce them (see Grosz, 2013, p. 228).

All of this suggests that skilled, habituated actions require less work to translate their past enactments into their future employment. The appropriate enactment of the movement comes to seem natural, even inevitable, due to the sheer weight and consistency of an individual's past experiences of them. When these movements employ a physical object, the physical attributes of the object can themselves play a role in this sense of naturalness and inevitability through their shaping of the process Bergson describes in terms of objects, bodies and recollections 'turning towards' one another.

Take the classic example of the hammer. There are all sorts of things one *could* do with a hammer, but there is one thing that is *best* to do with a hammer, and that is to bring its head forcefully down on some target. This is of course a result of the design of the hammer, but most correctly and specifically it is a result of the way in which the hammer interfaces with the human body. What I mean by this is that the rightness of hitting something with the hammer doesn't arise directly from the physical qualities of the hammer, but rather from what happens when the hammer is held in a human hand. The weight of the hammer is distributed in an intentionally unequal way; as an isolated artefact it is unbalanced and lopsided. If you wrap your fingers around its handle near the head, it feels weak and useless. But if you grasp the end of the handle, the human–hammer assemblage suddenly *wants* to hammer something. The weight of the hammer head begins to draw the hand downwards; the length of the handle and the weight at its end exaggerates and adds momentum to the arc made by swinging the arm; the potential energy we can feel being generated by this coupling is focused on a small, hard plane of steel that becomes its natural point of exchange with the environment.

I am not arguing that you can't do anything with a hammer except hammering—of course you can. But the hammer is a simple artefact whose design has been refined to maximise its applicability to a very specific action. The hammer invites a certain mode of interfacing, and it is a very effective mode because one particular way of interfacing with the hammer is immediately identifiable as right and appropriate, and immediately and satisfyingly produces a shift in the movements and capacities of the body using it.

This is because the hammer is a record of the countless instances of its previous use by human bodies. It has been shaped by these previous instances of use. Its interactions with moving human bodies has worn it into a certain shape, a certain set of contours. Countless gripping hands have worn its handle round and smooth, like waves working on a stone in the sea. The strained rocking back and forth of its head as its claws prise out nails has left it bowed in a way that records the trajectory of a levering arm. Just as the repetition of Bergson's learnt physical exercise has taught the body something, the repetition of these actions has taught the hammer something, something that it tells the human body that picks it up. Just like Bergson's memories, these past instances of hammer use are contracted and projected into now, producing its present use. Using Bergson's favoured metaphor of the kaleidoscope (e.g. Bergson, 2004, pp. 12–13, pp. 259–261, 1975, pp. 331–333), the hammer might be considered to have been imbued with planes that are intended to catch the light of human perception in certain ways, to some degree influencing the way in which hammer and human body orient themselves to produce a meeting of their surfaces. The hammer and the hammering body produce each other; in the words of Elizabeth Grosz, 'habits are how environments impact and transform the forms of life they accommodate and are themselves impacted and transformed by these forms of life' (2013, p. 219).

So memory is always also matter, given that it is always a part of a material body, and matter is at least sometimes like memory—certainly when we are talking about artefacts designed to interface with the human body in particular ways. Therefore, just as certain kinds of memories can be expected to articulate more immediately and smoothly with actions in the present, certain kinds of matter can be expected to do the reverse. And in the case of skilled, habituated actions using artefacts that are effectively designed to be effectively used in particular ways, both matter and memory can be expected to maximise smooth immediacy, both between body and artefact, and past and present.

Tool Time

The preceding account provides an explanation for why some relationships with artefacts are characterised by flow; furthermore, the experience of flow when playing video games suggests that it's possible to interface with a technology that is at least related to interactive computing in a way that creates flow rather than waiting or interruption. But if, as we've already seen, waiting and interruption are foundational principles of human–computer interaction, then how far can we move away from them?

A hand plane performs only one task. The user generally does not need to consciously interrogate the hand plane concerning its state of functioning, and the hand plane is incapable of interrogating the user, or responding to changes in the user's state even if it could. The woodworker planing a piece of wood takes up the plane and uses it in a direct way that might produce an experience of flow; but interactive computing would seem to have no equivalent experience. There is no moment in the woodworker's engagement with the hand plane at which the plane might need to await further information from its user before performing its role, or the woodworker might wait on some internal operation of the hand plane before continuing to use it. If the hand plane is in good working order and the user is habituated to its mode of use, the hand plane operates according to a logic of action, not inter-action.

The very interactivity that makes digital interfaces so useful would seem to sabotage any analogous experience of interfacing. If we return to the example of playing a video game, on further examination we can see that game-playing is often subject to interruption and waiting. While there can be periods of focused engagement, the player nevertheless waits for levels or saved games to load, or for a dead character to respawn, or for cut-scenes to play out, and various other things. At the same time, however, there can be experiences of flow, and where they do occur they seem similar to, for example, successfully writing in a word processor, where the writer fluidly and unreflectively engages with an input device to perform a task. But again, when writing in a word processor, these periods of successful interfacing are similarly interrupted with greater or lesser frequency by pauses to load and save, or perform other tasks.

These contrasting experiences highlight the limits of the approach to interfacing taken in this book. While previous work on human–computer interfaces has prioritised interactive software and largely ignored the foundational role of our embodied engagement with physical artefacts, it remains the case that, in the case of digital human–computer interfaces, our engagement with physical artefacts is directed towards the control of interactive software, and so is regularly interrupted by the rhythms of that software. Even if we can act *through* a device in a way that produces a successful human–machine assemblage, digital devices, unlike a hand plane, actually require us to periodically interrupt this acting *through* in order to act *on* the device.

There is a difference between acting *on* the device and acting *with* the device—the 'cut' that constitutes a discrete entity or assemblage can fall in different places (see Chapter 2). When acting *with* the device, at its best the extension of sensation and intention through the device facilitates the device's dropping out of conscious consideration. But what about when we act *on* the device? In this case, it is not possible for the device to drop out of conscious consideration, and it would not be possible to act on it if it did. This suggests that there is a base level at which we must remain separated from such devices. At the same time, it seems clear that there has been a trend over time towards the reduction of the need to act *on* the device. As noted previously, while interactive computing represents a break in the trajectory of automation, it is nevertheless dependent upon certain kinds of automation itself: the automation of processes that are not improved by human input and would break the flow of human–machine interaction.

Of course, some commentators are likely to decry this diminution in experiences of acting *on* devices: it is further evidence of Bolter and Gromala's ideology of transparency (see Chapter 1), robbing us of autonomy and individuality by naturalising a certain way of interacting with technology. And of course this is true; if the device functions independently in a predetermined way outside of my conscious awareness, then I do not have any capacity to influence that operation to suit my tastes or needs. At the same time, however, this is the price we pay with any device that readily extends our capacity for action and perception. Before the word processor, we wrote on typewriters, which ossified a particular set of historically specific ideas, practices and assumptions as an inescapable mode of user engagement, but the payoff was a ready-to-hand, habituated mode of action that produced writing. To illustrate the problems with the alternative, imagine that I created a product that allowed writers to create their own customised pens: it came with various colours and consistencies of ink, different kinds of nibs, ballpoints and felt tips for writing with, and a substance that could be moulded into any shape, size and weight of barrel before setting hard. Writers could make a pen that was perfect for their writing style, specific tasks or even moods; however, I think the reality is that most people would prefer to buy standard, ready-made pens, or if they created a customised pen of their own once, they would then simply continue to pick it up and use it without reflection every time they needed to write something, rather than engaging in an ongoing process of experimentation, refinement, or mercurial change. The reason for this is obvious: when we sit down to write, it's because we want to make words on a page, not because we want to make a pen. Having to set about creating or personalising a pen when you want to write—or creating your own paper, for that matter—would interfere with the process, making the writing implement the object of conscious focus rather than the words to be written.

As with the QWERTY keyboard, it's the fact that it's already a part of a vocabulary of habituated action and doesn't require any ongoing interpretation or negotiation that allows an artefact to be effectively utilised as an extension of the body. In Bergson's terms, the body has already come to understand it. The digital device, on the other hand, introduces more flexibility to the modes of interfacing it makes available at the cost of interrupting habituated action.

A hammer can be said to understand the body in the sense that it records and reflects the body's proportions and movements; the user knows how to engage physically with the hammer, but the hammer has also been imbued with a readiness to be engaged with. The keys of a typewriter similarly cup the fingertips to facilitate the engagement of the typist. But these engagements are, of course, inflexible, as they are fixed in the physical form of the artefact. If the user of a claw hammer shifts from hammering a nail in to pulling a nail out, the design of the hammer no longer seems optimised: when extracting a nail, it would be better if I could hold the handle horizontally, rather than vertically, and it might be necessary for me to put a wooden block under the head to improve leverage. The shape of the hammer can't be ideally suited to both hammering *and* extracting nails, and a hammer is likely to be used for hammering in far more than pulling out, so the first task is prioritised. An iPad, on the other hand, can change its operation to suit different applications, making it useful in a far wider variety of circumstances; but this very flexibility means that the iPad's physical form does not materialise any specific mode of bodily engagement beyond the most comfortable way to hold it, and also that it doesn't intrinsically 'understand' what its user wants from it. Again following the logic of interactive computing, it can't instantly leap into service, but must rather wait for a user to indicate how she wants to use it—for example by waking the device and selecting an app icon.

But there have been ongoing efforts to make devices and human–computer interfaces 'intuitive', with 'intuitive' effectively meaning able to pre-empt users' needs and so initiate the appropriate mode of functioning without waiting for input. Of course, these efforts can make the situation worse, taking the digital device further away from the instant usefulness of the hammer by making it actively initiate a mode of interaction that the user does not want; Clippit the paperclip, the helper character from past Microsoft Office versions, is probably the most infamous software feature ever created, precisely because of its constant, cack-handed attempts to pre-empt the user's needs, which only introduced more interruptions rather than flow.

In fact, all such efforts to create 'intuitive' user interfaces might seem innately conservative, even regressive, in their attempts to enforce a fixed relationship with artefacts. After all, they broadly follow the same logic seen in the idea of natural user interfaces (see Chapter 2). If a voice call is initiated by making the 'hang loose' sign with thumb and pinkie finger and putting them to the ear and mouth, this movement is intuitive and requires no negotiation with the technology because it follows a habituated vocabulary of physical action—it is precisely this intuitiveness that makes natural user interfaces seem desirable at first glance. But this approach need not be conservative as NUIs are; on the contrary, it can be far more radically progressive and individualised than the opposing idea of consciously shaping the operation of a digital device. But this potential for progressive and individualised experiences lies in a different understanding of its potential. New kinds of sensory experience created by new kinds of relationships with technology—discussed in the previous chapter—can produce new ways of engaging with the world around us, rather than simply reproducing what has gone before.

Conclusion

The development of interactive computing arose from an intentional effort to utilise automation and digital technologies to create tighter and more productive relationships between bodies and machines. While real-time human–computer interaction has come to be associated with the obsolescence of the body and the empowerment of inhuman technology, this is in fact its antithesis, as it rather seeks to articulate computer time and human time through a logic of waiting. Rather than destroying human time, all kinds of interfacing create new experiences of chronoception because the repeated use of an artefact embeds it in memory, creating close articulations between object and memory that make body and artefact operate smoothly together.

Despite the problems of interruption and waiting that it brings, real-time interaction is not evidence of digital technology's hostility towards embodied human perception and action. On the contrary, it has been successful precisely because it seeks to reconcile the time of the machine to that of human body. As we have seen, the human experience of time is central to the skilled, habituated use of all artefacts; the question is, can digital technologies sustain the most integrated forms of human–artefact assemblage, and what new forms of action and perception would be produced as a result if they can?

This book began with a critique of the idea that 'the interface' was a self-contained software feature 'given' to the user by a technology company. The critique of 'transparency' by Bolter and Gromala (2005) and others charges that, because such an interface is fixed and suited to use without modification or conscious awareness of its functioning, it disempowers the user and forces her to comply with a standardised logic of operation imposed from without. This argument implicitly maintains the logic of 'the interface' as isolated software feature, and makes this self-contained, externally imposed interface itself the site of a struggle over the user's autonomy. But if we shift to a discussion of *interfacing* that highlights the degree to which the human–computer interface exists *between* artefact and user, rather than 'inside' the artefact, and prioritises the ways in which the user acts *through* rather than *on* artefacts, our focus changes.

The hammer records (and dictates) a certain mode of action, but this need not be seen as restrictive or limiting. After all, rather than constraining the human body's range of interactions with its environment, it adds to it. The hammer's mode of action was not available to the hand before it hefted the hammer, and the hammer can always be put aside afterwards.

The hammer crystallises a new mode of human action, capturing it in an enduring form that, by virtue of being enduring rather than ephemeral and isolated as individual human actions must be, changes it relationship to time. Tools take action out of any specific set of temporal co-ordinates— the lateral curve of the hammer's handle or the concavity of the machine's button is both a mark of the bodies that have touched it in the past and a premonition of the those that will touch it in the future. They create new possibilities for human action, and embed those possibilities in the world in an enduring way, permanently changing our relationship with the world around us. Interfacing with the tool produces a body–tool assemblage that in turn creates a new way of interfacing with the wider environment. In the words of Drew Leder, 'To incorporate a tool is to redesign one's extended body until its extremities expressly mesh with the world' (1990, p. 34).

If we understand 'the interface' to be a fixed, external entity that the user must enter into some kind of negotiation with, then the question becomes, How can we maximise the user's conscious awareness of and control over the device? The relationship between user and device becomes the central concern, and there is a desire to maximise the user's authority over the device. But if we see 'the interface' as a plane across which is produced a collaborative engagement between user and artefact, and interfacing as the creation of a human–user assemblage oriented towards action upon its environment, then the problem becomes, not how the user acts on the machine, but rather how the user–machine assemblage acts on the world. And the user–machine assemblage's potential for new forms of action and experience are exponentially greater than any self-contained machine's potential to programmatically deliver new kinds of action and experience to a user, regardless of how much control the user has over it.

By the same token, the NUI gesture for making a voice call sees user and machine as separate from one another; rather than producing a new kind of user–machine assemblage, user and machine don't even come into physical contact. Rather than a way of acting directly through the device, the 'phone call' gesture is actually a sign: it's not a way of directly causing a voice call to happen, but is rather the gestural equivalent of saying 'telephone' to a voice-activated system. Significantly, while the discourse of natural user interfaces talks about catering to the natural behaviour of the user, this requires that the user 'perform' for the machine in order to be rewarded with a voice call. Placing your thumb and pinkie finger against ear and mouth does not *feel* like picking up a telephone—it only makes you *look* like you are picking up a telephone—but of course the user can't see herself doing this. Only the digital device 'sees' this, meaning that the system is designed from the perspective of the machine rather than the user, requiring the user to perform a game of charades in order to ask the device to do things for her.

In the case of both the natural user interface and the critique of transparency, the user is understood to be an isolated and autonomous entity with a fixed, enduring set of capacities, needs, and styles of action and perception to which the machine must be aligned—in the first case, by interface designers; in the second, by the user herself. But if we see the user–machine assemblage as the point of origin for styles of action and perception, then it is the pre-conscious, non-reflective and harmonious functioning of user and artefact together that produces what is new and individualised, because the transformative integration of the device into the user's sensorium and field of action facilitates entirely new kinds of experience.

Notes

1. David Wills has described Stiegler's conflation of a near-instantaneity of certain technical processes with an instantaneity of the events depicted or their reception as resulting from 'apparent lapses in critical rigor' (2006, p. 254).
2. Judy Wajcman notes research suggesting that we pass moral judgement on the tardiness of others' email responses (2015, p. 96).

Conclusion

We seem to be living at a time defined by the intensity of the relationships between bodies and machines that it has produced. Where once we might have been pressed into the service of a machine tool in a factory, or joined with a car to escape from home or work into the non-place of the highway, now machines can be with us constantly, regardless of where we are and what we are doing—perhaps rather than our relationships with them being independent of external context, we can say that they themselves provide a context for everything we do. We constantly carry and cradle them, attach them to our bodies or bed them down in our pockets; even as we sleep they wait at our bedside to be our first objects of attention upon waking, and in some cases they even watch over us as we sleep.

But the very power and extent of these relationships arises from their being a continuation of a much longer history. The idea that tool use defines or even inaugurates humanity, while problematic, nevertheless reflects an awareness that our relationships with technological artefacts have always been a part of who we are. While there are, of course, important differences between a stone hand-axe and a smartphone, they are both nevertheless dependent upon features of human embodiment that enable a productive engagement between body and object, and it is this engagement that I refer to as interfacing.

The human body is not a fixed, stable, discrete entity, nor is it simply a neurological fiction or product of social or cultural forces. It is an entity that is always implicated in that which lies outside itself, and is a living, productive part of the world by virtue of its ability to enter into dynamic relationships with features of its environment. This is why machines do not really extend or replace the functioning of the human body: the human body cannot function at all without always already being implicated in external matter, and so can never be isolated as a set of capacities to be extended or replaced. A body cannot breathe or speak or hear without the gases that swirl around it; cannot see without the torrents of light splashing off the objects before it; cannot jump or run without solid surfaces against which to brace its legs. As suggested by the perspective of Karen Barad, when investigating the interaction of body and machine, we mustn't forget that the boundaries of neither entity are stable or self-evident. Human beings have always created artefacts because to change something with which the body interacts is to change the potentiality of the body itself, and it is much easier to change the shape of a stone, for example, than to change the shape of one's own body.

Obversely, technological artefacts should not themselves be understood as self-contained aggregations of capacities. Of course, it is only common sense that the objects around us are generally of little human use without a human operator, and yet a habit of speaking of them as if they possessed abilities and values separate from us has become widespread, as reflected in the idea of machines independently having an interface discussed in Chapter 1. Interfacing produces a set of potentials that originates neither with the artefact nor the user in isolation; but it is also importantly not simply the adding of the potential of one to the potential of the other.

Our bodies function as nexuses in flows of sensation and movement, synthesising them into a coherent whole. But this should not be conceptualised as the brain being a computer into which various wires are plugged, carrying linear, discrete flows of inbound and outbound information about the world. Due to the far-reaching influence of computationalism, there is a tendency to believe that, if the body isn't a unified and fixed thing, this must be because it's a kind of illusion generated by the brain, whose information processing constitutes a real self inside the head. But sensation and action are not possible without a body, and it is over and through the body that sensations play, and from the body that the forces that produce action arise. The brain is clearly important in its capacity to negotiate harmonious relationships between these various flows, but the flows themselves are always arising as a friction generated by the interaction of body and world.

Our bodies have a great capacity to integrate different kinds of experience into a unity. The productiveness of our relationships with artefacts is dependent upon this capacity to assimilate novel sensory experiences produced through close engagement with objects into an immediate, pre-conscious whole. New technologies such as virtual reality might be sold to us in terms of complex technology's ability to 'trick' our brains into believing computer-generated illusions, but in reality our bodies and minds, rather than being dupes of the technology, are the most active and sophisticated components of the system, reconciling different kinds of fragmented and often contradictory perceptual information into a coherent experiential whole that intuitively 'makes sense' to a user. Without our bodies performing this synthetic role, the faltering and imperfect operations of the technology alone could not hope to succeed. The human body is a dense cloud of potential around which such technological artefacts orbit, and without which they would be inert, or at best shut into closed loops of meaningless activity.

Temporal relationships play a fundamental role in this process. Different kinds of sensory information are grouped together through synchronisation; when different kinds of sensory stimuli are coincident, there is a tendency to synthesise them into a unity and attribute them to a common source. The synchronisation of sensation between body and artefact, or shared and reciprocal rhythms in their activity, therefore function to integrate features of the environment into coherent human experience. This principle underlies the transfiguration of sensory experience using technological artefacts: the virtual reality display synchronises bodily movement and computer-generated image, and the sensory substitution device synchronises bodily movement with aural or tactile perception in order to produce sensory experiences that are novel but at the same time fit harmoniously and meaningfully within our existing understanding of body–environment interaction.

Not all of our relationships with artefacts are the same. Perhaps more than anything else, humanity is defined by the astonishing variety of physical objects it produces, and every single one of them, from the boomerang to the Reaper drone, generates a form of human engagement that is in some way unique. The employment of an artefact is never simply a matter of some plan or intention arising in an immaterial mental realm and then being imposed on an external tool; the physical qualities of the artefact itself are involved in the production of the acts and experiences in which it is employed, and, as a consequence, any difference in physical form will alter the relationships of which it becomes a part. But even physically identical artefacts can produce different relationships, given that these relationships are also dependent on the specificity of living bodies; when we factor in the flexibility of the human body's capacities for movement and sensation, and its ability to dynamically negotiate new modes of engagement with the material world, the variety of possible relationships generated by the coming together of body and object seems limitless.

At the same time, however, it is possible to draw some generalisations from this vast array of experiences. One reason for this is that human beings have developed specific attributes whose evolutionary value are partially or wholly dependent upon external objects, rather than the body in isolation. In the broadest sense, the entire human sensory apparatus can be said to fall into this category, given that senses have no value aside from producing dynamic relationships with the environment, but there is an important subset of these attributes that is keyed to the production of direct physical engagements that modify the body's range of perceptions and actions. As we saw in Chapter 2, this subset of human engagements has often been projected backwards onto particular kinds of artefacts to produce a loosely defined category of things: tools. The tool, an object that has been defined not by any physical qualities it might have in isolation, but rather by the actions and perceptual experiences of the human being who wields it, represents the particularity of a certain kind of bodily engagement with an object that is generated with the aid of particular natural human attributes.

When I use the term 'natural', I do not intend this to suggest the best or most efficient kind of relationship to have with an artefact, nor to suggest that there are natural or inevitable forms or outcomes for such relationships. Many existing accounts of the role of technological artefacts in human experience rely on a false opposition between the natural and artificial, and don't acknowledge the degree to which such relationships are always both natural *and* artificial. The experience of interfacing is always natural in that it is something that human beings have always and in all circumstances done, and will continue to do forever into the future, endlessly incorporating into such relationships any new object amenable to doing so. It is also natural in the sense that it can arise without instruction, planning or conscious forethought,[1] facilitated by evolutionarily organised features of the brain and body. But the experience of interfacing is also always artificial, in that there is no predetermined, inevitable form that individual artefacts will take, and each new relationship that arises from a new engagement between body and artefact is to some degree a surprise, a novel development that introduces something unprecedented into the world that is not defined by circumstances that predate it. But this simultaneously natural and artificial character of interfacing is precisely why explanations founded on assumptions about its either natural or artificial status always lead towards simplistic generalisations.

Attempts to leverage natural modes of engagement with artefacts—as exemplified by the natural user interface research discussed in Chapter 2— are constraining and intellectually moribund precisely because they look for the natural in existing patterns of use when the natural does not reside there. What is natural about interfacing is its ability to produce an endless variety of new engagements with artefacts by dynamically negotiating the specificity of particular bodies, particular physical objects and particular environmental contexts. Looking at what bodies already do for clues about natural modes of engagement means investigating the possible rather than the virtual, in Deleuze's terms, but those possibilities are derived from existing modes of engagement that have been actualised from the virtual and crystallised as stable forms. What is natural about interfacing is its engagement of the endless potential of the human body to produces these crystallisations of action and generate new possibilities in the first place, not the enduring artefacts or patterns of action that this process leaves in its wake. Picking over the by-products of this process in order to produce an endless series of sterile reproductions is the antithesis of its natural inclination towards the future.

On the other hand, treating interfacing as purely artificial tends to depict our engagement with artefacts as manufactured, as an expression of a particular ideology, philosophy or commercial agenda that is physically expressed in the artefact such that our interactions with it are defined by them. As we saw in Chapter 1, this is most apparent today in discussions of 'the interface', which portray the exemplary contemporary mode of engagement with technological artefacts as a system of representation that embodies a particular set of values. Both technological artefacts and human beings are real, physical things with sets of real—if varied and flexible—physical properties; our ways of engaging with artefacts are produced by these real physical properties more importantly than they are produced by ideas and representations. But even when that materiality is acknowledged, a tendency to collapse the distinction between the artefact as a physical object and 'the interface' as an interactionally produced phenomenon can still produce accounts that portray interfacing as a purely artificial, manufactured experience derived from mass-produced objects, rather than a contingent phenomenon generated by the interaction of bodies and artefacts. The recurrent theme of transparency versus opacity further reflects the imposition of binary value judgements onto our relationships with artefacts when in fact they are always more varied and ambiguous than that, and shift dynamically according to context.

Don Ihde's differentiation between embodiment and hermeneutic relationships with technological artefacts is important in this regard, as it shows that the value of a given mode of engagement with an artefact is importantly dependent upon context and aim. As I illustrated with the example of the steering wheel and the speedometer when driving in Chapter 2, the hermeneutic, non-tool-like relationship has value in contexts where the embodiment does not. The example of the car also highlights another issue: when considering many complex technological artefacts, at present it is hard for us to imagine the possibility of a pure embodiment relationship free from some reliance on conscious acts of planning and interpretation. Stephen Kercel, Arthur Reber and Wayne Manges have suggested that there remains a vast, and vastly under-appreciated, potential to remove conscious interpretation from our relationships with complex technological artefacts by employing devices such as Paul Bachy-Rita's 'brainport' tongue stimulator (2005; see Chapter 4), and I agree; at the same time, however, even if expert operators one day develop entirely new senses that give them a direct awareness of the health of a nuclear power plant or the stresses on the body of an aeroplane, such relationships will not achieve their full potential until these new kinds of perception are seamlessly married with new modes of action. And the question of how such an expert operator might modify the operation of a complex technological system in a fully embodied way remains not only unanswered, but largely unasked. Nevertheless, while my account of cutting-edge and speculative brain–machine interface research in Chapter 4 was largely critical in tone, that negativity does not arise from a belief in the impossibility or uselessness of the kinds of body–machine relationships it seeks to produce. Rather, it is a response to the false assumptions about the nature of human bodies and their relationships with artefacts that often inform the interpretation and formulation of their agendas.

A more detailed understanding of the kinds of body–machine engagements described by Ihde as embodiment relations, and by me as instances of interfacing—the ways in which they come to be, the nature of their operation, and their potential to produce new kinds of engagement in the future—has been my aim throughout this book. While it is true that this is not the only kind of productive human–artefact relationship, nor the only one that has value, I have focused on it for several reasons. First, interfacing represents the tightest possible coupling of body and artefact, and so illustrates most strikingly and provides the greatest insight into the degree to which human bodies perceive and act upon the world through physical objects. The very tightness and seamlessness of the join produced by interfacing generates experiences that are enigmatic to us precisely because they exist independently of conscious planning or interpretation, and thus investigating them provides valuable insights into the nature of human action and perception by excavating information that is otherwise unavailable to conscious reflection. Second, when we consider the important shifts in our relationships with technology brought about by the ongoing expansion and intensification of our engagement with digital technologies, we can see that new kinds of interfacing are key to many aspects of this development. In the nineteenth and on into the mid-twentieth centuries, the trajectory of body–machine relationships could be seen as eroding the power of interfacing, requiring that human beings effortfully maintain careful and contingent engagements with machines whose physical limitations could only support the most brittle of relationships. However, not only did the later development of new digital technologies facilitate the creation of machines capable of more flexible and responsive relationships with human users, but the interactive computing revolution of the late 1960s and early 1970s was actually driven by an intention to reshape this trajectory and re-establish a close articulation between body and artefact that had been disrupted by industrialisation—using the principle of real-time computing to create a 'man–computer symbiosis', in the words of Joseph Licklider (2003). Contemporary approaches such as natural user interface research are themselves inheritors of a set of values that see the seamless engagement of interfacing as user interface design's ideal—even as a subsequent, commercially driven obsession with ease of use has largely purged this of aspirations for expert operation or speculation concerning new models of control seen in the work of pioneers such as Doug Engelbart.

An important moment in the ongoing development of these tightly integrated relationships was the becoming-mobile of digital devices. This greatly expanded the range of possible engagements between both the digital machine and its surroundings, and the digital machine and its user. When the first iPhone was unveiled in 2007, its touchscreen was presented as a revolutionary user interface development, but, in reality, this only amounted to a more flexible instantiation of the principles of the mouse and keyboard, and was therefore not particularly revolutionary at all. What *was* revolutionary was its utilisation of a constellation of sensors that enabled it to respond to information not intentionally addressed to it by the user. Where the programs running on a personal computer might have been dependent upon a user delivering discrete instructions by typing or clicking a mouse, now factors such as the phone's orientation relative to the body of its user, or the phone–user assemblage's speed or trajectory through space, and even air pressure became meaningful input to which it could be programmed to respond without a need for intentional human direction. Suddenly the whole world was potentially a part of the device's user interface.

Consequently, understanding the nature of interfacing is important to understanding, not just the influence of these new technologies, but also how they can, might or should develop in the future. Rather than resulting directly from the invention of the digital computer itself, the impact of digital technologies on contemporary life results from the fact that, two decades or so after its invention, a group of researchers decided that the flexibility of the digital computer should be put to the service of creating new kinds of tightly articulated, tool-like relationships between human bodies and machines, and it was this development that has most importantly driven digital technology's subsequent role in society and culture, and will continue to do so into the future.

So what does an investigation of interfacing tell us about our relationships with technological artefacts? I have already discussed the first key insight: that interfacing is naturally artificial. It creates phenomena that are entirely new and result from directed human action, but that are simultaneously generated by biological capacities and drives that are older than the human race and independent of human planning or intention. The power of interfacing arises from the fact that it integrates an object into the human capacity for action and perception, creating a plane of articulation between an artefact that is produced by human industry and technologised culture and the stable biological properties of a human body. And this plane of articulation can produce a join so effective that it seems as if the human body has been tailored to the employment of that artefact despite the fact that it has been absent from the evolutionary history that made human bodies what they are. Interfacing is dependent upon natural human capacities, but natural human capacities for dynamic and adaptable engagement with the physical world, for generating previously unknown modes of action and perception by utilising the properties of external objects.

The second key insight is interfacing's transformation of action and perception itself. The transformation of human action and perception is the purpose of interfacing; this is the endlessly valuable property of interfacing that has driven the evolution of a set of innate human capacities keyed to its facilitation. The only indisputably natural and invariant quality of human bodies is their capacity to adapt and change, but this capacity is not itself generated by the body in isolation, but rather through its interactions with the material world. Examples of this are vast and varied, including neuroplasticity, the development of new skills, and a whole range of cultural influences on who we are and what we can do, but interfacing's generation of tight and relatively stable relationships between body and environment are particularly complex and significant. The physical properties of the human eye have remained largely fixed over a prolonged period of time, and yet the properties of human sight have changed and multiplied dramatically over the past 150 years as human vision has entered into relationships with a succession of new technological artefacts. The range of movement available to a human body has similarly remained stable while new modes of engagement with new artefacts have drastically altered the human capacity for action. Not only does interfacing produce flexibility and adaptability by allowing the parameters of human action and perception to be shifted at the scale of a human working on the environment, rather than the vastly slower scale of evolution's working on the human body, but it also produces a Swiss army knife effect, allowing different capacities for perception and action to be taken up and put aside, allowing us to move between different styles and postures in our engagement with the environment according to context.

The third insight is that these transformations transcend the logic of extension, substitution or augmentation to create new possibilities. Rather than simply modifying or redeploying existing possibilities, interfacing engages the virtual, actualising it to generate new ways of acting and perceiving that are crystallised in the physical form of artefacts. These artefacts add to a stock of possible human actions and perceptions that physically endure in the world.

Interfacing always creates something new, meaning that each instance can never be reduced to the alteration or replacement of something that predated it. In Chapter 3 we saw that the experience of virtual spaces is not simply about substituting one experience of space (the physical) with another (the simulated); nor is it about 'fooling' the brain into believing that the physical is not there and the simulated is. The body is a nexus that draws together different strands of sensory experience and plaits them into a coherent whole, and the result is a multiplication of experiences and a refraction of our sensed locus of action. Virtual environments do not take away one reality and substitute another; rather they create new experiences that our bodies bring into interaction with what is already there in order to produce a new unity.

In Chapter 4, I devoted some time to arguing the case for why prosthesis as trope neither captures the key attributes of our close engagement with artefacts nor leads us towards a better understanding of them. The logic of prosthesis is precisely one of replacement or augmentation, but most attempts to either conceptualise real physical prostheses or apply the term by extension to other body–technology relationships seek to eliminate or disavow an excess in body–machine relationships that is never reducible to these themes. An amputee with a prosthetic leg is not simply an incomplete person who has been completed, and a photograph is never simply an augmentation of human memory or a substitute for it.

Returning to the classic example of the blind person sensing with a cane, we can see that the model of extension, substitution or augmentation tells us nothing useful about what is happening. First, to say that the cane replaces sight is a gross mischaracterisation of what is happening. The sensory experience generated with the cane is clearly not vision; its capturing of spatial relations simply overlaps with vision in certain useful ways, even as both it and vision have important qualities that are not shared. It is also not simply an extension or augmentation of touch, even as the sense of touch facilitates the engagement of body and artefact. There is clearly tactile information—for example temperature or wetness—that is not captured by the cane, but, at the same time, the cane's ability to sweep across the environment to create a spatialised awareness of what lies beyond the physical limits of the user's body importantly exceeds the baseline capacities of touch. As with sensory substitution devices more generally, this is an example of a novel sensory capacity being generated by the productive coupling of body and artefact, an adding to existing sensory experience not in the sense of making what was there better, or replacing something that was missing, but rather the creation of something new through a novel combination of existing sensory and physical components.

Questions like 'Where does the user's body end, at the hand or the tip of the cane?' or 'Where does the sensing take place, in the hand or the cane?' are ultimately unproductive, precisely because interfacing transcends the logic of either/or, addition or substitution. Experientially, the user's body ends at the hand *and* the tip of the cane; her sensing takes place in hand *and* cane. Interfacing transcends the attributes of body and artefact; like the interface of fluid dynamics discussed in Chapter 1, this phenomenon is a third term that is generated by the coming together of two entities but is not reducible to them; it both defines and is defined by them in its capacity to sustain a perfect alignment and reciprocity between them, generating a new set of attributes as long as they are in contact, then vanishing when contact is broken.

The naturally artificial, the transformation of action and perception, and the creation of possibilities—these, I believe, are the three key defining attributes of interfacing. In order to concretise them some more, let's look at their role in the appearance of one of the first forms of human–artefact engagement. Because the following account takes our prehistoric ancestors as its subject, I'm aware that the details of this story must be to some extent speculative, and may be proven mistaken; but the literal truthfulness of the story is less important than its value as a narrativisation of the processes I'm seeking to illustrate.

Our primate ancestors developed the unusual capacity to rotate their shoulders in a 360-degree arc; the reason for this is that it allowed brachiation, a novel way of engaging with the environment roughly equivalent to walking upside-down on the sky, above the heads of predators and amongst the prized fruit and shelter in the tree foliage. This was an evolutionary change in the physical attributes of the human body brought about by a change in its mode of engagement with the environment, but this physical change also produced a shift in human potentiality. In 1995, Daniel J. Povinelli and John G. H. Cant suggested that this new mode of engagement with the environment initiated the development of self-awareness, as moving through a network of quite literally branching routes that would respond in varying ways to the weight of a relatively large hanging body required a greater awareness of the actions and physical attributes of that body than locomotion using the more stable and undifferentiated affordances of the ground (Povinelli and Cant, 1995). When later human ancestors abandoned brachiation, freeing both the new cognitive and perceptual abilities it had incited and the swinging and gripping arms it had required, they found them amenable to a new use: the modelling of physical properties and focused, spatialised vision that had allowed their ancestors to launch their bodies from one branch to another could also aim a rock held in a gripping hand and launched by a rotatable arm cocked beside the head. This ability to attack an enemy from a safe remove, only shared by close primate relatives and developed to a higher degree in humans, was a novel and very useful form of action at a distance (Corballis, 2002, pp. 76–80). In this case, particular physical properties of the body—the swinging and gripping arm—arose to facilitate a particular form of body–environment articulation, and this form of body–environment articulation required the development of a certain mode of sensing that could arise through the articulation itself; the swinging arm is also a mechanism for registering both the weight of the hanging body and the flexile qualities of the branch, and focused and spatialised vision combines with this appreciation of mass and movement to plot the body's possible trajectories through the air from one branch to another. The branch becomes a handle that the primate can grip so as to gain a purchase as it throws the world away from it and catches it again; when the branch is replaced with a stone, the same potentiality produces a new kind of action that changes the body from a fulcrum for moving the world to an engine for weaponising individual environmental features.

The shift from throwing one's own body to throwing a stone was therefore entirely new while nevertheless arising from existing natural, evolved bodily and cognitive capacities; it generated and relied upon ways of acting and perceiving that only arose through an engagement with a branch or stone; and it actualised a bodily potential that, while it had previously been there, was nonetheless entirely unheard of and without precedent. Admittedly, this change was a dramatic, long-term one, but it allows me to illustrate the broader principle in bold colours.

The appearance of modern technological artefacts tends to produce less radical shifts in human action and perception. There is more than one reason for this, but it importantly arises from the way existing instances of interfacing operate as a constraining set of possibilities. The nature of interfacing—the way in which it combines the properties of body and artefact to create a third, emergent set of properties—means that existing interfacing possibilities can be redeployed in new ways with new technologies even as they arise from a previously established logic. The development of technologies of spatialised visual representation provide a good example of this, given that they have tended to be motivated by a desire, not to create a new kind of sensory experience, but rather to simulate a previously existing one through attempts to attain visual realism.

Because the human eye functions by arresting the movement of light at the single physical point where it is situated, it doesn't have any innate capacity to register the spatial distribution of objects. As a result, the human perception of space is extrapolated using a variety of different sensory and cognitive operations. Putting aside the cognitive aspects as well as those that do not depend on vision on the grounds that they are outside the address of visual media, we are left with depth cues such as stereopsis (triangulation by comparing the perspective of each eye), perspective and parallax (variation in objects' visual qualities according to distance), and vergence and accommodation (variations in the orientation of the eyes and the deformation of their lenses). Looking at the development of technologies of realistic spatialised visual representation, we see first the attempt to simulate perspective without space (perspectival artistic and then mechanical visual representation). Then the moving perspective of parallax is added by the technology of film; however, because this technology cannot actually move the body's viewing position (at least until the head-mounted display intensifies the effect by reintroducing bodily movement), the capacity for movement is introduced to the machine instead, producing a body–artefact assemblage with an aggregate effect that is roughly the same. To this can be added stereopsis through stereoscopic images, but again the location of the key attributes are shifted: because the technology cannot simulate the multiplicity of relations given to objects by their arrangement in physical space, the screen itself becomes multiple rather than the spatial relationships—or at least double. That leaves accommodation and vergence, which are not currently simulated by any commercially available technology, although the market for VR and mixed reality devices is driving development in this area.[2] The development of these successive technologies represents a conservative approach to interfacing because each new technology is intended to contribute to the reassembly of an originary set of sensory possibilities: visual spatial perception. At the same time, however, the hopes of technology developers and the claims of marketers could only ever convince the most naïve observer that each new development simply replaces another missing piece of our visual experience of space. Even as these technologies are defined by existing possibilities, and seek to do no more than reintroduce components of an existing mode of environmental engagement, the results are always something importantly different. No matter how constrained by a previously established set of possible interfacing experiences, new forms of interfacing always articulate with the realm of the virtual to introduce something new. The invention of the car might have been motivated simply by a desire to replace the horse-drawn carriage, but the mode of sensation and action produced by the articulation of hands on steering wheel and feet on pedals is a form of embodiment completely alien to driving a carriage. The typewriter might have appeared as a mechanised replacement for the intricacies of penmanship, but the mode of sensation and action produced by the articulation of touch-typist's fingers and keys is utterly unlike that of calligraphy. Even if the creators of these newer artefacts understood themselves to be reproducing or replacing the older, the resulting ways of interfacing with them are nevertheless fundamentally different, richly embodied modes of experience in their own right.

To harness the full potential of interfacing, therefore, human–machine interfaces should not be developed or evaluated using previously established ways of interfacing as a guide or benchmark. While engaging bodily with a new artefact will always generate new possibilities whether the artefact's designers want it to or not, the exploration of new potentialities can be the aim of interfacing rather than an unintentional by-product of efforts to reproduce or extend what has come before. Interfacing brings the human body into contact with a limitless potentiality, but each successive instance should seek to reactivate this moment of contact, rather than simply drawing on the set of possibilities left behind by previous ones. Furthermore, when seeking to understand interfacing, and through this its future development, the focus needs to be on what it is doing, not what it is. It is easier to deal with fixed sets of stable attributes, whether they be of a human body, a technological artefact, or an interface itself understood as a mediating entity, but it is the very fact that interfacing transcends discrete categories to produce a dynamic set of emergent attributes that gives it its value, and these things can only be investigated through experiment and speculation. The purpose of interfacing is always to produce new ways of perceiving and acting upon the environment and thus cannot be adequately understood by breaking the assemblage of body and artefact apart; rather, it requires that we consider how the body–artefact assemblage engages productively with the world around it.

When seeking to understand our relationships with technological artefacts or imagine new ones, the focus must be on, not what an artefact can do, or even on what a human body can do, but rather on what a given artefact–body assemblage can do. The focus must be, not on the relationship between user and artefact, but that between user–artefact assemblage and environment. Useful artefacts should seek to maximise action and minimise interaction in order to produce a body–machine assemblage that can maximally generate and harness new possibilities. Action can never completely supplant interaction—the more complex and flexible an artefact becomes, the more moments of conscious interaction it is likely to generate—but the flexibility of digital user interfaces and the proliferation of sensors that can generate feedback loops of reciprocal transformation of perception and action nonetheless create a potential that has not yet been fully explored.

The minimising of conscious planning or control in our interactions with artefacts need not be restrictive or conservative, because it generates new human capacities. Even if the aim of creating a new mode of body–artefact engagement *is* conservative—for example, creating a natural user interface designed to reproduce existing ways of interacting with older physical objects, or a prosthetic limb designed to make an 'incomplete' body function like the 'complete' bodies around it—a new experience of interfacing will unavoidably create a new set of possibilities. The only difference is whether these new possibilities are seen as unwanted side effects that interfere with the efficient operation of the system, or this generation of the unexpected, this unavoidable branching off into new productive energies and potentialities, is harnessed to produce new models of engagement with our environment, and through them new human experiences of action and perception.

Notes

1. Which is not to say that particular skills regarding, or prescribed, normative uses of, individual artefacts do not arise from these things, only that interfacing can arise without them.
2. For example using light-field displays (Lanman and Luebke, 2013), which escalate the stereoscopic display's multiplication of images to a large number of 'slices' of spatial representation, or simpler eye-tracking devices that can extrapolate focal distance from vergence.

Bibliography

Armstrong, D. and Ma, M. (2013). Researcher Controls Colleague's Motions in 1st Human Brain-to-Brain Interface. [Online] Available at: www.washington. edu/news/2013/08/27/researcher-controls-colleagues-motions-in-1st-human-brain-to-brain-interface/ [Accessed 6 June 2018].

Arns, I. (2011). Transparent World: Minoritarian Tactics in the Age of Transparency. In: *Interface Criticism: Aesthetics Beyond the Buttons*, C. U. Andersen and S. B. Pold, eds. Aarhus: Aarhus University Press, pp. 253–276.

Ars Staff. (2018). Inbox Zero and the Search for the Perfect Email Client. [Online] *Ars Technica*. Available at: https://arstechnica.com/information-technology/2018/05/inbox-zero-and-the-search-for-the-perfect-email-client/ [Accessed 16 May 2018].

Auvray, M. and Myin, E. (2009). Perception with Compensatory Devices: From Sensory Substitution to Sensorimotor Extension. *Cognitive Science*, 33(6), pp. 1036–1058.

Bach-y-Rita, P. (1972). *Brain Mechanisms in Sensory Substitution*. New York: Academic Press.

Bach-y-Rita, P. and Kercel, S. W. (2003). Sensory Substitution and the Human-Machine Interface. *Trends in Cognitive Sciences*, 7(12), pp. 541–546.

Balasubramanian, K. et al. (2017). Changes in Cortical Network Connectivity with Long-Term Brain-Machine Interface Exposure After Chronic Amputation. *Nature Communications*, 8(1), pp. 1–10.

Barad, K. M. (2007). *Meeting the Universe Halfway: Quantum Physics and the Entanglement of Matter and Meaning*. Durham: Duke University Press.

Barlow, J. P. (1996). A Declaration of the Independence of Cyberspace. [Online] *Electronic Frontier Foundation*. Available at: www.eff.org/cyberspace-independence [Accessed 7 May].

Baudrillard, J. (1988). *The Ecstasy of Communication*. Trans. S. Lotringer. New York: Semiotext(e).

Bayne, T. and Spence, C. (2015). Multisensory Perception. In: *The Oxford Handbook of Philosophy of Perception*, M. Matthen, ed. Oxford: Oxford University Press, pp. 603–620.

Beal, V. (n.d.) Real Time. [Online] *Webopedia*. Available at: www.webopedia. com/TERM/R/real_time.html [Accessed 6 June 2018].

Beck, B. B. (1980). *Animal Tool Behavior: The Use and Manufacture of Tools by Animals*. New York: Garland STPM.

Bedini, S. A. (1964). The Role of Automata in the History of Technology. *Technology and Culture*, 5(1), pp. 24–42.

Bentley-Condit, V. K. and Smith, E. O. (2010). Animal Tool Use: Current Definitions and an Updated Comprehensive Catalog. *Behaviour*, 147(2), pp. 185–221.

Bergson, H. (1975). *Creative Evolution*. Trans. A. Mitchell. Westport: Greenwood Press.

Bergson, H. (2004). *Matter and Memory*. Trans. N. M. Paul and W. S. Palmer. Mineola: Dover Publications.

Berti, A. and Frassinetti, F. (2000). When Far Becomes Near: Remapping of Space By Tool Use. *Journal of Cognitive Neuroscience*, 12(3), pp. 415–420.

Black, D. (2014). *Embodiment and Mechanisation: Reciprocal Understandings of Body and Machine from the Renaissance to the Present*. Farnham: Ashgate.

Bolter, J. D. and Gromala, D. (2005). *Windows and Mirrors*. Cambridge, MA: MIT Press.

Bolter, J. D. and Grusin, R. A. (1999). *Remediation: Understanding New Media*. Cambridge, MA: MIT Press.

Boothroyd, D. (2009). Touch, Time and Technics: Levinas and the Ethics of Haptic Communications. *Theory, Culture & Society*, 26(2–3), pp. 330–345.

Borell, M. (1987). Instrumentation and the Rise of Modern Physiology. *Science & Technology Studies*, 5(2), pp. 53–62.

Breuer, T., Ndoundou-Hockemba, M. and Fishlock, V. (2005). First Observation of Tool Use in Wild Gorillas. *PLoS Biology*, 3(11), pp. 241–243.

Brooker, W. (2009). Camera-Eye, CG-Eye: Videogames and the 'Cinematic.' *Cinema Journal*, 48(3), pp. 122–128.

Bryant, L. R. (2010). Onticology—A Manifesto for Object-oriented Ontology, Part I. [Online] *Larval Subjects*. Available at: https://larvalsubjects.wordpress.com/2010/01/12/object-oriented-ontology-a-manifesto-part-i/ [Accessed 29 June 2018].

Bryant, L. R. (2014). *Onto-cartography: An Ontology of Machines and Media*. Edinburgh: Edinburgh University Press.

Calleja, G. (2007). Digital Game Involvement a Conceptual Model. *Games and Culture*, 2(3), pp. 236–260.

Card, S. K., Newell, A. and Moran, T. P. (1983). *The Psychology of Human-computer Interaction*. Hillsdale: Lawrence Erlbaum Associates.

Chesher, C. (2004). Neither Gaze nor Glance, But Glaze: Relating to Console Game Screens. *SCAN Journal of Media Arts and Culture*, 1(1), pp. 98–117.

Chun, W.H.K. (2008). On 'Sourcery,' or Code as Fetish. *Configurations*, 16(3), pp. 299–324.

Chun, W.H.K. (2011). *Programmed Visions*. Cambridge, MA: MIT Press.

Clark, A. (1997). *Being There: Putting Brain, Body, and World Together Again*. Cambridge, MA: MIT Press.

Clark, A. (2001). *Mindware: An Introduction to the Philosophy of Cognitive Science*. Oxford: Oxford University Press.

Clark, A. (2003). *Natural-born Cyborgs: Minds, Technologies, and the Future of Human Intelligence*. Oxford: Oxford University Press.

Clark, A. (2008a). Pressing the Flesh: A Tension in the Study of the Embodied, Embedded Mind. *Philosophy and Phenomenological Research*, 76(1), pp. 37–59.

Clark, A. (2008b). *Supersizing the Mind: Embodiment, Action, and Cognitive Extension*. Oxford: Oxford University Press.

Clark, A. and Chalmers, D. J. (1998). The Extended Mind. *Analysis*, 58(1), pp. 7–19.

Corballis, M. C. (2002). *From Hand to Mouth: The Origins of Language*. Princeton: Princeton University Press.

Cramer, F. (2011). What Is Interface Aesthetics, Or What Could It Be (Not)? In: *Interface Criticism: Aesthetics Beyond the Buttons*, C. U. Andersen and S. B. Pold, eds. Aarhus: Aarhus University Press, pp. 117–129.

Crary, J. (2014). *24/7: Late Capitalism and the Ends of Sleep*. London: Verso.

Crawford, C. S. (2014). *Phantom Limb: Amputation, Embodiment, and Prosthetic Technology*. New York: New York University Press.

Csikszentmihalyi, M. (1992). *Flow*. London: Rider.

Dactyl Nightmare. (n.d.). [Online] *Gaming History*. Available at: www.arcade-history.com/?n=dactyl-nightmare&page=detail&id=12493 [Accessed 30 July 2017].

Danilov, Y. and Tyler, M. (2005). Brainport: An Alternative Input to the Brain. *Journal of Integrative Neuroscience*, 4(4), pp. 537–550.

Davis, L. J. (2006). Stumped by Genes: Lingua Gataca, DNA and Prosthesis. In: *The Prosthetic Impulse*, M. Smith and J. Morra, eds. Cambridge, MA: MIT Press, pp. 91–106.

Deleuze, G. (1988). *Bergsonism*. Trans. H. Tomlinson and B. Habberjam. New York: Zone Books.

Deleuze, G. (1994). *Difference and Repetition*. Trans. P. Patton. New York: Columbia University Press.

Denisova, A. and Cairns, P. (2015). First Person vs. Third Person Perspective in Digital Games. *The 33rd Annual ACM Conference*, pp. 145–148.

Deroy, O. and Auvray, M. (2015). A Crossmodal Perspective on Sensory Substitution. In: *Perception and Its Modalities*, D. Stokes, M. Matthen and S. Biggs, eds. Oxford: Oxford University Press, pp. 327–349.

de Vignemont, F. (2011). Embodiment, Ownership and Disownership. *Consciousness and Cognition*, 20(1), pp. 82–93.

Dexta Robotics. (2018). [Online] *Dexta Robotics*. Available at: www.dextarobotics.com [Accessed 28 June 2017].

Doom. (1993). iD Software.

Dourish, P. (2004 [2001]). *Where the Action Is*. Cambridge, MA: MIT Press.

Dourish, P. (2017). *The Stuff of Bits: An Essay on the Materialities of Information*. Cambridge, MA: MIT Press.

Elbert, T. et al. (1995). Increased Cortical Representation of the Fingers of the Left Hand in String Players. *Science*, 270(5234), pp. 305–307.

Emerson, L. (2014). *Reading Writing Interfaces: From the Digital to the Bookbound*. Minneapolis: University of Minnesota Press.

Endo, T. and Kawasaki, H. (2015). A Fine Motor Skill Training System Using Multi-Fingered Haptic Interface Robot. *International Journal of Human-Computer Studies*, 84, pp. 41–50.

Endo, T. et al. (2011). Five-Fingered Haptic Interface Robot: Hiro III. *Haptics, IEEE Transactions On*, 4(1), pp. 14–27.

Engelbart, D. (2003). Augmenting Human Intellect: A Conceptual Framework. In: *The New Media Reader*, N. Wardrip-Fruin and N. Montfort, eds. Cambridge, MA: MIT Press, pp. 95–108.

Farina, M. (2013). Neither Touch nor Vision: Sensory Substitution as Artificial Synaesthesia? *Biology and Philosophy*, 28(4), pp. 639–655.

Flusser, V. (1999). *The Shape of Things: A Philosophy of Design*. Trans. A. Mathews. London: Reaktion.

Foley, K. E. (2016). Ideas in Movement: The Next Wave of Brain-Computer Interfaces. *Nature Medicine*, 22(1), pp. 2–5.

Foucault, M. (1973). *The Birth of the Clinic: An Archaeology of Medical Perception*. Trans. A. Sheridan. New York: Vintage Books.

Foucault, M. (1975). *Discipline and Punish: The Birth of the Prison*. Trans. A. Sheridan. London: Allen Lane.

Foucault, M. (1978). *The History of Sexuality, Volume 1: An Introduction*. Trans. R. Hurley. New York: Vintage Books.

Freud, S. (2015). *Civilization and Its Discontents*. Ed. T. Dufresne. Trans. G. C. Richter. Peterborough: Broadview Press.

Friedberg, A. (2006). *The Virtual Window: From Alberti to Microsoft*. Cambridge, MA: MIT Press.

Gallagher, S. (2005). *How the Body Shapes the Mind*. Oxford: Oxford University Press.

Gallagher, S. and Zahavi, D. (2013). *The Phenomenological Mind*. London: Routledge.

Gallese, V. and Lakoff, G. (2005). The Brain's Concepts: The Role of the Sensory-Motor System in Conceptual Knowledge. *Cognitive Neuropsychology*, 22(3/4), pp. 455–479.

Galloway, A. R. (2006). *Gaming: Essays on Algorithmic Culture*. Minneapolis: University of Minnesota Press.

Galloway, A. R. (2009). The Unworkable Interface. *New Literary History*, 39(4), pp. 931–955.

Galloway, A. R. (2012). *The Interface Effect*. Cambridge: Polity.

Gegenfurtner, K. R., Bloj, M. and Toscani, M. (2015). The Many Colours of 'the Dress.' *Current Biology*, 25(13), pp. R543–R544.

George, R. and Blake, J. (2010). Objects, Containers, Gestures, and Manipulations: Universal Foundational Metaphors of Natural User Interfaces. [Online] *CHI 2010*. Available at: www.semanticscholar.org/paper/Objects%2C-Containers%2C-Gestures%2C-and-Manipulations%3A-George-Blake/20f558 1f9b7b1be9f9b2c7942a5dd6f83e0e6b23 [Accessed 29 June 2018].

Gibson, J. J. (1986). *The Ecological Approach to Visual Perception*. Hillsdale: Lawrence Erlbaum Associates.

Goodall, J. (1968). The Behaviour of Free-Living Chimpanzees in the Gombe Stream Reserve. *Animal Behaviour Monographs*, 1(3), pp. 161–311.

Grand Theft Auto. (1997). Rockstar Games.

Granter, E. (2008). A Dream of Ease: Situating the Future of Work and Leisure. *Futures*, 40(9), pp. 803–811.

Greenfeld, K. T. (1994). *Speed Tribes*. New York: HarperCollins Publishers.

Grosz, E. (2013). Habit Today: Ravaisson, Bergson, Deleuze and Us. *Body & Society*, 19(2–3), pp. 217–239.

Guterstam, A. and Ehrsson, H. H. (2012). Disowning One's Seen Real Body During an Out-of-body Illusion. *Consciousness and Cognition*, 21(2), pp. 1037–1042.

Hansell, M. and Ruxton, G. D. (2008). Setting Tool Use Within the Context of Animal Construction Behaviour. *Trends in Ecology & Evolution*, 23(2), pp. 73–78.

Hansen, M.B.N. (2000). *Embodying Technesis: Technology Beyond Writing.* Ann Arbor: University of Michigan Press.

Hansen, M.B.N. (2004). *New Philosophy for New Media.* Cambridge, MA: MIT Press.

Hansen, M.B.N. (2006). *Bodies in Code: Interfaces with Digital Media.* New York: Routledge.

Hansen, M.B.N. (2015). *Feed-forward: On the Future of Twenty-first-century Media.* Chicago: University of Chicago Press.

Hardcore Henry. (2016). Bazelevs Production/Versus Pictures.

Hassan, R. (2003). Network Time and the New Knowledge Epoch. *Time & Society,* 12(2–3), pp. 225–241.

Hassan, R. (2007). Network Time. In: *24/7: Time and Temporality in the Network Society,* ed. Stanford: Stanford Business Books, pp. 37–61.

Hassan, R. (2009). *Empires of Speed.* Leiden: Brill.

Hayles, N. K. (1999). *How We Became Posthuman: Virtual Bodies in Cybernetics, Literature, and Informatics.* Chicago: University of Chicago Press.

Hayles, N. K. (2017). *Unthought: The Power of the Cognitive Nonconscious.* Chicago: University of Chicago Press.

Heidegger, M. (1996). *Being and Time: A Translation of Sein und Zeit.* Trans. J. Stambaugh. Albany: SUNY Press.

Heim, M. (1993). *The Metaphysics of Virtual Reality.* Oxford: Oxford University Press.

Hookway, B. (2014). *Interface.* Cambridge, MA: MIT Press.

Hope, W. (2006). Global Capitalism and the Critique of Real Time. *Time & Society,* 15(2–3), pp. 275–302.

Hurley, S. and Noë, A. (2003). Neural Plasticity and Consciousness. *Biology and Philosophy,* 18(1), pp. 131–168.

Husserl, E. (1991). *On the Phenomenology of the Consciousness of Internal Time (1893–1917).* Trans. J. B. Brough. Dordrecht: Kluwer.

Hutchins, E. (1995). *Cognition in the Wild.* Cambridge, MA: MIT Press.

Ihde, D. (1979). *Technics and Praxis.* Dordrecht: D. Reidel.

Ihde, D. (1983). *Existential Technics.* Albany: SUNY Press.

Ihde, D. (1990). *Technology and the Lifeworld: From Garden to Earth.* Bloomington and Indianapolis: Indiana University Press.

Ihde, D. (2010). *Embodied Technics.* New York: Automatic Press.

Ihde, D. (2011a). Husserl's Galileo Needed a Telescope. *Philosophy & Technology,* 24(1), pp. 69–82.

Ihde, D. (2011b). Stretching the in-Between: Embodiment and Beyond. *Foundations of Science,* 16(2–3), pp. 109–118.

Ingold, T. (1995). Work, Time and Industry. *Time & Society,* 4(1), pp. 5–28.

Ingold, T. (1999). 'Tools for the Hand, Language for the Face': An Appreciation of Leroi-Gourhan's Gesture and Speech. *Studies in History and Philosophy of Science,* 30(4), pp. 411–453.

Ingold, T. (2000). *The Perception of the Environment: Essays on Livelihood, Dwelling and Skill.* London: Routledge.

Iversen, M. (2005). The Discourse of Perspective in the Twentieth Century: Panofsky, Damisch, Lacan. *Oxford Art Journal,* 28(2), pp. 191–202.

Jain, S. S. (1999). The Prosthetic Imagination: Enabling and Disabling the Prosthesis Trope. *Science, Technology & Human Values,* 24(1), pp. 31–54.

Johnson, S. (1997). *Interface Culture: How New Technology Transforms the Way We Create and Communicate*. New York: Basic Books.

Jørgensen, K. (2009). "I'm Overburdened!" an Empirical Study of the Player, the Avatar, and the Gameworld. [Online] *DiGRA '09*. Available at: http://citeseerx. ist.psu.edu/viewdoc/download?doi=10.1.1.190.2037&rep=rep1&type=pdf [Accessed 29 June 2018].

Jütte, R. (2005). *A History of the Senses: From Antiquity to Cyberspace*. Cambridge: Polity.

Kauffmann, O. (2011). Brain Plasticity and Phenomenal Consciousness. *Journal of Consciousness Studies*, 18(7–8), pp. 46–70.

Kay, A. (1990). User Interface: A Personal View. In: *The Art of Human-computer Interface Design*, B. Laurel, ed. Reading: Addison-Wesley, pp. 191–207.

Keeley, B. L. (2015). Nonhuman Animal Senses. In: *The Oxford Handbook of Philosophy of Perception*, M. Matthen, ed. Oxford: Oxford University Press, pp. 853–870.

Kemp, M. (2006). *Seen/unseen: Art, Science, and Intuition from Leonardo to the Hubble Telescope*. Oxford: Oxford University Press.

Kercel, S. W., Reber, A. S. and Manges, W. W. (2005). Some Radical Implications of Bach-y-Rita's Discoveries. *Journal of Integrative Neuroscience*, 4(4), pp. 551–565.

Kittler, F. A. (1990). *Discourse Networks 1800/1900*. Trans. M. Metteer and C. Cullens. Stanford: Stanford University Press.

Kittler, F. A. (1999). *Gramophone, Film, Typewriter*. Trans. G. Winthrop-Young and M. Wutz. Stanford: Stanford University Press.

Kiverstein, J. and Clark, A. (2009). Introduction: Mind Embodied, Embedded, Enacted: One Church or Many? *Topoi*, 28(1), pp. 1–7.

Kiverstein, J., Farina, M. and Clark, A. (2015). Substituting the Senses. In: *The Oxford Handbook of Philosophy of Perception*, M. Matthen, ed. Oxford: Oxford University Press, pp. 659–675.

Klevjer, R. (2013). Representation and Virtuality in Computer Games. [Online] *The Philosophy of Computer Games Conference 2013*. Available at: http:// gamephilosophy2013.b.uib.no/files/2013/10/Klevjer_RepresentationAndVirtuality. pdf [Accessed 29 June 2018].

König, W. A., Rädle, R. and Reiterer, H. (2009). Squidy: A Zoomable Design Environment for Natural User Interfaces. *CHI '09 Extended Abstracts on Human Factors in Computing Systems*, pp. 4561–4566.

Krueger, M. W. (1977). Responsive Environments. [Online] *Proceedings of the 1977 National Computer Conference*. Available at: https://dl.acm.org/citation. cfm?id=1499476 [Accessed 29 June 2018].

Krueger, M. W. (1991). *Artificial Reality II*. Reading: Addison-Wesley.

Kurzman, S. L. (2001). Presence and Prosthesis: A Response to Nelson and Wright. *Cultural Anthropology*, 16(3), pp. 374–387.

Lady in the Lake. (1947). MGM.

Lafer-Sousa, R., Hermann, K. L. and Conway, B. R. (2015). Striking Individual Differences in Color Perception Uncovered By 'the Dress' Photograph. *Current Biology*, 25(13), pp. R545–R546.

Lanier, J. (2017). *Dawn of the New Everything: A Journey Through Virtual Reality*. London: The Bodley Head.

Lanier, J. and Biocca, F. (1992). An Insider's View of the Future of Virtual Reality. *Journal of Communication*, 42(4), pp. 150–172.

Lanman, D. and Luebke, D. (2013). Near-Eye Light Field Displays. *ACM Transactions on Graphics (TOG)*, 32(6), pp. 220–210.

Latour, B. (2005). *Reassembling the Social: An Introduction to Actor-network-theory*. Oxford: Oxford University Press.

Latour, B. and Venn, C. (2002). Morality and Technology: The End of the Means. *Theory, Culture & Society*, 19(5–6), pp. 247–260.

Laurel, B. (1993). *Computers as Theatre*. Reading: Addison-Wesley.

Lawnmower Man. (1992). New Line Cinema.

Lebedev, M. A. and Nicolelis, M.A.L. (2006). Brain—Machine Interfaces: Past, Present and Future. *TRENDS in Neurosciences*, 29(9), pp. 536–546.

Leder, D. (1990). *The Absent Body*. Chicago: University of Chicago Press.

Leroi-Gourhan, A. (1993). *Gesture and Speech*. Trans. A. B. Berger. Cambridge, MA: MIT Press.

Lévy, P. (1998). *Becoming Virtual: Reality in the Digital Age*. Trans. R. Bononno. New York: Plenum.

Licklider, J.C.R. (2003). Man—Computer Symbiosis. In: *The New Media Reader*, N. Wardrip-Fruin and N. Montfort, eds. Cambridge, MA: MIT Press, pp. 74–82.

Liu, W. (2010). Natural User Interface—Next Mainstream Product User Interface. *2010 IEEE 11th International Conference on Computer-Aided Industrial Design & Conceptual Design (CAIDCD)*, 1, pp. 203–205.

Lo Verde, L., Morrone, M. C. and Lunghi, C. (2017). Early Cross-Modal Plasticity in Adults. *Journal of Cognitive Neuroscience*, 29(3), pp. 520–529.

Manovich, L. (2001). *The Language of New Media*. Cambridge, MA: MIT Press.

Manovich, L. (2013). *Software Takes Command*. New York: Bloomsbury.

Martin, P. (2012). A Phenomenological Account of the Playing-body in Avatar-based Action Games. [Online] *Philosophy of Computer Games Conference 2012*. Available at: www.academia.edu/download/31325524/Phenomenology Games.pdf [Accessed 29 June 2018].

Marx, K. (1976). *Capital: A Critique of Political Economy*. Trans. B. Fowkes. Harmondsworth: Penguin Books in association with New Left Review.

Marx, K. (1980). *Marx's Grundriss*. London: Macmillan.

Maslow, A. H. (1966). *The Psychology of Science: A Reconnaissance*. New York: Harper and Row.

Max Payne. (2001). Rockstar Games.

McGarry, B. (2015). This Woman Flew an F-35 Simulator with Her Mind. [Online] Available at: http://defensetech.org/2015/03/02/this-woman-flew-an-f-35-simulator-with-her-mind/ [Accessed 6 June 2018].

McGlone, F. and Reilly, D. (2010). The Cutaneous Sensory System. *Neuroscience & Biobehavioral Reviews*, 34(2), pp. 148–159.

McLuhan, M. (1964). *Understanding Media: The Extensions of Man*. London: Routledge and Kegan Paul.

McLuhan, M. and McLuhan, E. (1988). *Laws of Media: The New Science*. Toronto: University of Toronto Press.

Meijer, P.B.L. (1992). An Experimental System for Auditory Image Representations. *Biomedical Engineering, IEEE Transactions On*, 39(2), pp. 112–121.

Meltzoff, A. N. and Moore, M. K. (1983). Newborn Infants Imitate Adult Facial Gestures. *Child Development*, 54(3), pp. 702–709.

Menary, R. (2009). Intentionality, Cognitive Integration and the Continuity Thesis. *Topoi*, 28(1), pp. 31–43.

Mendelson, E. (2016). In the Depths of the Digital Age. *The New York Review of Books*.

Merleau-Ponty, M. (2002). *Phenomenology of Perception*. Trans. C. Smith. London: Routledge.

Metz, C. (2017). Facebook's Race to Link Your Brain to a Computer Might Be Unwinnable. [Online] *Wired*. Available at: www.wired.com/2017/04/facebooks-race-link-brain-computer-might-unwinnable/ [Accessed 27 April].

Minority Report. (2002). Twentieth Century Fox.

Modern Times. (1936). Charles Chaplin Productions.

Moggridge, B. (2007). *Designing Interactions*. Cambridge, MA: MIT Press.

Morra, J. and Smith, M. (2006). Introduction. In: *The Prosthetic Impulse*, M. Smith and J. Morra, eds. Cambridge, MA: MIT Press, pp. 1–14.

Mulder, A. (2006). Media. *Theory, Culture & Society*, 23(2–3), pp. 289–296.

Mumford, L. (1963). *Technics and Civilization*. New York: Harcourt.

Munster, A. (2006). *Materializing New Media: Embodiment in Information Aesthetics*. Hanover: Dartmouth College Press.

Nagel, S. K. et al. (2005). Beyond Sensory Substitution—Learning the Sixth Sense. *Journal of Neural Engineering*, 2(4), pp. R13–R26.

Noë, A. (2004). *Action in Perception*. Cambridge, MA: MIT Press.

Noë, A. and O'Regan, J. K. (2000). Perception, Attention, and the Grand Illusion. *Psyche*, 6(15), pp. 6–15.

Noë, A., Pessoa, L. and Thompson, E. (2000). Beyond the Grand Illusion: What Change Blindness Really Teaches Us About Vision. *Visual Cognition*, 7(1), pp. 93–106.

Norimoto, H. and Ikegaya, Y. (2015). Visual Cortical Prosthesis with a Geomagnetic Compass Restores Spatial Navigation in Blind Rats. *Current Biology*, 25(8), pp. 1091–1095.

Norman, D. A. (1999). *The Invisible Computer*. Cambridge, MA: MIT Press.

Norman, D. A. (2010). Natural User Interfaces Are Not Natural. *Interactions*, 17(3), pp. 6–10.

Nørskov, M. (2015). Revisiting Ihde's Fourfold 'Technological Relationships': Application and Modification. *Philosophy & Technology*, 28(2), pp. 189–207.

Norton, Q. (2006). A Sixth Sense for a Wired World. [Online] *Wired*. Available at: www.wired.com/gadgets/mods/news/2006/06/71087?currentPage=all [Accessed 6 June 2018].

Oddo, C. M. et al. (2016). Intraneural Stimulation Elicits Discrimination of Textural Features by Artificial Fingertip in Intact and Amputee Humans. [Online] *eLife*. Available at: www.ncbi.nlm.nih.gov/pmc/articles/PMC4798967/ [Accessed 29 June 2018].

O'Doherty, J. E. et al. (2012). Virtual Active Touch Using Randomly Patterned Intracortical Microstimulation. *IEEE Transactions on Neural Systems and Rehabilitation Engineering*, 20(1), pp. 85–93.

Össur Sport Solutions. (2016). [Online] *Össur America*. Available at: www.ossur.com/prosthetic-solutions/products/sport-solutions?view=products [Accessed 6 June 2018].

Pais-Vieira, M. et al. (2013). A Brain-to-brain Interface for Real-Time Sharing of Sensorimotor Information. *Nature Scientific Reports*, 3(1319).

Panofsky, E. (1991). *Perspective as Symbolic Form*. New York: Zone Books.

Paterson, M. (2007). *The Senses of Touch*. Oxford: Berg.

Peirce, C. S. (1955). *Philosophical Writings of Peirce*. Ed. J. Buchler. New York: Dover Publications.

Petkova, V. I. and Ehrsson, H. H. (2008). If I Were You: Perceptual Illusion of Body Swapping. *PLoS ONE*, 3(12), pp. e3832.

Pias, C. (2011). The Game Player's Duty: The User as the Gestalt of the Ports. In: *Media Archaeology: Approaches, Applications, and Implications*, E. Huhtamo and J. Parikka, eds. Berkeley: University of California Press, pp. 164–183.

Pickrell, J. E., Bernstein, D. M. and Loftus, E. F. (2004). Misinformation Effect. In: *Cognitive Illusions: A Handbook on Fallacies and Biases in Thinking, Judgement and Memory*, R. Pohl, ed. New York: Psychology Press, pp. 345–361.

Povinelli, D. J. and Cant, J.G.H. (1995). Arboreal Clambering and the Evolution of Self-Conception. *The Quarterly Review of Biology*, 70(4), pp. 393–421.

Price, S. (2012). Alvaro Cassinelli: You Really Can Use a Banana as a Telephone. [Online] *The Guardian*. Available at: www.theguardian.com/technology/2012/jan/01/invoked-computing-household-objects-cassinelli [Accessed 6 June 2018].

Ptito, M. and Kupers, R. (2005). Cross-Modal Plasticity in Early Blindness. *Journal of Integrative Neuroscience*, 4(4), pp. 479–488.

Rao, R.P.N. et al. (2014). A Direct Brain-to-brain Interface in Humans. *PLoS ONE*, 9(11), pp. e111332.

Rehak, B. (2003). Playing at Being: Psychoanalysis and the Avatar. In: *The Video Game Theory Reader*, M.J.P. Wolf and B. Perron, eds. London: Routledge, pp. 103–127.

Rheingold, H. (1991). *Virtual Reality*. New York: Touchstone.

Rizzolatti, G., Sinigaglia, C. and Anderson, F. (2008). *Mirrors in the Brain: How Our Minds Share Actions, Emotions, and Experience*. Oxford: Oxford University Press.

Roe, A. W. et al. (1992). Visual Projections Routed to the Auditory Pathway in Ferrets: Receptive Fields of Visual Neurons in Primary Auditory Cortex. *The Journal of Neuroscience*, 12(9), pp. 3651–3664.

Rosa, H. (2013). *Social Acceleration: A New Theory of Modernity*. Trans. J. Trejo-Mathys. New York: Columbia University Press.

Rousseau, J.-J. (2007). *Discourse on the Origin of Inequality*. Minneapolis: Filiquarian Publishing.

Salen, K. and Zimmerman, E. (2004). *Rules of Play: Game Design Fundamentals*. Cambridge, MA: MIT Press.

Sawday, J. (2007). *Engines of the Imagination: Renaissance Culture and the Rise of the Machine*. London: Routledge.

Schacter, D. L. (1996). *Searching for Memory: The Brain, the Mind, and the Past*. New York: Basic Books.

Schilder, P. (1950). *The Image and Appearance of the Human Body: Studies in the Constructive Energies of the Psyche*. New York: International Universities Press.

Schivelbusch, W. (1980). *The Railway Journey: Trains and Travel in the 19th Century*. Trans. A. Hollo. Oxford: Blackwell.

Schüll, N. D. (2012). *Addiction by Design: Machine Gambling in Las Vegas.* Princeton: Princeton University Press.

Scott, D. (2006). The 'Concept of Time' and the 'Being of the Clock': Bergson, Einstein, Heidegger, and the Interrogation of the Temporality of Modernism. *Continental Philosophy Review,* 39(2), pp. 183–213.

Seed, A. and Byrne, R. (2010). Animal Tool-Use. *Trends in Ecology & Evolution,* 20(23), pp. R1032–R1039.

Sega V. R. (n.d.). [Online] *Wikipedia.* Available at: https://en.wikipedia.org/wiki/Sega_VR [Accessed 30 July 2017]

Shaw, A. (2010). *Identity, Identification, and Media Representation in Video Game Play: An Audience Reception Study.* PhD. University of Pennsylvania.

Shedroff, N. and Noessel, C. (2012). *Make It So: Interaction Design Lessons from Science Fiction.* Brooklyn: Rosenfeld Media.

Shields, R. (2005). *The Virtual.* London: Routledge.

Shumaker, R. W., Walkup, K. R. and Beck, B. B. (2011). *Animal Tool Behavior: The Use and Manufacture of Tools by Animals.* Baltimore: Johns Hopkins University Press.

Slater, M. et al. (2008). Towards a Digital Body: The Virtual Arm Illusion. *Frontiers in Human Neuroscience,* 2(6), pp. 1–8.

Smith, A. (2009). *An Inquiry into the Nature and Causes of the Wealth of Nations.* Lawrence: Digireads.com Publishing.

Smith, D. C. (1975). *Pygmalion: A Creative Programming Environment.* PhD. Stanford University.

Sobchack, V. (1992). *The Address of the Eye: A Phenomenology of Film Experience.* Princeton: Princeton University Press.

Sobchack, V. (2004). *Carnal Thoughts.* Berkeley: University of California Press.

Sobchack, V. (2010). Living a 'Phantom Limb': On the Phenomenology of Bodily Integrity. *Body & Society,* 16(3), pp. 51–67.

St Amant, R. and Horton, T. E. (2008). Revisiting the Definition of Animal Tool Use. *Animal Behaviour,* 75(4), pp. 1199–1208.

Sterne, J. (2001). A Machine to Hear for Them: On the Very Possibility of Sound's Reproduction. *Cultural Studies,* 15(2), pp. 259–294.

Stetson, C., Fiesta, M. P. and Eagleman, D. M. (2007). Does Time Really Slow Down During a Frightening Event? *PLoS ONE,* 2(12), pp. e1295.

Steuer, J. (2006). Defining Virtual Reality: Dimensions Determining Telepresence. *Journal of Communication,* 42(4), pp. 73–93.

Stiegler, B. (1998). *Technics and Time, 1: The Fault of Epimetheus.* Trans. R. Beardsworth and G. Collins. Stanford: Stanford University Press.

Stiegler, B. (2009). *Technics and Time, 2: Disorientation.* Trans. S. Barker. Stanford: Stanford University Press.

Stiegler, B. (2011). *Technics and Time, 3: Cinematic Time and the Question of Malaise.* Trans. S. Barker. Stanford: Stanford University Press.

Suchman, L. A. (2007). *Human-machine Reconfigurations: Plans and Situated Actions.* Cambridge: Cambridge University Press.

Sutherland, I. E. (1968). A Head-Mounted Three Dimensional Display. [Online] *Proceedings of the 1968 Fall Joint Computer Conference.* Available at: https://dl.acm.org/citation.cfm?id=1476686 [Accessed 29 June 2018].

Synnott, A. (1992). Tomb, Temple, Machine and Self: The Social Construction of the Body. *The British Journal of Sociology,* 43(1), pp. 79–110.

Thacker, E. (2004). *Biomedia*. Minneapolis: University of Minnesota Press.

The Brain as Tape Recorder. (1957). *Time*, pp. 37.

Thompson, E. P. (1967). Time, Work-Discipline, and Industrial Capitalism. *Past and Present*, 38, pp. 56–97.

Tomb Raider. (1996). Eidos Interactive.

Travieso, D. et al. (2015). Body-Scaled Affordances in Sensory Substitution. *Consciousness and Cognition*, 38, pp. 130–138.

Trendacosta, K. and Gonzalez, B. (2015). The 'What Color Is This Goddamn Dress?' Debate Explained By Science. [Online] *io9*. Available at: http://io9.com/the-what-color-is-this-goddamn-dress-debate-explaine-1688378120 [Accessed 6 June 2018].

Trivedi, B. (2010). Sensory Hijack: Rewiring Brains to See with Sound. *New Scientist*, 2773, pp. 42–45.

Turkle, S. (1984). *The Second Self: Computers and the Human Spirit*. London: Granada.

Turner, J. (1992). Myron Krueger Live. [Online] *CTheory*. Available at: https://journals.uvic.ca/index.php/ctheory/article/view/14583/5428 [Accessed 29 June 2018].

Turner, P. (2009). The End of Cognition? *Human Technology: An Interdisciplinary Journal on Humans in ICT Environments*, 5(1), pp. 5–11.

Ubisoft. (2007). Assassin's Creed.

Upson, S. (2014). Cyborg Confidential. *Scientific American Mind*, 25(6), pp. 30–35.

Utterson, A. (2013). Early Visions of Interactivity: The in(put)s and Out(put)s of Real-Time Computing. *Leonardo*, 46(1), pp. 67–72.

Valli, A. (2007). Natural Interaction White Paper. [Online] Available at: http://citeseerx.ist.psu.edu/viewdoc/download?doi=10.1.1.98.9153&rep=rep1&type=pdf [Accessed 6 June 2018].

van der Hoort, B., Guterstam, A. and Ehrsson, H. H. (2011). Being Barbie: The Size of One's Own Body Determines the Perceived Size of the World. *PLoS ONE*, 6(5), pp. e20195.

van Dijk, J. (2009). Cognition Is Not What It Used to Be: Reconsidering Usability From an Embodied Embedded Cognition Perspective. *Human Technology: An Interdisciplinary Journal on Humans in ICT Environments*, 5(1), pp. 29–46.

Verbeek, P. (2005). *What Things Do: Philosophical Reflections on Technology, Agency, and Design*. University Park, PA: Pennsylvania State University Press.

Virilio, P. (1995a). *The Art of the Motor*. Trans. J. Rose. Minneapolis: University of Minnesota Press.

Virilio, P. (1995b). Speed and Information: Cyberspace Alarm! [Online] *CTheory*. Available at: http://journals.uvic.ca/index.php/ctheory/article/view/14657/5523 [Accessed 29 June 2018].

Virilio, P. (1997). *Open Sky*. Trans. J. Rose. London: Verso.

Virilio, P. (2005). *Negative Horizon: An Essay in Dromoscopy*. Trans. M. Degener. London: Continuum.

Virtual Boy. (n.d.). [Online] *Wikipedia*. Available at: https://en.wikipedia.org/wiki/Virtual_Boy [Accessed 30 June 2017].

von Melchner, L., Pallas, S. L. and Sur, M. (2000). Visual Behaviour Mediated By Retinal Projections Directed to the Auditory Pathway. *Nature*, 404(6780), pp. 871–876.

Wajcman, J. (2015). *Pressed for Time: The Acceleration of Life in Digital Capitalism*. Chicago: University of Chicago Press.

Walker, J. (1990). Through the Looking Glass. In: *The Art of Human-computer Interface Design*, B. Laurel, ed. Reading: Addison-Wesley, pp. 439–447.

Ward, J. and Meijer, P. (2010). Visual Experiences in the Blind Induced By an Auditory Sensory Substitution Device. *Consciousness and Cognition*, 19(1), pp. 492–500.

Weber, D. (n.d.). Hand Proprioception and Touch Interfaces (haptix). [Online] *DARPA*. Available at: www.darpa.mil/program/hand-proprioception-and-touch-interfaces [Accessed 19 June 2017].

Weiser, M. (1994). The World Is Not a Desktop. *Interactions*, 1(1), pp. 7–8.

Weiskrantz, L. (1990). *Blindsight*. Oxford: Oxford University Press.

Wheeler, M. (2015). Not What It's Like But Where It's Like: Phenomenal Consciousness, Sensory Substitution, and the Extended Mind. *Journal of Consciousness Studies*, 22(3–4), pp. 129–147.

Wills, D. (2006). Techneology or the Discourse of Speed. In: *The Prosthetic Impulse*, M. Smith and J. Morra, eds. Cambridge, MA: MIT Press, pp. 237–263.

Winkler, A. D. et al. (2015). Asymmetries in Blue–Yellow Color Perception and in the Color of 'the Dress.' *Current Biology*, 25(13), pp. R547–R548.

Winograd, T. and Flores, F. (2003). Using Computers: A Direction for Design. In: *The New Media Reader*, N. Wardrip-Fruin and N. Montfort, eds. Cambridge, MA: MIT Press, pp. 551–561.

Winter, A. (2012). *Memory: Fragments of a Modern History*. Chicago: University of Chicago Press.

Wood, G. (2002). *Edison's Eve: A Magical History of the Quest for Mechanical Life*. New York: Alfred A. Knopf.

World of Warcraft. (2004). Blizzard Entertainment.

Year 2000 Problem. (n.d.). [Online] *Wikipedia*. Available at: https://en.wikipedia.org/wiki/Year_2000_problem [Accessed 10 May 2018].

Yonck, R. (2010). The Age of the Interface. *The Futurist*, pp. 14–19.

Zettl, H. (2014). *Sight, Sound, Motion: Applied Media Aesthetics*. Boston: Wadsworth Cengage Learning.

Index

Printed in the United States
by Baker & Taylor Publisher Services